101
Made-to-Fit
Quilts
For Your
Home

Edited by Jeanne Stauffer & Sandra L. Hatch

HOUSE of
WHITE
BIRCHES

101 Made-to-Fit Quilts for Your Home

Editors: Jeanne Stauffer & Sandra L. Hatch
Design Manager: Vicki Blizzard
Project Supervisor: Barb Sprunger
Copy Editors: Mary Nowak, Nicki Lehman, Sue Harvey
Publications Coordinator: Tanya Turner

Photography: Tammy Christian, Jeff Chilcote, Justin Wiard
Photography Stylist: Arlou Wittwer
Photography Assistant: Linda Quinlan

Production Coordinator: Brenda Gallmeyer
Book Design: Vicki's Design Studio
Technical Artist: Connie Rand
Production Artist: Pam Gregory
Production Assistants: Janet Bowers, Marj Morgan
Traffic Coordinator: Sandra Beres

Publishers: Carl H. Muselman, Arthur K. Muselman
Chief Executive Officer: John Robinson
Marketing Director: Scott Moss
Product Development Director: Vivian Rothe
Publishing Services Manager: Brenda R. Wendling

Printed in the United States of America
First Printing: 2000
Library of Congress Number: 00-132494
ISBN: 1-882138-62-7

Every effort has been made to ensure the accuracy and completeness of the instructions
in this book. However, we cannot be responsible for human error or for the results when using
materials other than those specified in the instructions, or for variations in individual work.

Welcome!

What a delight it has been to put this book together for you. We spent many enjoyable hours searching for quilt designs that were old and not recently published or at least different in some way from those you already have in your quilt books.

All the quilts in this collection are lap-size or larger. We know you will find many quilts that you will want to stitch to decorate your home or to give as gifts to family and friends.

To make your quilting even more enjoyable, we have taken the drudgery out of adjusting the patterns to fit your use. We know that many times you need to change the size or shape of a quilt to fit a specific person or place. Or you want to change a full-size quilt to a lap quilt or the reverse. We have done the work for you! We've given each quilt design in two or three sizes, so you can make a quilt in just the right size to fit your needs.

We've also taken the work out of adjusting the instructions because we give you the instructions for all three sizes! You'll find the instructions for the quilt in the photo given first, with the instructions for the other designs given in parentheses, the smaller size first. We know you will appreciate this added bonus!

All of us who worked together to bring you this book wish you many relaxing and rewarding hours spent piecing, appliquéing and quilting.

Warmest regards,

Jeanne Stauffer

Sandra L. Hatch

Contents

Patchwork Garden

Quilt Upon a Star

General Instructions

Chapter One

Shortcut Quilts

What a way to spend a weekend!

Yes, you really can complete the quilts

in this chapter in 20 hours or less

if you have already selected and

prepared the fabric and use the

shortcut methods suggested in our

easy-to-follow instructions.

Have a great quilting weekend!

Whirlybird Bed Quilt

By Holly Daniels

My first love in quilting is the scrap quilt. I wanted this quilt to have a scrappy feel, but be quick to sew. The multicolored sashing is staggered to create the scrappy illusion. Two different color blocks add to the feel.

Whirligig
12" x 12" Block

Quilt Sizes			
	Twin	**Queen**	**King**
Finished Quilt Size	68" x 92"	86" x 92"	104" x 92"
Block Size	12" x 12"	12" x 12"	12" x 12"
Number of Blocks	21	28	35
Materials			
Nine dark prints (each)	1/4 yard	1/3 yard	1/3 yard
Blue-on-blue print	1 yard	1 1/8 yards	1 1/4 yards
Pink print	1 yard	1 1/8 yards	1 1/4 yards
Blue print	2 1/2 yards	2 1/2 yards	3 yards
White solid	2 1/4 yards	3 yards	3 1/2 yards
Backing	72" x 96"	90" x 96"	108" x 96"
Batting	72" x 96"	90" x 96"	108" x 96"
Self-made or purchased binding	9 1/2 yards	10 1/2 yards	11 1/2 yards
Neutral color all-purpose thread			
White and navy all-purpose thread			
Basic sewing supplies and tools			

Instructions

Instructions are given for the size shown in photo, with other sizes in parentheses. When only 1 number is given, it applies to all sizes.

Step 1. From fabric length, cut two strips each 4 1/2" x 84 1/2" (4 1/2" x 84 1/2") (4 1/2" x 84 1/2") and 4 1/2" x 68 1/2" (4 1/2" x 86 1/2") (4 1/2" x 104 1/2") blue print for borders; set aside.

Step 2. Cut three (4) (4) strips from each of the nine dark prints, the pink print and the blue-on-blue print 2 1/2" by fabric width. Join one strip of each color with right sides together along length to form a strip set; press seams in one direction. Repeat for three (4) (4) strip sets, sewing strips in a different order for each set.

Step 3. Cut each strip set into 6 1/2" segments as shown in Figure 1. Sew segments together on short ends to make one continuous strip.

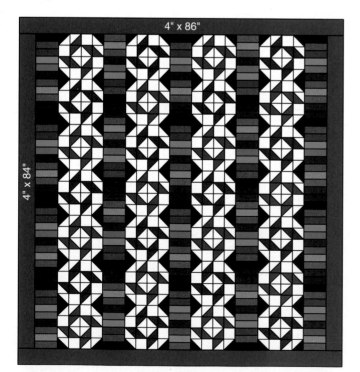

Whirlybird Bed Quilt
Placement Diagram
86" x 92"

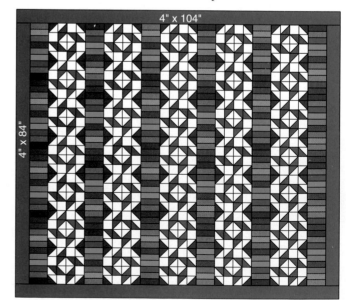

Whirlybird Bed Quilt
Placement Diagram
104" x 92"

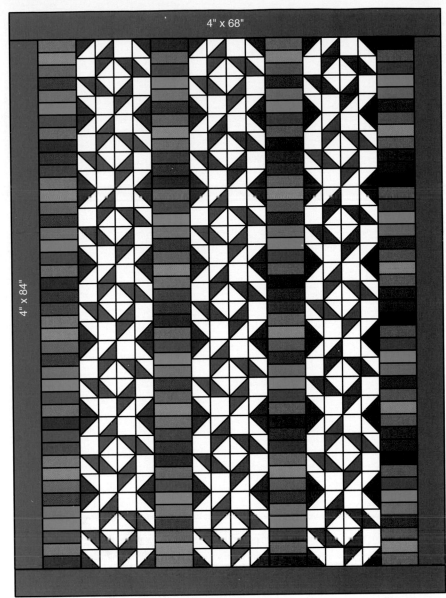

Whirlybird Bed Quilt
Placement Diagram
68" x 92"

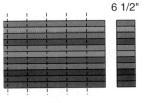

6 1/2"

Figure 1
Cut each strip set into 6 1/2" segments.

Step 4. Starting at one end of the strip, count out 42 segments; remove stitches between segment 42 and segment 43; repeat for four (5) (6) 42-segment strips. Set aside for later use; discard remaining segments to your scrap bag.

Step 5. Cut 126 (168) (210) squares white solid 3 7/8" x 3 7/8"; set aside one set of 40 (56) (68) squares and one set of 42 (56) (70) squares. Cut 44 (56) (72) squares pink print 3 7/8" x 3 7/8".

Step 6. Layer a pink print square with a white solid square with right sides together; mark a diagonal line on the white solid square side. Sew 1/4" on each side of the diagonal line as shown in Figure 2.

1/4"

Figure 2
Sew 1/4" on each side
of the diagonal line.

Step 7. Cut apart on the drawn line and clip off corners as shown in Figure 3; press open to reveal a triangle/square as shown in Figure 4. Repeat for all pink print and white solid squares.

Figure 3
Cut apart on the drawn
line and clip off corners.

Figure 4
Press open to reveal
a triangle/square.

Step 8. Cut 40 (56) (68) squares blue print and 42 (56) (70) squares blue-on-blue print 3 7/8" x 3 7/8". Layer each of these squares with the remaining white solid squares and make triangle/squares as in Steps 6 and 7.

Step 9. Cut 84 (112) (140) squares white solid 3 1/2" x 3 1/2". Arrange eight white/pink triangle/squares with four white solid squares and four blue-on-blue/white triangle/squares to form a Whirligig block as shown in Figure 5. Join units in rows; join to complete one block. Press seams in one direction. Repeat for 11 (14) (18) pink/white blocks and 10 (14) (17) blue/white blocks as shown in Figure 6.

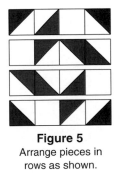

Figure 5
Arrange pieces in
rows as shown.

Make 10 (14) (17)   Make 11 (14) (18)

Figure 6
Join to complete 1 block.

Step 10. Join four pink/white blocks with three blue/white blocks to make a row as shown in Figure 7; repeat for two (2) (3) pink/white rows. Join four blue/white blocks with three pink/white blocks to

Continued on page 26

Two-Patch Quilt

By Carla Schwab

Burgundy and blue prints and solids combine to make this quick-to-stitch country-look quilt for your baby or small child.

Two-Patch
3" x 3" Block

Instructions

Instructions are given for the size shown in photo, with other sizes in parentheses. When only 1 number is given, it applies to all sizes.

Step 1. Cut two (5) (13) strips each 2" by fabric width from burgundy and blue prints.

Step 2. Sew a burgundy print strip to a blue print strip with right sides together along length; press seams in one direction. Repeat for two (5) (13) strip sets.

Step 3. Cut each strip set into 3 1/2" Two-Patch blocks as shown in Figure 1; you will need 20 (50) (150) blocks.

Figure 1
Cut each strip set into 3 1/2"
Two-Patch blocks.

Step 4. Cut two (5) (14) strips burgundy solid 3 1/2" by fabric width. Cut each strip into 2" segments; you will need 31 (85) (275) segments for sashing strips.

Step 5. Cut one (2) (6) strips dark blue solid 2" by fabric width. Cut each strip into 2" segments; you will need 12 (36) (126) segments for sashing squares.

Step 6. Join four (5) (10) blocks with three (4) (9) sashing strips to make an A block row as shown in Figure 2; repeat for three (5) (8) A block rows.

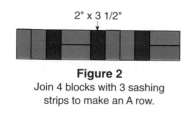

Figure 2
Join 4 blocks with 3 sashing
strips to make an A row.

Quilt Sizes

	Cradle	Crib	Youth
Finished Quilt Size	28 1/2" x 33"	33" x 55 1/2"	55 1/2" x 78"
Block Size	3" x 3"	3" x 3"	3" x 3"
Number of Blocks	20	50	150

Materials

Blue solid	1/4 yard	1/2 yard	3/4 yard
Dark blue solid	1/3 yard	1/2 yard	1 yard
Burgundy print	1/3 yard	1/2 yard	1 yard
Burgundy solid	1/2 yard	3/4 yard	1 3/4 yards
Blue print	1/2 yard	3/4 yard	1 1/8 yards
Backing	33" x 37"	37" x 60"	60" x 82"
Batting	33" x 37"	37" x 60"	60" x 82"
Neutral color all-purpose thread			
White quilting thread			
Basic sewing supplies and tools			

Step 7. Join four (5) (10) blocks with three (4) (9) sashing strips to make a B block row as shown in Figure 3; repeat for two (5) (7) B block rows.

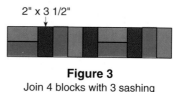

Figure 3
Join 4 blocks with 3 sashing
strips to make a B row.

Step 8. Join four (5) (10) sashing strips with three (4) (9) sashing squares to make a sashing row as shown in Figure 4; repeat for four (9) (14) sashing rows.

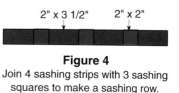

Figure 4
Join 4 sashing strips with 3 sashing
squares to make a sashing row.

Step 9. Arrange A and B block rows with sashing rows referring to the Placement Diagram for positioning of rows. Join rows to complete the pieced center.

Step 10. Cut (and piece) two strips each blue solid 3" x 17" (3" x 21 1/2") (3" x 44") and 3" x 26 1/2" (3" x 49") (3" x 71 1/2"). Sew the shorter strips to the top and bottom and longer strips to opposite sides of the pieced center; press seams toward strips.

Step 11. Cut (and piece) two strips each dark blue solid 4" x 22" (4" x 26 1/2") (4" x 49") and 4" x

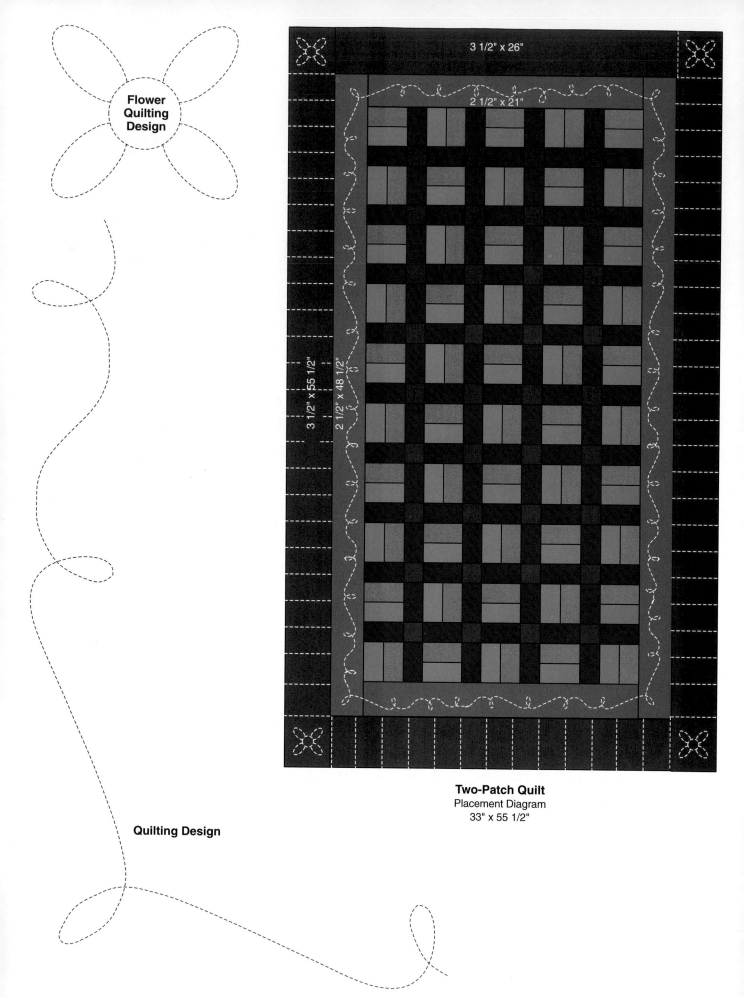

**Flower
Quilting
Design**

3 1/2" x 26"

2 1/2" x 21"

3 1/2" x 55 1/2"

2 1/2" x 48 1/2"

Quilting Design

Two-Patch Quilt
Placement Diagram
33" x 55 1/2"

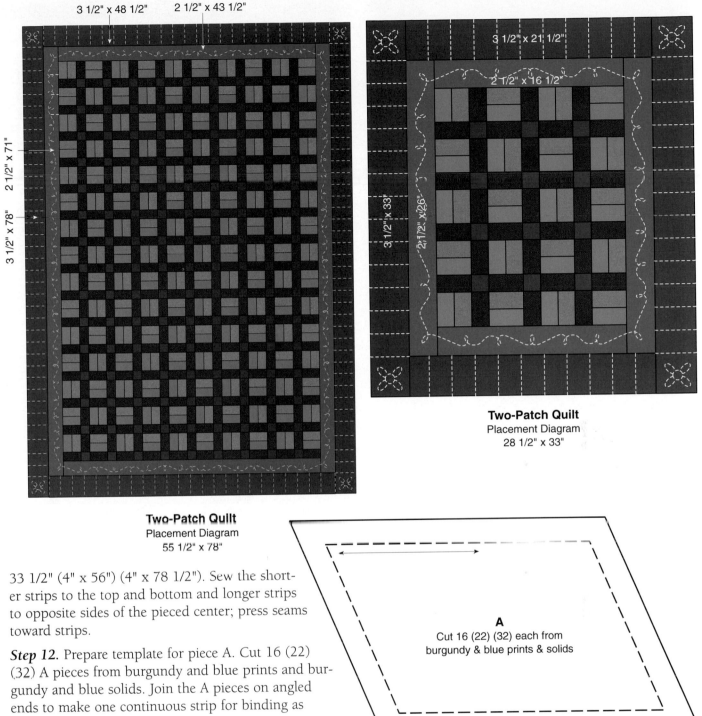

Two-Patch Quilt
Placement Diagram
28 1/2" x 33"

3 1/2" x 48 1/2"   2 1/2" x 43 1/2"

2 1/2" x 71"

3 1/2" x 78"

3 1/2" x 21 1/2"

2 1/2" x 16 1/2"

3 1/2" x 33"

2 1/2" x 26"

Two-Patch Quilt
Placement Diagram
55 1/2" x 78"

33 1/2" (4" x 56") (4" x 78 1/2"). Sew the shorter strips to the top and bottom and longer strips to opposite sides of the pieced center; press seams toward strips.

Step 12. Prepare template for piece A. Cut 16 (22) (32) A pieces from burgundy and blue prints and burgundy and blue solids. Join the A pieces on angled ends to make one continuous strip for binding as shown in Figure 5.

A
Cut 16 (22) (32) each from
burgundy & blue prints & solids

Figure 5
Join the A pieces on angled ends to
make 1 continuous strip for binding.

Step 13. Prepare top for quilting and finish using pieced binding strip referring to the General Instructions. **Note:** *The quilt shown was hand-quilted in the ditch of seams, with the design given on the inside border, with the flower design given in each outside border corner, and in 2" intervals on outside border strip (refer to Placement Diagram) using white quilting thread.* ❧

Garden Friends

By Leslie Hartsock

Make this happy quilt in three sizes, crib, youth or twin, and brighten up any child's room.

Project Notes

To make the two larger-size quilts you will have to prepare a pieced background. It is recommended that the fabric be cut with the lengthwise grain running up and down on the quilt, rather than crosswise. Try to hide the lengthwise seam under a stem where possible.

Instructions

Instructions are given for the size shown in photo, with other sizes in parentheses. When only 1 number is given, it applies to all sizes.

Step 1. Prepare a bright green mottled rectangle referring to Figure 1 for sizes.

Step 2. Cut (and piece) two strips each hot pink mottled 3 1/2" x 38 1/2" (4 1/2" x 68 1/2") (4 1/2" x 79 1/2") and 3 1/2" x 37 1/2" (4 1/2" x 58 1/2") (4 1/2" x 63 1/2") for borders; set aside.

Step 3. Cut dark green mottled into two (6) (6) 2" by fabric width strips. Subcut strips to make lengths as shown in Figure 1.

Step 4. Cut 2"-wide strips of fusible transfer web to fit dark green mottled strips. Fuse to wrong side of each strip; remove paper backing.

	Quilt Sizes		
	Crib	**Youth**	**Twin**
Finished Quilt Size	37" x 44"	58" x 76"	63" x 87"
Materials			
Bright green mottled	1 yard	4 yards	4 1/2 yards
Hot pink mottled	1/2 yard	1 1/4 yards	1 1/4 yards
Medium green mottled	1/4 yard	3/8 yard	3/8 yard
Dark green mottled	1/8 yard	3/8 yard	3/8 yard
10" x 20" rectangle orange and purple prints	1 each	1 each	1 each
10" x 20" rectangle pink and yellow prints	1 each	2 each	2 each
Black, yellow and red solids	scraps	scraps	scraps
Orange, pink, white, red and yellow prints	scraps	scraps	scraps
Red-with-white polka dot	scrap	scrap	scrap
Yellow/black stripe	scrap	scraps	scraps
Backing	41" x 48"	62" x 80"	67" x 91"
Batting or quilter's fleece	41" x 48"	62" x 80"	67" x 91"
Batting or quilter's fleece (for flowers)	20" x 20"	30" x 30"	30" x 30"
Self-made or purchased binding	5 yards	8 yards	9 yards
White all-purpose thread			
White machine-quilting thread			
Black, yellow, white, pink, green, orange and red rayon thread			
Fusible transfer web	1 1/2 yards	2 1/2 yards	2 3/4 yards
Tear-off fabric stabilizer	2 yards	6 yards	6 1/2 yards
Basic sewing supplies and tools			

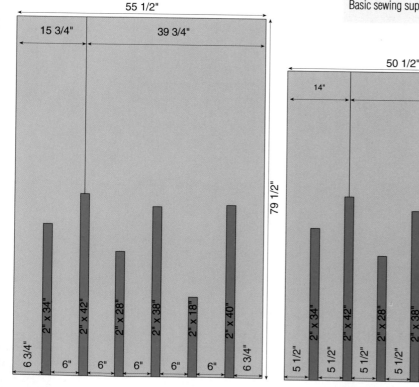

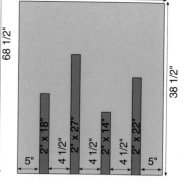

Figure 1
Arrange stem pieces on background pieces.

Step 5. Arrange stem pieces on background pieces again referring to Figure 1; fuse in place.

Step 6. Prepare templates for appliqué shapes except flowers. Trace shapes on the paper side of the fusible transfer web as directed on pattern pieces for number to cut. Cut out shapes, leaving a margin around each one. Fuse shapes to the wrong side of fabrics as directed on pattern pieces for color. Cut out shapes on traced lines; remove paper backing.

Step 7. Trace four (5) (5) flower shapes onto quilter's fleece; cut loosely around each one.

Step 8. Fold each 10" x 20" fabric rectangle in half with right sides together. Pin fleece to one side. Sew directly on traced line on fleece. Trim away excess fabric; clip corners and curves. Make a small slit in the center of each flower; turn right side out and press.

Step 9. Arrange leaves along stems, bee(s) on background and ladybug on bottom corner referring to the Placement Diagram for positioning suggestions. Fuse shapes in place. Fuse flower centers on flowers.

Step 10. Pin flowers to top of stems. Pin tear-off fabric stabilizer behind background piece. Using rayon thread to match fabrics in the top of the machine and white all-purpose thread in the bobbin, machine zigzag-stitch around ladybug and bee shapes, along stem edges, around leaves and around flower centers (leaving flower edges free). Zigzag-stitch antennae on ladybug and bee(s) using black rayon thread in the top of the machine and all-purpose thread in the bobbin and referring to the Placement Diagram for positioning.

Step 11. When all stitching is complete, remove fabric stabilizer.

Step 12. Sew a 3 1/2" x 38 1/2" (4 1/2" x 68 1/2") (4 1/2" x 79 1/2") hot pink mottled strip to each long side and a 3 1/2" x 37 1/2" (4 1/2" x 58 1/2") (4 1/2" x 63 1/2") hot pink mottled strip to the top and bottom; press seams toward strips.

Step 13. Prepare top for quilting and finish using self-made or purchased binding referring to the General Instructions. **Note:** *The quilt shown was machine-quilted in the ditch of border seams and 1/8" from all appliqué pieces using white machine-quilting thread.* ❧

3" x 37"

Garden Friends
Placement Diagram
37" x 44"

Flower Center
Cut 1 (1) (1) each orange & pink scraps &
1 (2) (2) each red & yellow scraps

Ladybug Head
Cut 1 (1) (1) black solid

Bee Head
Cut 1 (2) (3) yellow solid

Garden Friends
Placement Diagram
58" x 76"

Garden Friends
Placement Diagram
63" x 87"

Place line on fold

Ladybug
Cut 1 (1) (1) red-with-white polka dot

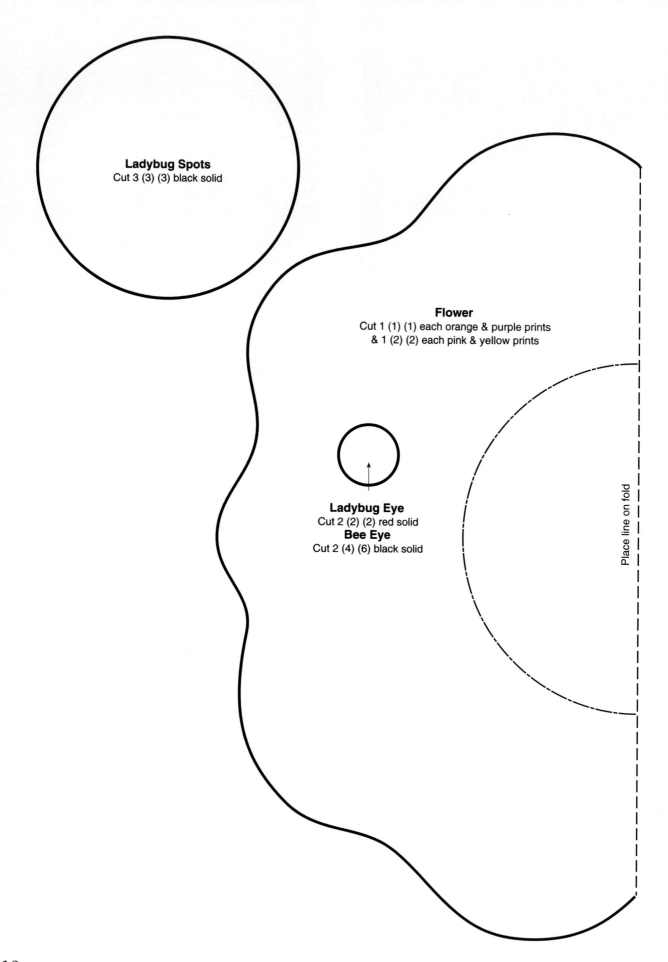

Ladybug Spots
Cut 3 (3) (3) black solid

Flower
Cut 1 (1) (1) each orange & purple prints
& 1 (2) (2) each pink & yellow prints

Ladybug Eye
Cut 2 (2) (2) red solid
Bee Eye
Cut 2 (4) (6) black solid

Place line on fold

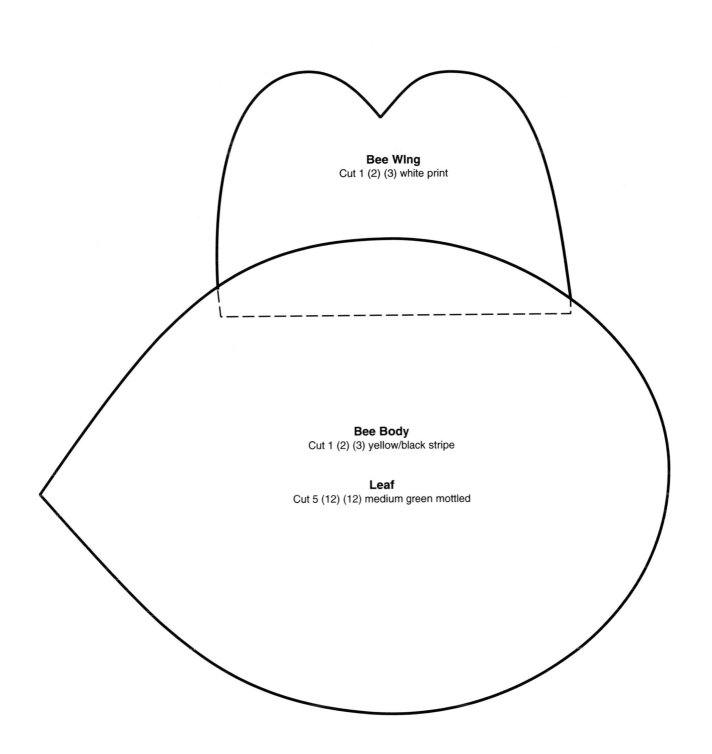

Bee Wing
Cut 1 (2) (3) white print

Bee Body
Cut 1 (2) (3) yellow/black stripe

Leaf
Cut 5 (12) (12) medium green mottled

Nine-Patch Rectangle

By Sandra L. Hatch

I like the idea of taking a traditional square block and turning it into a rectangle. Although the block has similar pieces, it really does look stretched in rectangular form. The Nine-Patch is an easy one to change and to stitch.

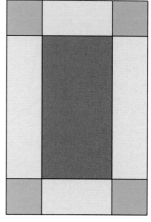

Nine-Patch Rectangle
6" x 9" Block

Project Notes

The sample quilt was made with a large variety of scraps, but cutting strips of four–six pastel prints to create the Nine-Patch blocks is also an option. The instructions are given for cutting individual pieces for the scrap method.

Instructions

Instructions are given for the size shown in photo, with other sizes in parentheses. When only 1 number is given, it applies to all sizes.

Step 1. Cut 25 (36) (49) rectangles pastel scraps 3 1/2" x 6 1/2" for A.

Step 2. Cut 50 (72) (98) rectangles pastel scraps 2" x 3 1/2" for B. **Note:** *Each block requires two same-fabric B and C pieces.*

Step 3. Cut 50 (72) (98) rectangles pastel scraps 2" x 6 1/2" for C.

Step 4. Cut eight (10) (13) strips green print 2" by fabric width; subcut into 2" squares for D. You will need 148 (205) (272) green print D squares.

Step 5. Cut two (2) (3) strips cream-on-cream print 9 1/2" by fabric width; subcut into 2" segments for E. You will need 30 (42) (56) E pieces.

Step 6. Cut two (2) (3) strips cream-on-cream print 6 1/2" by fabric width; subcut into 2" segments for F. You will need 30 (42) (56) F pieces.

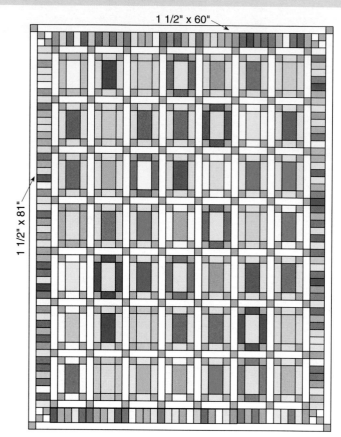

1 1/2" x 60"

1 1/2" x 81"

Nine-Patch Rectangle
Placement Diagram
63" x 84"

Quilt Sizes			
	Lap	**Youth**	**Twin**
Finished Quilt Size	48" x 63"	55 1/2" x 73 1/2"	63" x 84"
Block Size	6" x 9"	6" x 9"	6" x 9"
Number of Blocks	25	36	49

Materials			
Green print	1/2 yard	2/3 yard	1 yard
Cream-on-cream print	1 1/4 yards	1 1/2 yards	2 yards
Light and medium pastel scraps	2 1/2 yards	3 yards	3 1/2 yards
Backing	52" x 67"	60" x 78"	67" x 88"
Batting	52" x 67"	60" x 78"	67" x 88"
Self-made or purchased binding	6 3/4 yards	7 3/4 yards	9 1/4 yards
White all-purpose thread			
Clear nylon monofilament			
Basic sewing supplies and tools			

Step 7. To piece one block, sew two same-fabric C rectangles to opposite sides of an A rectangle. Sew D to each end of two B rectangles; sew to remaining sides of

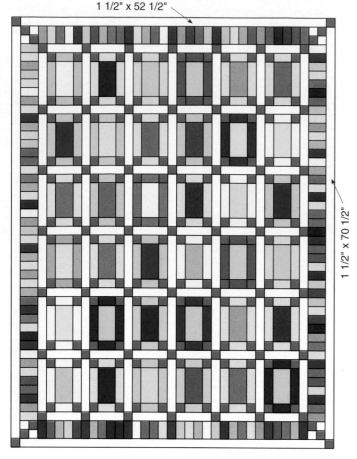

1 1/2" x 52 1/2"

1 1/2" x 70 1/2"

Nine-Patch Rectangle
Placement Diagram
55 1/2" x 73 1/2"

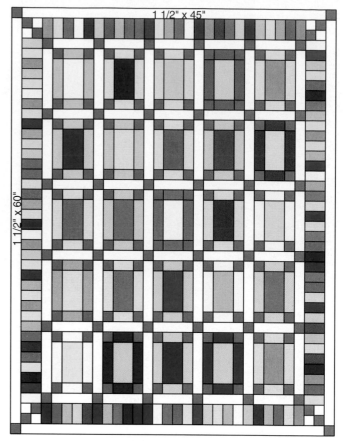

1 1/2" x 45"

1 1/2" x 60"

Nine-Patch Rectangle
Placement Diagram
48" x 63"

A referring to Figure 1 to complete one block. Press; repeat for 25 (36) (49) blocks. *Note: Use lighter B and C pieces with medium-colored A pieces and medium B and C pieces with lighter-colored A pieces.*

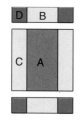

Figure 1
Join pieces as shown
to complete 1 block.

Step 8. Join five (6) (7) blocks with six (7) (8) E pieces to make a block row as shown in Figure 2; repeat for five (6) (7) block rows. Press seams toward E.

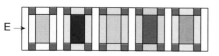

Figure 2
Join 5 blocks with 6 E pieces to make
a block row as shown.

Step 9. Join five (6) (7) F pieces with six (7) (8) D squares to make a sashing row as shown in Figure 3; repeat for six (7) (8) sashing rows. Press seams toward F.

Figure 3
Join 5 F pieces with 6 D squares
to make a sashing row.

Step 10. Join sashing rows with block rows, beginning and ending with sashing rows; press seams toward blocks.

Step 11. Cut 124 (148) (172) B rectangles 2" x 3 1/2" from a variety of pastel scraps. Join 26 (31) (36) B rectangles to make a strip as shown in Figure 4; repeat for two strips. Sew a strip to the top and bottom of the pieced center; press seams toward pieced strips. Repeat for two strips with 36 (43) (50) B rectangles each; set aside.

Figure 4
Join 26 B rectangles to make a strip.

Step 12. Cut eight 2" x 2" D squares cream-on-cream print. Join two cream-on-cream print D squares with two green print D squares to make a Four-Patch unit as shown in Figure 5; repeat for four Four-Patch units.

Figure 5
Join D squares as shown
to make a Four-Patch unit.

Continued on page 26

22 ◆ *101 Made-to-Fit Quilts for Your Home*

Flying Geese Strippy

By Sandra L. Hatch

Plaids, checks and stripes combine to make this scrappy quilt for a country accent as a den throw or in a masculine bedroom.

Project Notes

The sample quilt was made using sample scraps which were cut and used in a random placement. Choose at least 15 or more fabrics for your quilt to give it this scrappy look.

Instructions

Instructions are given for the size shown in photo, with other sizes in parentheses. When only 1 number is given, it applies to all sizes.

Step 1. Cut 17 (24) (30) 4 1/2" by fabric width strips from a variety of plaids, checks and stripe fabrics. Subcut strips into 2 1/2" segments for 270 (374) (468) A rectangles.

Step 2. Cut 15 (22) (27) 2 1/2" by fabric width strips from a variety of plaids, checks and stripe fabrics. Subcut strips into 2 1/2" segments for 240 (340) (432) B squares.

Step 3. Place a contrasting B square right sides together with an A rectangle and stitch on one diagonal referring to Figure 1. Trim excess beyond seam to 1/4" as shown in Figure 2. Press remaining B triangle section with seam away from A to make a unit as shown in Figure 3; repeat for 120 (170) (216) units.

Figure 1
Place a contrasting B square right sides together with an A rectangle and stitch on 1 diagonal.

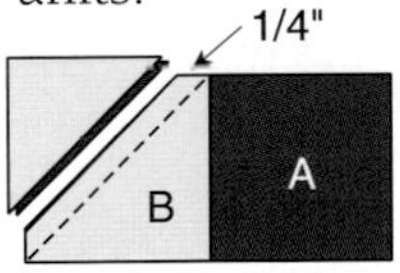

Figure 2
Trim excess beyond seam to 1/4".

Figure 3
Press remaining B triangle section with seam away from A to make a unit.

Step 4. Place a matching B square right sides together with a pieced A-B unit and stitch on the diagonal as shown in Figure 4. Trim excess beyond seam to 1/4" as in Step 3 and press to complete a Flying Geese unit as shown in Figure 5; repeat for 120 (170) (216) units.

Figure 4
Place a matching B square right sides together with a pieced A-B unit and stitch on the diagonal.

Quilt Sizes

	Twin	Double	Queen
Finished Quilt Size	63" x 79"	78" x 87"	89" x 91"
Block Size	2" x 4"	2" x 4"	2" x 4"
Number of Blocks	120	170	216

Materials

Brown solid	1 3/4 yards	2 yards	2 1/4 yards
Cream check	1/2 yard	1/2 yard	1/2 yard
Green plaid	2 yards	2 1/4 yards	2 1/2 yards
Plaids, checks and stripes	3 1/2 yards	5 yards	6 yards
Backing	67" x 83"	82" x 91"	93" x 95"
Batting	67" x 83"	82" x 91"	93" x 95"
Self-made or purchased binding	8 1/2 yards	9 1/2 yards	10 1/2 yards

- Neutral color all-purpose thread
- Clear nylon monofilament
- Basic sewing supplies and tools

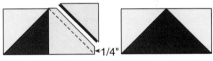

Figure 5
Trim excess beyond seam to 1/4"; press to complete a Flying Geese unit.

Step 5. Join 30 (34) (36) A rectangles to make a strip as shown in Figure 6; repeat for five (6) (7) strips. Press seams in one direction.

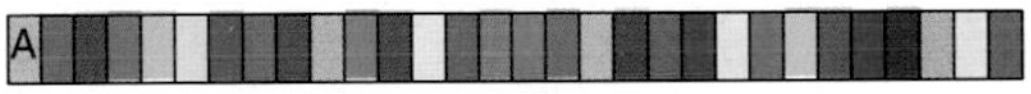

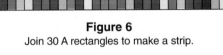

Figure 6
Join 30 A rectangles to make a strip.

Step 6. Cut 10 (12) (14) strips along length of brown solid 2" x 60 1/2" (68 1/2") (72 1/2"). Sew a brown solid strip to opposite long sides of each A strip as shown in Figure 7; press seams toward strips.

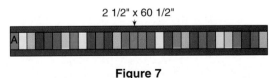

2 1/2" x 60 1/2"

Figure 7
Sew a brown solid strip to opposite long sides of each A strip.

Step 7. Join 30 (34) (36) Flying Geese units to make a strip; repeat for four (5) (6) strips.

Step 8. Join the A strips with the Flying Geese strips to complete the pieced center, referring to the Placement Diagram.

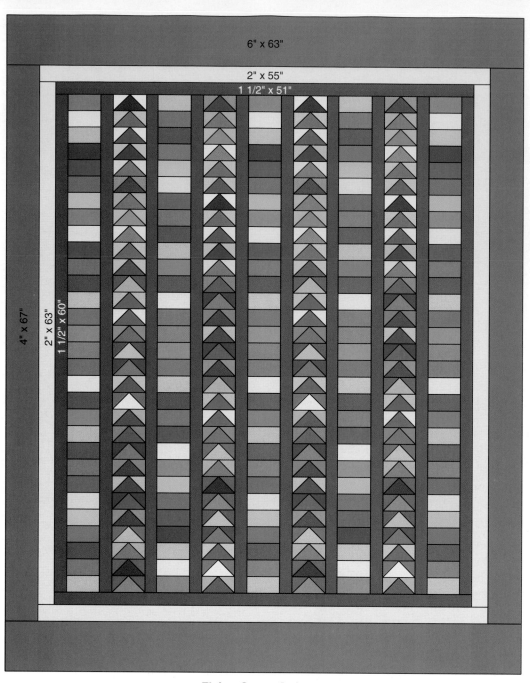

6" x 63"

2" x 55"

1 1/2" x 51"

4" x 67"

2" x 63"

1 1/2" x 60"

Flying Geese Strippy
Placement Diagram
63" x 79"

Step 9. Cut two strips along length of brown solid 2" x 51 1/2" (62 1/2") (73 1/2"). Sew a strip to the top and bottom of the pieced center; press seams toward strips.

Step 10. Cut and piece two strips each cream check 2 1/2" x 63 1/2" (71 1/2") (75 1/2") and 2 1/2" x 55 1/2" (66 1/2") (77 1/2"). Sew the longer strips to opposite long sides and the shorter strips to top and bottom of the pieced center; press seams toward strips.

Step 11. Cut two strips along length of green plaid 4 1/2" x 66 1/2" (6 1/2" x 75 1/2") (6 1/2" x 79 1/2"); sew a strip to opposite long sides of the pieced center. Press seams toward strips.

Step 12. Cut two strips along length of green plaid 6 1/2" x 63 1/2" (78 1/2") (89 1/2"); sew a strip to the top and bottom of the pieced center. Press seams toward strips.

Step 13. Prepare top for quilting and finish as desired referring to the General Instructions. **Note:** *The quilt shown was machine-quilted in the ditch of seams using clear nylon monofilament in the top of the machine and all-purpose thread in the bobbin.* ❧

Continued on page 26

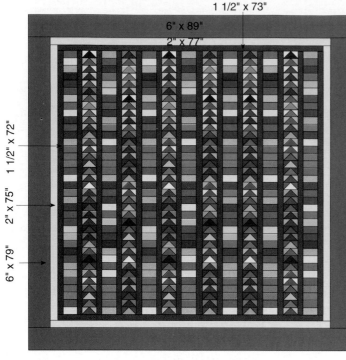

1 1/2" x 73"

6" x 89"

2" x 77"

1 1/2" x 72"

2" x 75"

6" x 79"

Flying Geese Strippy
Placement Diagram
89" x 91"

6" x 78"

2" x 66"

6" x 75"

2" x 71"

Flying Geese Strippy
Placement Diagram
78" x 87"

Whirlybird Bed Quilt

Continued from page 9

make a row, referring to Figure 8; repeat for one (2) (2) blue/white rows. Press seams in one direction.

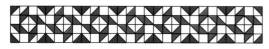

Figure 7
Join blocks to make a pink/white row.

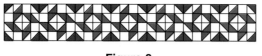

Figure 8
Join blocks to make a blue/white row.

Step 11. Join the block rows with the strip rows referring to the Placement Diagram; press seams toward pieced strips.

Step 12. Sew the 84 1/2"-long blue print strips cut in Step 1 to opposite long sides and the remaining blue print strips cut in Step 1 to the top and bottom of the pieced center; press seams toward strips.

Step 13. Prepare top for quilting and finish as desired referring to the General Instructions. *Note: The quilt shown was machine-quilted in a meandering pattern inside blocks using white all-purpose thread in the top of the machine and in the bobbin, and in straight lines on borders and strips using navy all-purpose thread in the top of the machine and in the bobbin.* ❧

Nine-Patch Rectangle

Continued from page 22

Step 13. Sew a Four-Patch unit to each end of the remaining pieced B strips as shown in Figure 6; press. Sew one of these pieced strips to each opposite long side of the pieced center; press seams toward strips.

Figure 6
Sew a Four-Patch unit to each
end of the pieced B strips.

Step 14. Cut and piece two strips each 2" x 60 1/2" (2" x 71") (2" x 81 1/2") and 2" x 45 1/2" (2" x 53") (2" x 60 1/2") cream-on-cream print. Sew the longer strips to opposite long sides; press seams toward strips. Sew a green print D square to each end of each shorter strip and sew to the top and bottom; press seams toward strips.

Step 15. Prepare top for quilting and finish as desired referring to the General Instructions. *Note: The quilt shown was machine-quilted in the ditch of seams using clear nylon monofilament in the top of the machine and all-purpose thread in the bobbin.* ❧

Flannel Four-Patch

By Holly Daniels

Today's flannel fabrics are suitable for projects other than baby quilts or nightgowns. Flannel quilts have a cuddly appeal no other fabric can match.

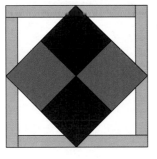

Flannel Four-Patch
12" x 12" Block

Instructions

Instructions are given for the size shown in photo, with other sizes in parentheses. When only 1 number is given, it applies to all sizes.

Step 1. From length of fabric, cut two strips each dark tan check 4 1/2" x 68 1/2" (4 1/2" x 86 1/2") (4 1/2" x 104 1/2") and 4 1/2" x 84 1/2" (4 1/2" x 84 1/2") (4 1/2" x 84 1/2"), four (5) (6) strips cream solid 2 1/2" x 84 1/2" and eight (10) (12) strips tan solid 2 1/2" x 84 1/2". Set aside for borders.

Step 2. Cut six (7) (9) strips tan plaid 4 3/4" by fabric width. From the remaining dark tan check cut 12 (14) (18) strips 4 3/4" x 21". Sew a tan plaid strip to two dark tan check strips with right sides together along length to make a strip set as shown in Figure 1; press seams toward dark tan check.

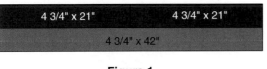

Figure 1
Sew a tan plaid strip to 2 dark tan check strips with right sides together along length to make a strip set.

Step 3. Cut each strip set into 4 3/4" segments. You will need 42 (56) (70) segments.

Step 4. Join two segments to make a Four-Patch unit as shown in Figure 2; press seams in one direction. Repeat for 21 (28) (35) Four-Patch units.

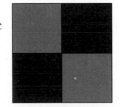

Figure 2
Join 2 segments to make a Four-Patch unit.

6 7/8"

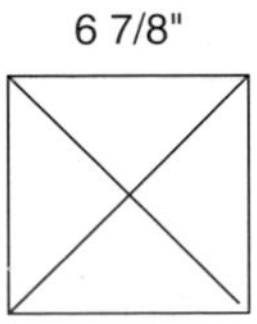

Figure 3
Cut 6 7/8" squares on both diagonals to make triangles.

Quilt Sizes

	Twin	Queen	King
Finished Quilt Size	68" x 92"	86" x 92"	104" x 92"
Block Size	12" x 12"	12" x 12"	12" x 12"
Number of Blocks	21	28	35

Materials

Tan plaid flannel	1 yard	1 yard	1 1/4 yards
Dark tan check flannel	2 1/2 yards	2 3/4 yards	3 yards
Tan solid flannel	3 yards	3 1/4 yards	5 yards
Cream solid flannel	2 1/2 yards	2 1/2 yards	2 1/2 yards
Backing	72" x 96"	90" x 96"	108" x 96"
Batting	72" x 96"	90" x 96"	108" x 96"
Self-made or purchased binding	9 1/2 yards	10 1/2 yards	11 1/2 yards
Neutral color and tan all-purpose thread			
Basic sewing supplies and tools			

Step 5. Cut 21 (28) (35) squares cream solid 6 7/8" x 6 7/8". Cut each square on both diagonals to make triangles as shown in Figure 3.

Step 6. Cut 84 (112) (140) strips tan solid 1 1/2" x 16"; cut each strip into two 8" segments. Sew one 8" segment to one short side of a cream solid triangle as shown in Figure 4; press seam toward segment. Trim segment even with angled edge of the triangle as shown in Figure 5; repeat for all cream solid triangles.

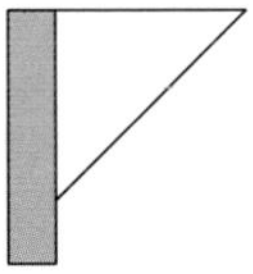

Figure 4
Sew 1 segment to 1 short side of a cream solid triangle.

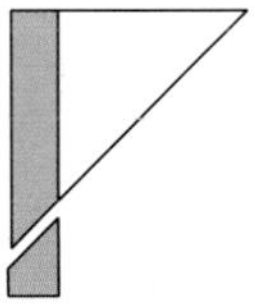

Figure 5
Trim segment even with angled edge of the triangle.

Step 7. Sew an 8" segment to the remaining short side of a cream solid triangle as shown in Figure 6; press seams toward segment. Trim segment even with angled edge of the triangle as in Step 6; repeat for all cream solid triangles.

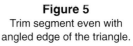

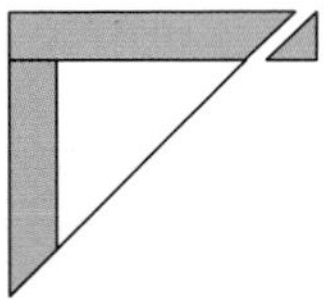

Figure 6
Sew a segment to the remaining short side of a cream solid triangle.

Step 8. Sew a tan/cream triangle unit to each side of a Four-Patch unit to complete one block as shown in Figure 7; press seams toward triangle units. Repeat for 21 (28) (35) blocks.

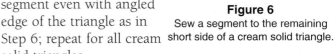

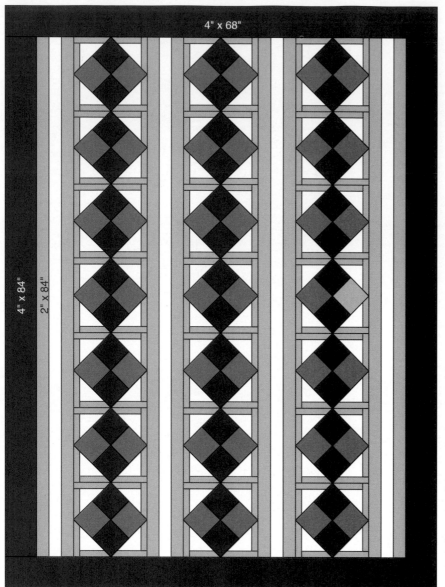

Flannel Four-Patch
Placement Diagram
68" x 92"

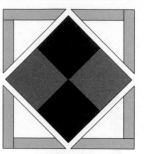

Figure 7
Sew a tan/cream triangle unit to
each side of a Four-Patch unit to
complete 1 block.

Step 9. Sew a cream solid border strip between two tan solid strips with right sides together along length to make a strip set; press seams toward tan solid strips. Repeat for four (5) (6) strip sets.

Step 10. Join seven pieced blocks to make a block row; press seams in one direction. Repeat for three (4) (5) block rows.

Step 11. Join the strip sets with the block rows, beginning and ending with a strip set; press seams toward strip sets.

Step 12. Sew a 4 1/2" x 84 1/2" border strip dark tan check to each long side of the pieced center; press seams toward strips. Sew the remaining dark tan check border strips to the top and bottom of the pieced center.

Step 13. Prepare top for quilting and finish as desired referring to the General Instructions. *Note: The quilt shown was machine-quilted in a meandering design using tan all-purpose thread.* ❧

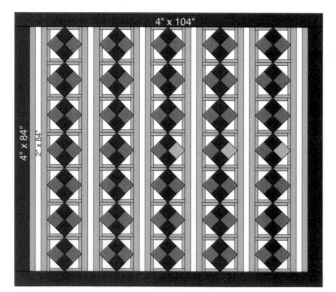

Flannel Four-Patch
Placement Diagram
104" x 92"

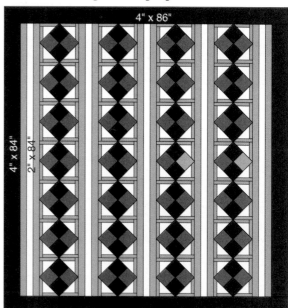

Flannel Four-Patch
Placement Diagram
86" x 92"

Chapter Two

Growing Up With Quilts

You'll find a variety of quilts in this chapter, beginning with a soft cuddly flannel quilt for your favorite baby and ending with a masculine quilt featuring bears and fishing. It's just right for decorating a college dorm room or guy's bedroom. You'll find quilts for everyone in between as well.

Baton Rouge Baby Quilt

By Holly Daniels

Soft pastel colors are used to make this pretty baby quilt. Hearts are appliquéd in the center of each block to show the love stitched into this little treasure.

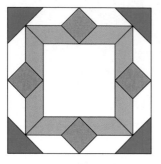

Baton Rouge
12" x 12" Block

Instructions

Instructions are given for the size shown in photo, with other sizes in parentheses. When only 1 number is given, it applies to all sizes.

Step 1. Prepare template for piece A using pattern piece given.

Step 2. Cut eight (20) (34) strips each white-on-white print and light green print 2" by fabric width. Sew a white-on-white print strip to a light green print strip along length with right sides together; press seams toward light green print. Repeat for eight (20) (34) strip sets.

Step 3. Place the A template on one strip as shown in Figure 1 and cut; repeat for 36 (96) (168) A1 units. Turn template over and cut 36 (96) (168) A2 units as shown in Figure 2.

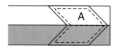 

Figure 1
Place the A template on 1 strip to make A1 units.

Figure 2
Reverse the A template to make A2 units.

Step 4. Cut three (6) (11) strips light pink print 2 5/8" by fabric width. Cut each strip into 2 5/8" segments to make 36 (96) (168) B squares.

Step 5. Join an A1 unit to an A2 unit with B, setting in seams as shown in Figure 3; press seams away from B. Repeat for 36 (96) (168) units.

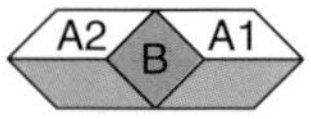

Figure 3
Join an A1 unit to an A2 unit with B, setting in seams.

Quilt Sizes

	Crib	Twin	Queen
Finished Quilt Size	42" x 42"	62" x 86"	86" x 98"
Block Size	12" x 12"	12" x 12"	12" x 12"
Number of Blocks	9	24	42

Materials

Dusty pink print	1/4 yard	3/8 yard	2/3 yard
Light pink print	5/8 yard	1 1/3 yards	2 yards
Light green print	5/8 yard	1 1/4 yards	2 1/4 yards
Medium green print	5/8 yard	1 1/2 yards	2 1/4 yards
White-on-white print	1 yard	2 yards	2 1/2 yards
Backing	46" x 46"	66" x 90"	66" x 90"
Batting	46" x 46"	66" x 90"	66" x 90"
Self-made or purchased binding	4 3/4 yards	8 3/4 yards	10 3/4 yards
White all-purpose thread			
Pink rayon thread			
Fusible transfer web	3/8 yard	3/4 yard	1 1/4 yards
Tear-off fabric stabilizer	3/8 yard	3/4 yard	1 1/4 yards
Basic sewing supplies and tools			

Step 6. Cut nine (24) (42) squares white-on-white print 6 1/2" x 6 1/2" for C. Sew an A-B unit to each side of C as shown in Figure 4; miter corner seams. Repeat for nine (24) (42) units.

Step 7. Cut 18 (48) (84) squares medium green print 3 7/8" x 3 7/8". Cut each square in half on one diagonal to make D triangles. Sew a D triangle to each corner of the unit to complete one Baton Rouge block as shown in Figure 5; press. Repeat for nine (24) (42) blocks.

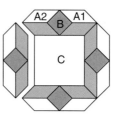 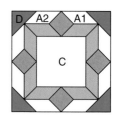

Figure 4
Sew an A-B unit to each side of C.

Figure 5
Sew a D triangle to each corner of the unit to complete 1 block.

Step 8. Prepare template for heart shape using pattern given. Prepare for machine appliqué referring to the General Instructions and referring to pattern for color and number to cut.

Step 9. Center and fuse a heart shape on each block referring to the manufacturer's instructions and the

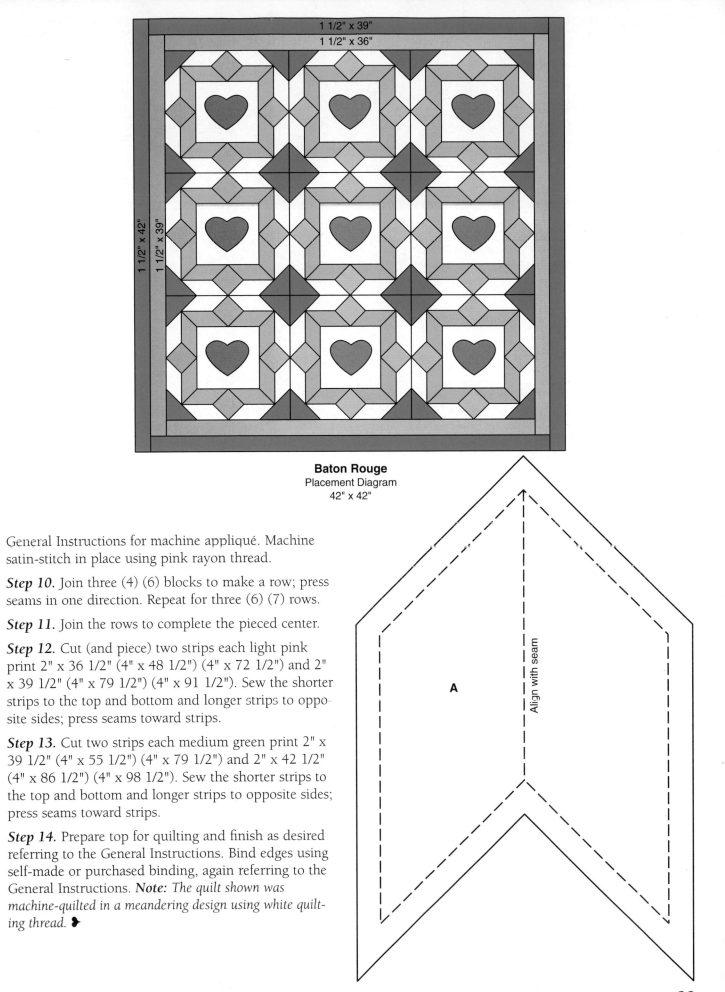

Baton Rouge
Placement Diagram
42" x 42"

General Instructions for machine appliqué. Machine satin-stitch in place using pink rayon thread.

Step 10. Join three (4) (6) blocks to make a row; press seams in one direction. Repeat for three (6) (7) rows.

Step 11. Join the rows to complete the pieced center.

Step 12. Cut (and piece) two strips each light pink print 2" x 36 1/2" (4" x 48 1/2") (4" x 72 1/2") and 2" x 39 1/2" (4" x 79 1/2") (4" x 91 1/2"). Sew the shorter strips to the top and bottom and longer strips to opposite sides; press seams toward strips.

Step 13. Cut two strips each medium green print 2" x 39 1/2" (4" x 55 1/2") (4" x 79 1/2") and 2" x 42 1/2" (4" x 86 1/2") (4" x 98 1/2"). Sew the shorter strips to the top and bottom and longer strips to opposite sides; press seams toward strips.

Step 14. Prepare top for quilting and finish as desired referring to the General Instructions. Bind edges using self-made or purchased binding, again referring to the General Instructions. ***Note:*** *The quilt shown was machine-quilted in a meandering design using white quilting thread.* ❧

A

Align with seam

3 1/2" x 55"

3 1/2" x 48"

3 1/2" x 86"

3 1/2" x 79"

Baton Rouge
Placement Diagram
62" x 86"

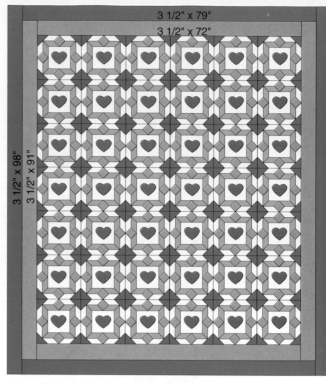

3 1/2" x 79"

3 1/2" x 72"

3 1/2" x 98"

3 1/2" x 91"

Baton Rouge
Placement Diagram
86" x 98"

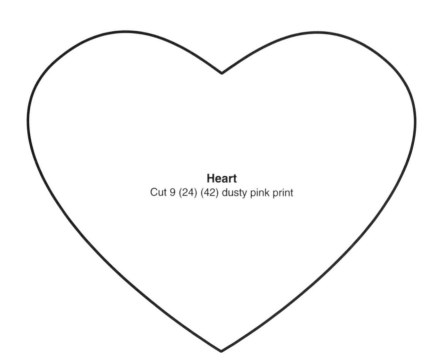

Heart
Cut 9 (24) (42) dusty pink print

Bears Gone Fishing

By Barbara Clayton

Make this outdoor-lover's quilt for the sportsman in your family. It is rugged and will withstand lots of wear and tear.

Bear
9" x 9" Block

Trees
9" x 9" Block

Fish
4" x 4" Block

Quilt Sizes			
	Twin	**Youth**	**Double**
Approximate Finished Quilt Size	64" x 90"	51" x 77"	77" x 90"
Block Size	9" x 9"	9" x 9"	9" x 9"
Number of Blocks	24	15	30

Materials			
Light brown print	1/8 yard	1/8 yard	1/8 yard
Red print	1/3 yard	1/3 yard	3/8 yard
Green print 1 and green print 2	5/8 yard each	3/8 yard each	5/8 yard each
Brown print	1/2 yard	1/2 yard	1/2 yard
Dark blue denim (60" wide)	1/2 yard	1/2 yard	1/2 yard
Medium blue denim (60" wide)	1 yard	3/4 yard	1 yard
Light blue denim (60" wide)	1 3/4 yards	1 1/4 yards	2 yards
Navy/red plaid	2 yards	1 1/2 yards	2 1/4 yards
Backing	68" x 94"	55" x 81"	81" x 94"
Batting	68" x 94"	55" x 81"	81" x 94"
Self-made or purchased denim binding	9 yards	7 1/2 yards	9 3/4 yards
Fusible transfer web	3 1/4 yards	2 yards	4 yards
Tear-off fabric stabilizer	3 1/4 yards	2 yards	4 yards
Navy all-purpose thread			
Green, brown, red and black rayon thread			
Navy quilting thread			
Basic sewing supplies and tools			

Instructions

Instructions are given for the size shown in photo, with other sizes in parentheses. When only 1 number is given, it applies to all sizes.

Step 1. Prepare templates for appliqué motifs. Prepare for machine appliqué as directed in the General Instructions and referring to patterns for color and number to cut.

Step 2. Cut 24 (15) (30) background squares light blue denim 9 1/2" x 9 1/2".

Step 3. Arrange the bear motif on 12 (8) (15) of the background squares referring to the Placement Diagram and block drawing for positioning and layering pieces in numerical order referring to circled numbers on pattern. Fuse in place referring to manufacturer's instructions.

Step 4. Machine-appliqué bears and ears in place and add detail lines inside bear using brown rayon thread in the top of the machine and all-purpose thread in the bobbin. Repeat for trees using green rayon thread. Machine satin-stitch the nose, eyes and claws with black rayon thread.

Step 5. Repeat Step 3 and 4 with with large and medium tree motifs on 12 (7) (15) background squares and machine-appliqué in place using green rayon thread.

Step 6. Cut 35 (24) (42) squares medium blue denim 4 1/2" x 4 1/2". Center a fish shape on 17 (12) (21) of these squares and repeat Steps 3 and 4 to complete appliqué using red rayon thread.

Step 7. Cut 58 (38) (71) sashing strips navy/red plaid 4 1/2" x 9 1/2".

Step 8. Join two (2) (3) Bear blocks and two (1) (2) Tree blocks with five (4) (6) sashing strips to make a row as shown in Figure 1; press seams toward strips. Repeat for three (3) (3) rows.

4 1/2" x 9 1/2"

Figure 1
Join blocks and sashing strips to make a row.

Step 9. Join two (1) (2) Bear blocks and two (2) (3) Tree blocks with five (4) (6) sashing strips to make a row as shown in Figure 2; press seams toward strips. Repeat for three (2) (3) rows.

4 1/2" x 9 1/2"

Figure 2
Join blocks and sashing strips to make a row.

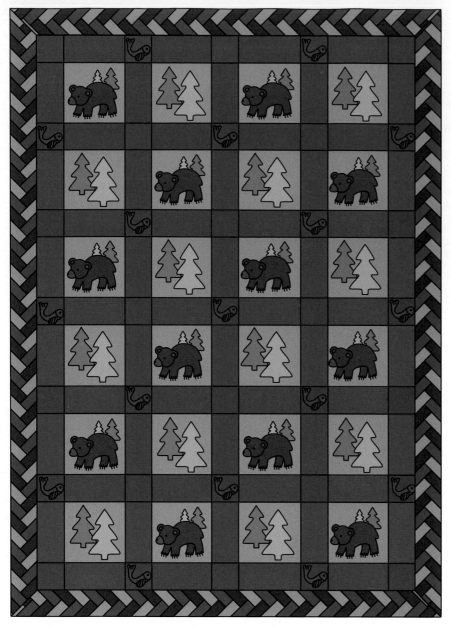

Bears Gone Fishing
Placement Diagram
Approximately 64" x 90"

Fish
Cut 17 (12) (21) red print

Step 10. Join two (2) (3) Fish blocks with three (3) (3) 4 1/2" x 4 1/2" medium blue denim squares and four (3) (5) sashing strips to make a sashing row as shown in Figure 3; press seams toward squares. Repeat for four (3) (4) sashing rows.

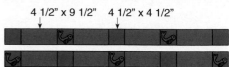

4 1/2" x 9 1/2"   4 1/2" x 4 1/2"

Figure 3
Join Fish blocks, squares and sashing strips to make a sashing row.

Step 11. Join three (2) (3) Fish blocks with two (2) (3) 4 1/2" x 4 1/2" medium blue denim squares and four (3) (5) sashing strips to make a sashing row again referring to Figure 3; press seams toward squares. Repeat for three (3) (3) sashing rows.

Step 12. Join the block rows with the sashing rows referring to the Placement Diagram for arrangement; press seams in one direction.

Step 13. Cut three (4) (4) strips each 4" by fabric width from light, medium and dark blue denims. Subcut each strip into 2" segments.

Step 14. Begin piecing border strips by sewing a dark blue segment to a light blue segment as shown in Figure 4. Add a medium blue segment then a light blue segment referring to Figure 5. Continue this pattern to make two strips with 72 (60) (84) segments and two strips with 96 (72) (96) segments as shown in Figure 6. Press each strip.

Figure 4
Begin piecing border strips by sewing a dark blue segment to a light blue segment.

Figure 5
Add a medium blue segment then a light blue segment.

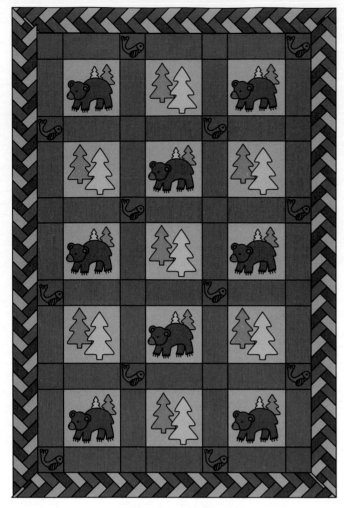

Bears Gone Fishing
Placement Diagram
Approximately 51" x 77"

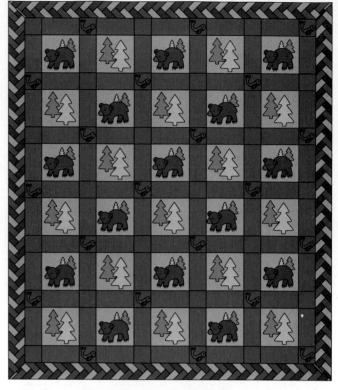

Bears Gone Fishing
Placement Diagram
Approximately 77" x 90"

Step 15. Trim both long sides of each strip even with the outside intersection of the segments as shown in Figure 7. Square-off the top and bottom edges as shown in Figure 8.

Step 16. Center and sew the shorter strips to the top and bottom and the longer strips to opposite long sides of the pieced center; miter corners. Press corner seams open.

Step 17. Prepare top for quilting and finish as desired referring to the General Instructions. Bind edges using denim binding, again referring to the General Instructions. *Note: The quilt shown was hand-quilted 1/4" away from all appliqué motifs and from edges of background blocks using navy quilting thread.* ❧

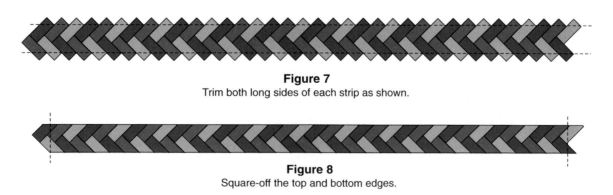

Figure 6
Continue this pattern to make 2 strips with 72 (60) (84) pieces and 2 strips with 96 (72) (96) pieces as shown.

Figure 7
Trim both long sides of each strip as shown.

Figure 8
Square-off the top and bottom edges.

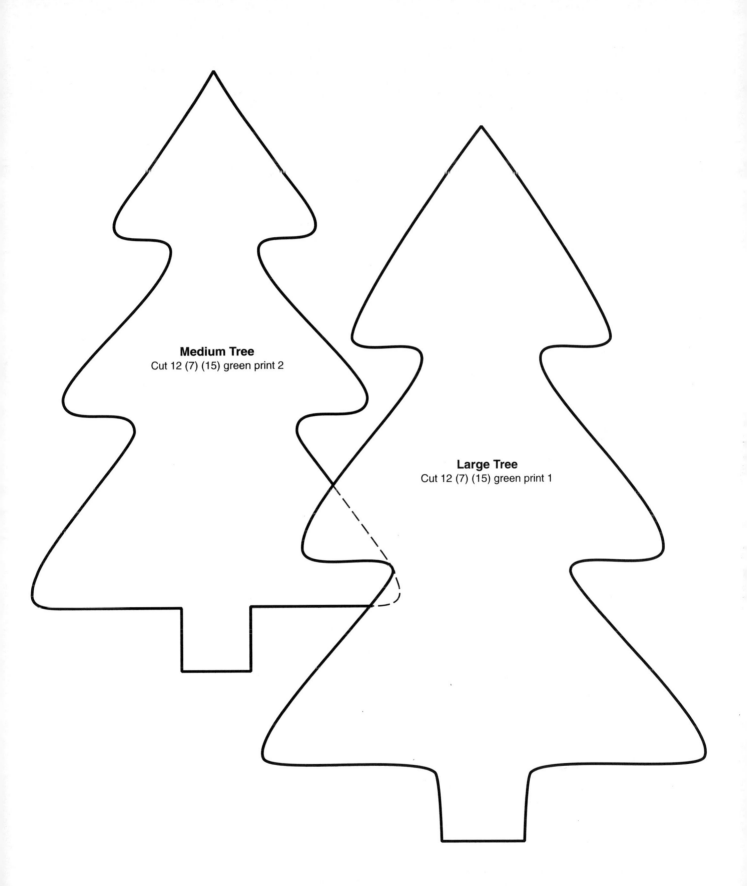

Medium Tree
Cut 12 (7) (15) green print 2

Large Tree
Cut 12 (7) (15) green print 1

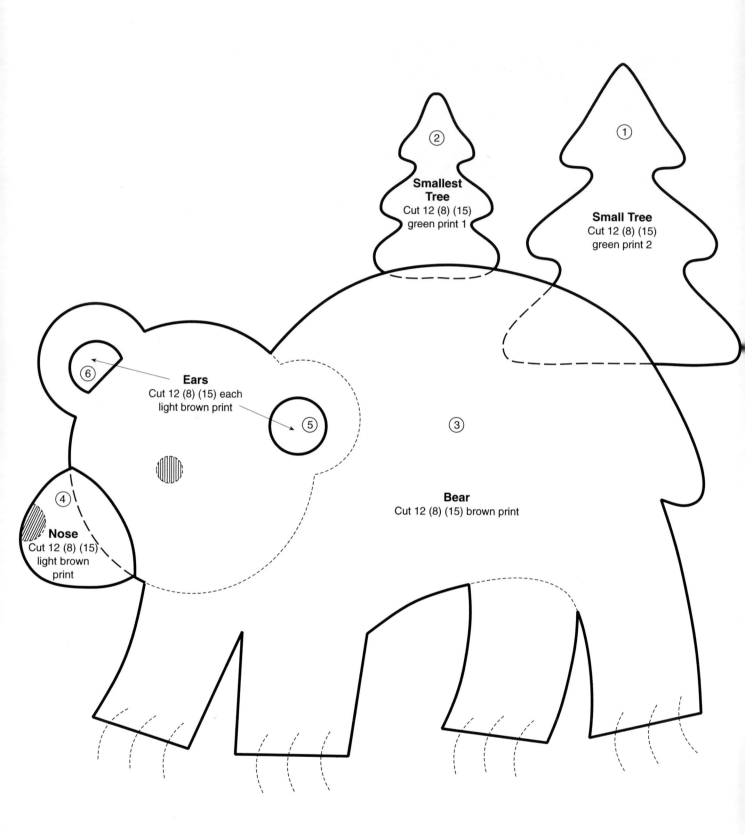

②
Smallest Tree
Cut 12 (8) (15)
green print 1

①
Small Tree
Cut 12 (8) (15)
green print 2

⑥
Ears
Cut 12 (8) (15) each
light brown print
⑤

③

Bear
Cut 12 (8) (15) brown print

④
Nose
Cut 12 (8) (15)
light brown
print

Rocket in Outer Space

By Leslie Hartsock

A future astronaut may be dreaming under this quilt which shines with fabric showing the outer galaxies.

Instructions

Instructions are given for the size shown in photo, with other sizes in parentheses. When only 1 number is given, it applies to all sizes.

Step 1. Cut along length of fabric two 6" x 60 1/2" (5 1/2" x 51 1/2") (6" x 60 1/2") strips, two 8" x 39" (6" x 33") (8" x 39") strips, two 6" x 30" (5 1/2" x 24") (6" x 30") strips, two 5" x 5" (3" x 3") (5" x 5") squares and two 5 1/2" x 5 1/2" (3 1/2" x 3 1/2") (5 1/2" x 5 1/2") squares from planet print. **Note:** *For twin-size quilt, also cut one strip 8" x 47", two strips 8" x 87" and one strip 13 1/2" x 47" from planet print.*

Step 2. Cut one each 12" x 12" (10" x 10") (12" x 12") squares orange and red marbled and two 8" x 8" (6" x 6") (8" x 8") squares red marbled.

Step 3. Cut two 12" x 12" (10" x 10") (12" x 12") squares purple marbled.

Step 4. Cut (and piece) two 2" x 30" (2" x 24") (2" x 30") strips, two 2" x 46 1/2" (2" x 38 1/2") (2" x 46 1/2") strips and four 7" x 7" (7" x 7") (7" x 7") squares lime green mottled. **Note:** *For twin-size quilt, also cut two strips each 3 1/2" x 47" and 3 1/2" x 60 1/2" lime green mottled.*

Step 5. Pin a 5" x 5" (3" x 3") (5" x 5") square planet print to one corner of each 8" x 8" (6" x 6") (8" x 8") square red marbled. Sew on one diagonal of each square referring to Figure 1; trim seam to 1/4" beyond stitching line. Fold open and press to complete rocket base squares as shown in Figure 2.

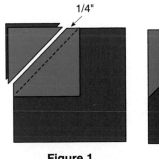

Figure 1
Sew on 1 diagonal of each square; trim seam to 1/4" beyond stitching line.

Figure 2
Fold open and press to complete rocket base squares.

Step 6. Sew a 5 1/2" x 5 1/2" (3 1/2" x 3 1/2") (5 1/2" x 5 1/2") square planet print to two adjacent corners of the remaining red marbled square; trim, fold and press

Quilt Sizes

	Youth	Crib	Twin
Finished Quilt Size	40 1/2" x 60"	33 1/2" x 51"	61 1/2" x 86 1/2"

Materials

Purple and orange marbled	1/2 yard	1/3 yard	1/2 yard
Red marbled	3/8 yard	1/3 yard	3/8 yard
Lime green mottled	5/8 yard	3/8 yard	3/4 yard
Planet print	2 yards	1 3/4 yards	4 yards
Backing	44" x 64"	37" x 55"	65" x 91"
Batting or quilter's fleece	44" x 64"	37" x 55"	65" x 91"
Quilter's fleece for fire	12" x 12"	10" x 10"	12" x 12"
Self-made or purchased binding	6 yards	5 1/4 yards	8 3/4 yards
Neutral color all-purpose thread			
Lime rayon thread			
Clear nylon monofilament			
Fusible transfer web	1/2 yard	1/2 yard	1/2 yard
Tear-off fabric stabilizer	1/2 yard	1/2 yard	1/2 yard
Basic sewing supplies and tools			

as for rocket base squares to complete rocket top as shown in Figure 3.

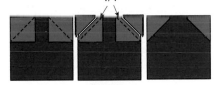

Figure 3
Complete rocket top as shown.

Step 7. Prepare template for the star shape. Prepare for machine-appliqué referring to the General Instructions and template for color and number to cut. **Note:** *Use small star pattern for crib-size quilt.*

Step 8. Center and fuse a star shape on the rocket top, each rocket bottom and the orange marbled square; appliqué in place using lime rayon thread referring to the General Instructions.

Step 9. Join the rocket top with the purple and orange marbled squares referring to Figure 4; press seams in one direction.

Step 10. Sew the rocket bottom blocks to one end of each 8" x 39" (6" x 33") (8" x 39") planet print strip as shown in Figure 5. Sew a pieced strip to each side of the pieced center section referring to Figure 6; press seams toward strips.

Step 11. Prepare template for fire shape; cut as directed on piece. Place two shapes right sides together; pin

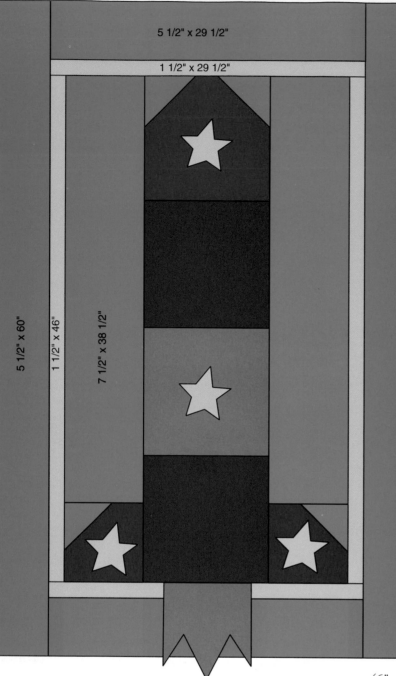

5 1/2" x 29 1/2"

1 1/2" x 29 1/2"

5 1/2" x 60"

1 1/2" x 46"

7 1/2" x 38 1/2"

Rocket in Outer Space
Placement Diagram
40 1/2" x 60"

Figure 4
Join the rocket top with
the purple and orange
marbled squares.

Figure 5
Sew the rocket bottom
blocks to 1 end of each 8" x
39" (6" x 33") (8" x 39")
planet print strip.

Figure 6
Sew a pieced strip to
each side of the
pieced center section.

quilter's fleece square to one side. Stitch all around, leaving top straight edge open. Trim batting close to seam; turn right side out and press. Baste top edge closed.

Step 12. Stitch three vertical lines through all layers using thread to match fabric and referring to Figure 7 for placement of stitching lines.

Figure 7
Stitch 3 vertical lines on
fire shape as shown.

Step 13. Center and pin quilted fire piece to bottom of pieced center referring to Figure 8.

Figure 8
Center and pin quilted
fire piece to bottom of
pieced center.

Step 14. Sew a 2" x 46 1/2" (2" x 38 1/2") (2" x 46 1/2") strip lime green mottled to opposite long sides and a 2" x 30" (2" x 24") (2" x 30") strip to the top and bottom; press seams toward strips.

Step 15. Sew a 6" x 30" (5 1/2" x 24") (6" x 30") strip planet print to the top and bottom and a 6" x 60 1/2" (5 1/2" x 51 1/2") (6" x 60 1/2") strip to opposite long sides of the pieced center; press seams toward strips. **Note:** *For twin-size quilt, also sew 3 1/2" x 60 1/2" and 3 1/2" x 47" lime green mottled strips to opposite long sides and the top and bottom. Sew the 8" x 47" planet print strip to the bottom, the 13 1/2" x 47" strip to the top and the 8" x 87" strips to opposite long sides.*

Step 16. Prepare top for quilting and finish as desired referring to the General Instructions. Bind edges using self-made or purchased binding, again referring to the General Instructions. **Note:** *The quilt shown was machine-quilted in a random pattern and with a few of the star designs using clear nylon monofilament in the top of the machine and all-purpose thread in the bobbin.* ❧

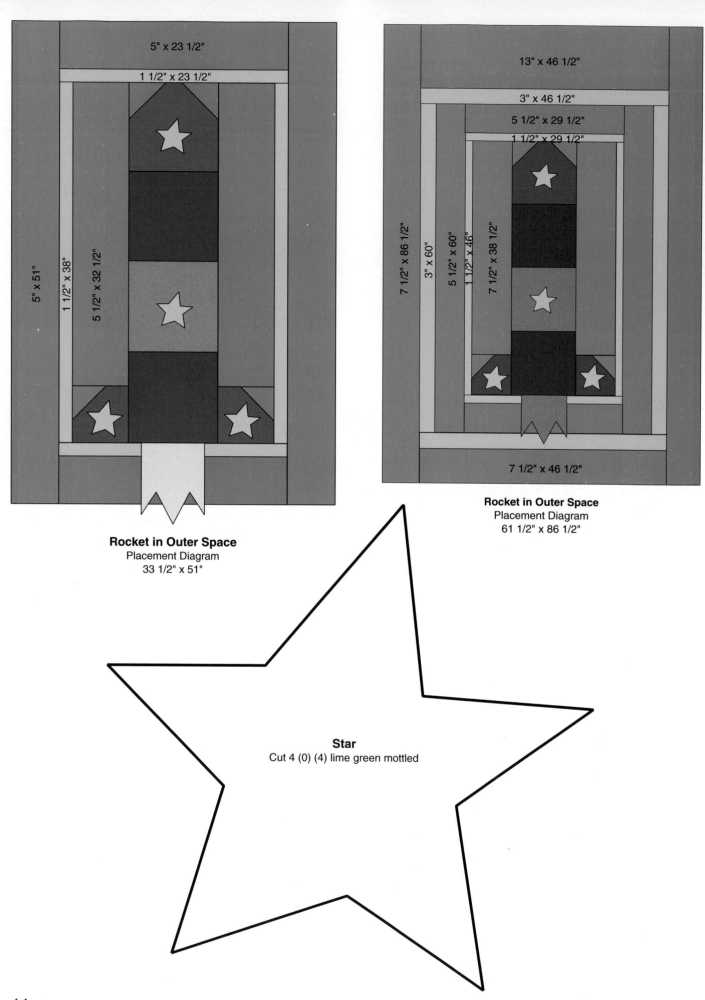

5" x 23 1/2"

1 1/2" x 23 1/2"

5" x 51"

1 1/2" x 38"

5 1/2" x 32 1/2"

Rocket in Outer Space
Placement Diagram
33 1/2" x 51"

13" x 46 1/2"

3" x 46 1/2"

5 1/2" x 29 1/2"

1 1/2" x 29 1/2"

7 1/2" x 86 1/2"

3" x 60"

5 1/2" x 60"

1 1/2" x 46"

7 1/2" x 38 1/2"

7 1/2" x 46 1/2"

Rocket in Outer Space
Placement Diagram
61 1/2" x 86 1/2"

Star
Cut 4 (0) (4) lime green mottled

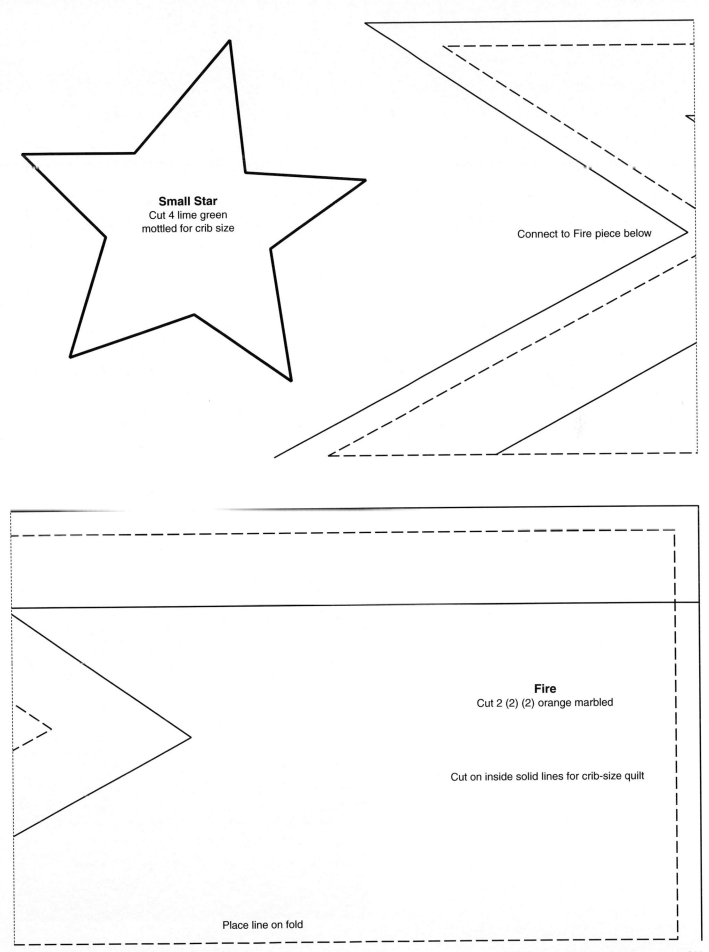

Small Star
Cut 4 lime green
mottled for crib size

Connect to Fire piece below

Fire
Cut 2 (2) (2) orange marbled

Cut on inside solid lines for crib-size quilt

Place line on fold

Bugs in My House

By Kathy Brown

One large Log Cabin block is all it takes to make this quilt. It can be any size you want— just keep adding logs to the outside. The quilt will always be square unless you make side strips narrower and top and bottom strips wider.

Instructions

Instructions are given for the size shown in photo, with other sizes in parentheses. When only 1 number is given, it applies to all sizes.

Step 1. Cut a square white bug print for center 8 1/2" x 8 1/2".

Step 2. Cut one strip 4 1/2" x 8 1/2" lime green print; sew to one side of the square; press seams toward strip. Cut another strip lime green print 4 1/2" x 12 1/2"; sew to the adjacent side of the square as shown in Figure 1. Cut a same-size strip yellow mottled and add to top; cut a yellow mottled strip 4" x 16 1/2" and sew to the remaining side.

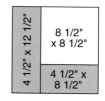

Figure 1
Sew the strip to the adjacent
side of the square.

Step 3. Continue to cut and piece as necessary 4 1/2"-wide strips referring to Figure 2 for length of each strip and starting with green bug print, then orange mottled; blue/green mottled and orange/purple mottled; blue bug print and red/orange print; purple print and red print.

Step 4. Sew strips to center in the sequence given and referring to the Placement Diagram for positioning of colors and to Figure 2 for size of strips. Press all seams away from the center. *Note: For king-size quilt, repeat Steps 1–4 to make four blocks. Join the blocks as shown in the Placement Diagram for larger quilt.*

Step 5. Prepare template for bug; prepare for machine-appliqué referring to the General Instructions. *Note: If you choose to put bugs on the king-size quilt, make number desired and purchase buttons and supplies for machine appliqué as needed.*

Step 6. Arrange bugs on completed top in a random pattern referring to the Placement Diagram for positioning suggestions.

Quilt Sizes		
	Lap	**King**
Finished Quilt Size	52" x 52"	100" x 100"
Center Size	8" x 8"	8" x 8"

Materials		
White bug print	8 1/2" x 8 1/2"	1/3 yard
Lime green print	1/6 yard	1/3 yard
Yellow mottled	1/6 yard	5/8 yard
Green bug print	1/6 yard	5/8 yard
Orange mottled	1/3 yard	7/8 yard
Blue/green mottled	1/3 yard	1 1/8 yards
Orange/purple mottled	1/3 yard	1 1/8 yards
Blue bug print	1/3 yard	1 1/8 yards
Red/orange print	1/3 yard	1 1/8 yards
Purple print	1/2 yard	1 1/4 yards
Red print	1/2 yard	1 1/4 yards
Bright bug print	1/2 yard	3/4 yard
Backing	52" x 52"	100" x 100"
Batting	52" x 52"	100" x 100"
Lime green, blue, purple, yellow, black and red all-purpose thread		
Fusible transfer web	1/2 yard	
Tear-off fabric stabilizer	1/2 yard	
7/8" black buttons	27	
Basic sewing supplies and tools		

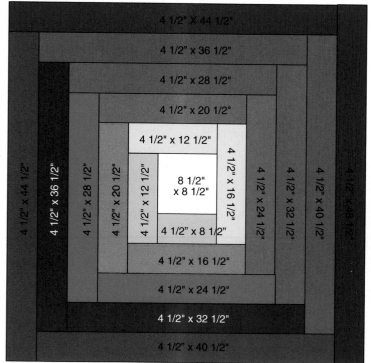

Figure 2
Sew strips to sides as shown.

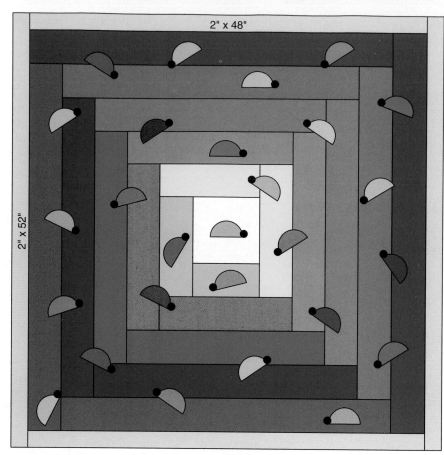

Bugs in My House
Placement Diagram
52" x 52"

Step 7. Machine-appliqué in place using a variety of bright thread colors referring to the General Instructions.

Step 8. Sew a 7/8" black button to one end of the bugs for heads using black all-purpose thread.

Step 9. Cut and piece two strips each bright bug print 2 1/2" x 48 1/2" (2 1/2" x 96 1/2") and 2 1/2" x 52 1/2" (2 1/2" x 100 1/2"). Sew the shorter strips to the top and bottom and longer strips to opposite sides; press seams toward strips.

Step 10. Place backing right sides together with quilt top; place batting on wrong side of backing.

Step 11. Stitch all around, leaving a 5" opening on one side. Turn right side out; press. Hand-stitch opening closed. Quilt as desired by hand or machine. *Note: The quilt shown was machine-quilted 1/4" from seams of each log with thread to match each fabric.* ❧

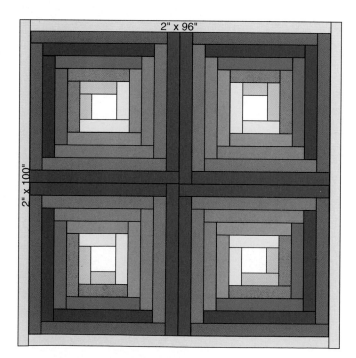

Bugs in My House
Placement Diagram
100" x 100"

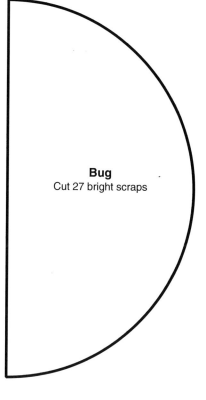

Bug
Cut 27 bright scraps

Tied With a Bow

By Sue Harvey

Traditional Jack-in-the-Box blocks surrounded by a pieced ribbon and bow border combine to make a warm and cuddly flannel quilt for your baby or toddler.

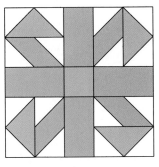

Jack-in-the-Box
7 1/2" x 7 1/2" Block

Quilt Sizes			
	Crib	**Youth**	**Twin**
Finished Quilt Size	32 1/2" x 44 1/2"	56 1/2" x 74 1/2"	65 1/2" x 83 1/2"
Block Size	7 1/2" x 7 1/2"	7 1/2" x 7 1/2"	7 1/2" x 7 1/2"
Number of Blocks	12	35	48
Materials			
Mint green print flannel	1/2 yard	1 yard	1 1/2 yards
White print flannel	1 yard	3 yards	3 3/4 yards
Mint green solid flannel	1 yard	2 3/4 yards	3 1/2 yards
Backing	36" x 48"	61" x 80"	71" x 89"
Batting	36" x 48"	61" x 80"	71" x 89"
Self-made or purchased binding	4 3/4 yards	8 yards	9 yards
White all-purpose thread			
Basic sewing supplies and tools			

Instructions

Instructions are given for the size shown in photo, with other sizes in parentheses. When only 1 number is given, it applies to all sizes.

Step 1. Cut five (14) (19) 3 1/2" by fabric width strips mint green solid flannel; subcut into 2" segments for A. You will need 96 (280) (384) A rectangles. Cut one (3) (4) 8" by fabric width strip; subcut into 2" segments for sashing strips. You will need 17 (58) (82) sashing strips.

Step 2. Cut three (7) (10) 3 1/2" by fabric width strips mint green print flannel; subcut into 2" segments for B. You will need 48 (140) (192) B rectangles. Cut one (3) (4) 2" by fabric width strip; subcut into 2" segments for D and sashing squares. You will need 12 (35) (48) D squares and six (24) (35) sashing squares.

Step 3. Cut 10 (27) (37) 2" by fabric width strips white print flannel; subcut into 2" segments for C. You will need 192 (560) (768) C squares.

Step 4. To make one block, place C right sides together on one end of A as shown in Figure 1; sew on the diagonal of C. Trim 1/4" from the stitching line as shown in Figure 2; press C open. Repeat on the opposite end of A as shown in Figure 3. Repeat for four A-C units.

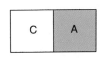

Figure 1
Place C on 1 end of A.

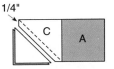

Figure 2
Sew on the diagonal of C;
trim seam allowance to 1/4".

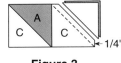

Figure 3
Place C on the opposite end
of A; sew on the diagonal of C
and trim seam allowance.

Step 5. Repeat Step 4 to make four B-C units referring to Figure 4 for correct placement of C on the B rectangle.

Step 6. Join an A-C unit with a B-C unit as shown in Figure 5; press seam toward the B-C unit. Repeat for four A-B-C units.

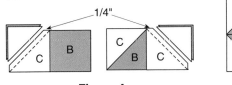

Figure 4
Place C on B as shown.

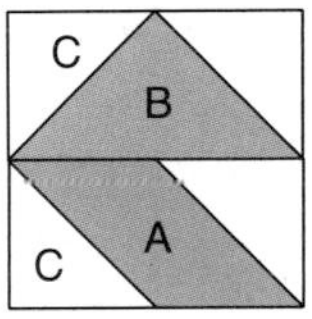

Figure 5
Join A-C with B-C.

Step 7. Join two A-B-C units with one A rectangle as shown in Figure 6; repeat. Join two A rectangles with one D square. Arrange the units in rows as shown in Figure 7; join rows to complete one Jack-in-the-Box block. Repeat to make 12 (35) (48) blocks.

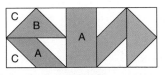

Figure 6
Join 2 A-B-C units with A.

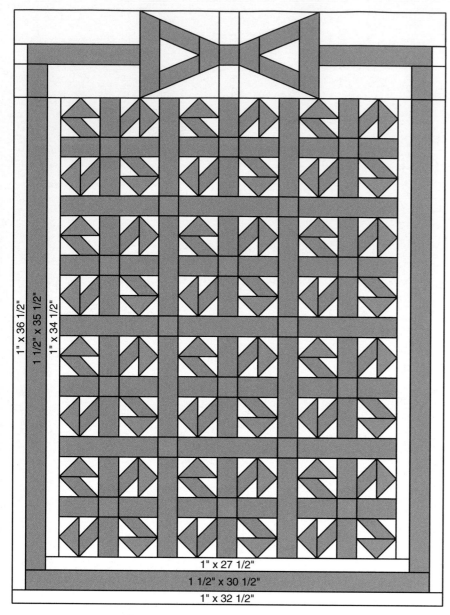

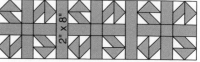

Figure 8
Join 3 blocks with 2 sashing strips
to make a block row.

Figure 9
Join 3 sashing strips with 2 sashing
squares to make a sashing row.

Step 10. Join block rows with sashing rows, beginning and ending with a block row.

Step 11. Cut one strip white print flannel 1 1/2" x 28" (3" x 49") (3" x 58") and two strips 1 1/2" x 35" (3" x 62") (3" x 71"). Sew the longer strips to opposite long sides and the shorter strip to the bottom of the pieced center.

Step 12. Cut one strip mint green solid flannel 2" x 31" (2" x 52") (2" x 61") and two strips 2" x 36" (2" x 64 1/2") (2" x 73 1/2"). Sew the longer strips to opposite long sides and the shorter strip to the bottom of the pieced center.

Step 13. Cut one strip white print flannel 1 1/2" x 33" (3" x 57") (3" x 66") and two strips 1 1/2" x 37 1/2" (3" x 66") (3" x 75"). Sew the longer strips to opposite long sides and shorter strip to the bottom of the pieced center.

Tied With a Bow
Placement Diagram
32 1/2" x 44 1/2"

Step 14. Prepare templates for pieces E–I; cut as directed on each piece. Cut one 2" x 2" square mint green solid flannel for J and two 2" x 3" rectangles white print flannel for K.

Step 15. Sew H and HR to opposite sides of F as shown in Figure 10; add E and G. Sew I and IR to opposite sides to complete one half-bow unit. Repeat to make two half-bow units.

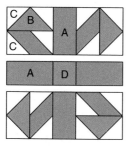

Figure 7
Arrange block units in rows; join units to
complete 1 Jack-in-the-Box block.

Step 8. Join three (5) (6) blocks with two (4) (5) sashing strips to make a block row as shown in Figure 8; repeat for four (7) (8) block rows.

Step 9. Join three (5) (6) sashing strips with two (4) (5) sashing squares to make a sashing row as shown in Figure 9. Repeat for three (6) (7) sashing rows.

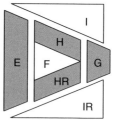

Figure 10
Sew H and HR to opposite
sides of F; add E and G. Sew
I and IR to opposite sides.

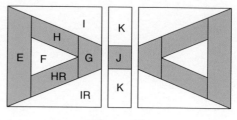

Step 16. Sew J between two K rectangles. Arrange units as shown in Figure 11; join units to complete one bow unit.

Figure 11
Arrange units to make 1 bow unit.

Step 17. Cut two each white print flannel rectangles 1 1/2" x 2" (2" x 3") (2" x 3"), 1 1/2" x 3" (3" x 3") (3" x 3"), 3" x 7 1/2" (3" x 18") (3" x 22 1/2") and 3" x 10" (3" x 22") (3" x 26 1/2"). Cut two each mint green solid flannel rectangles 2" x 3" (2" x 3") (2" x 3") and 2" x 9" (2" x 19 1/2") (2" x 24").

Step 18. Arrange white print flannel rectangles in rows with mint green solid rectangles as shown in Figure 12; join rows. Sew one pieced section to each side of the bow unit referring to the Placement Diagram for positioning. Sew to the top edge of the pieced and bordered quilt.

Step 19. Prepare top for quilting and finish as desired referring to the General Instructions. *Note: The quilt shown was machine-quilted in the ditch of the mint green solid pieces using white all-purpose thread in the top of the machine and in the bobbin.* ❧

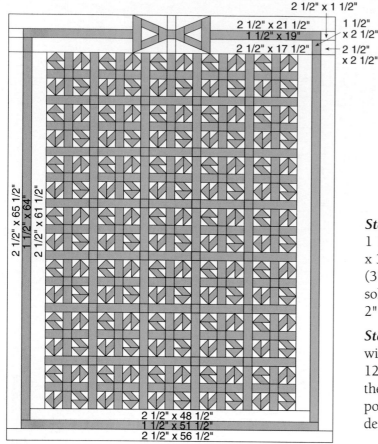

Tied With a Bow
Placement Diagram
56 1/2" x 74 1/2"

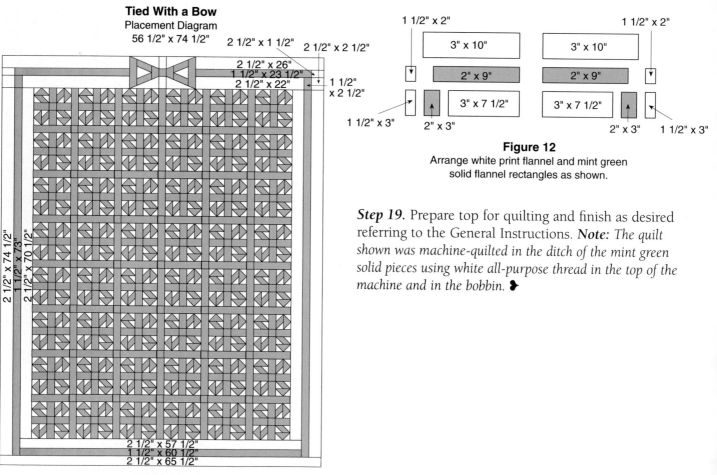

Figure 12
Arrange white print flannel and mint green
solid flannel rectangles as shown.

Tied With a Bow
Placement Diagram
65 1/2" x 83 1/2"

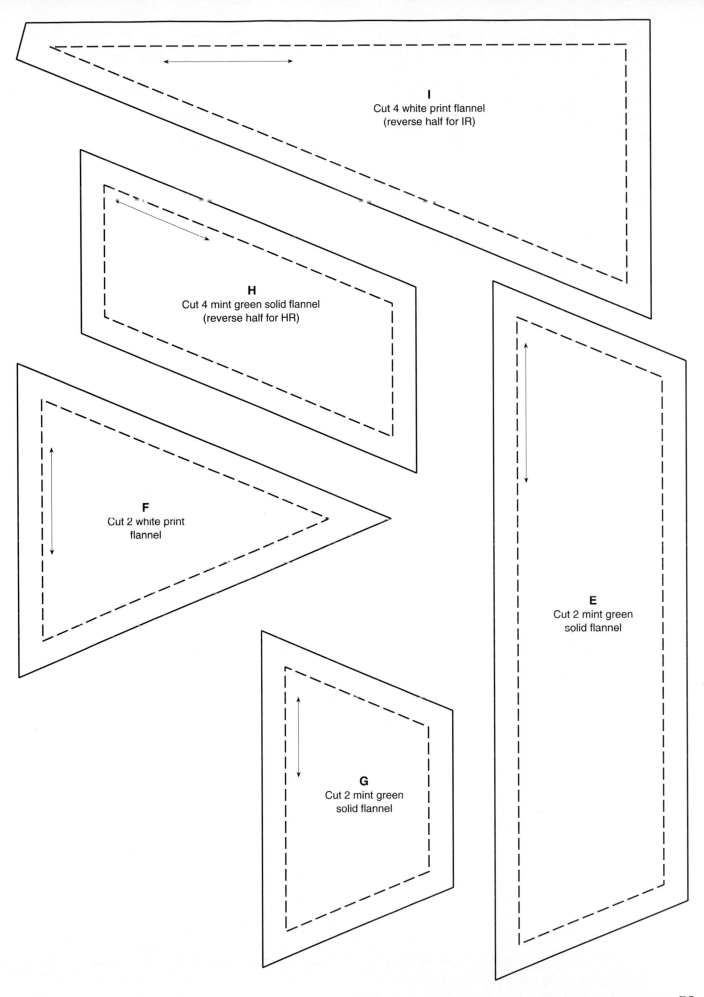

I
Cut 4 white print flannel
(reverse half for IR)

H
Cut 4 mint green solid flannel
(reverse half for HR)

F
Cut 2 white print
flannel

E
Cut 2 mint green
solid flannel

G
Cut 2 mint green
solid flannel

Good Night Good Earth

By Carla Schwab

Night colors and stars work together with the appliquéd earth to make this unique quilt in two different sizes.

Large Pinwheel
8" x 8" Block

Small Pinwheel
4" x 4" Block

Project Note

Separate instructions for putting together a larger quilt are given because the basic quilt is quite different when enlarged. Follow Steps 1–11 for both sizes, Steps 12–18 for the lap-size quilt and the separate instructions given for the twin-size quilt. The twin-size quilt has a pillow-tuck section which is included in the background.

Instructions

Instructions are given for the size shown in photo, with other sizes in parentheses. When only 1 number is given, it applies to all sizes.

Step 1. Cut a 32 1/2" x 36 1/2" (40 1/2" x 65 1/2") rectangle blue print for center background.

Step 2. Prepare templates for pieces E–L using patterns given; cut as directed on each piece. Do not add a seam allowance to each piece when cutting.

Step 3. Arrange cut pieces on the fusible side of the lightweight fusible interfacing with edges of pieces touching to make the earth design referring to Figure 1. Fuse shapes in place being careful not to touch iron on outside edges of fusible interfacing. Trim excess interfacing even with edges of fused area. Fuse again to secure fully.

Step 4. Apply fusible bias tape to all inner seams fusing all horizontal lines first. Using thread to match bias tape, stitch along both edges of tape to secure.

Step 5. Center the earth shape on the background rectangle; baste in place. Apply fusible bias tape all around, folding under end and overlapping beginning. Stitch in place as in Step 4. *Note: Center earth shape 18" from bottom edge of background rectangle for twin-size quilt.*

Step 6. Prepare templates for Large Pinwheel blocks using A and B patterns given. Cut as directed on each piece for one block; repeat for four (12) blocks.

Step 7. To piece one block, sew a blue print A to a yellow print A as shown in Figure 2; repeat for four units. Sew B to each A unit as shown in Figure 3; repeat for four units.

Quilt Sizes

	Lap	Twin
Finished Quilt Size	48" x 52"	64" x 97"
Block Size	8" x 8"	8" x 8"
	4" x 4"	4" x 4"
Number of Blocks	4 large	12 large
	2 small	2 small

Materials

	Lap	Twin
Variety of yellow prints	1/4 yard total	1/2 yard total
Green solid	5/8 yard	1 3/4 yards
Variety of green prints	1 yard total	1 yard total
Blue print	1 1/2 yards	3 yards
Green print	5/8 yard	1 yard
Backing	52" x 56"	68" x 101"
Batting	52" x 56"	68" x 101"
Self-made or purchased binding	6 yards	9 1/2 yards
All-purpose thread to match fabrics		
Lightweight fusible interfacing	1 yard	1 yard
1/4"-wide fusible green bias tape	5 1/2 yards	5 1/2 yards
Basic sewing supplies and tools		

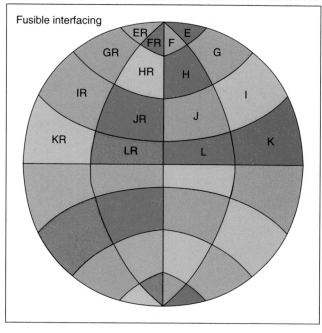

Figure 1
Arrange cut pieces on the fusible side of the lightweight fusible interfacing with edges of pieces touching to make the earth design.

Step 8. Join the A-B units as shown in Figure 4 to complete one Large Pinwheel block; repeat for four (12) blocks.

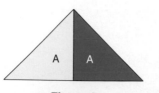

Figure 2
Sew a blue print A to a yellow print A.

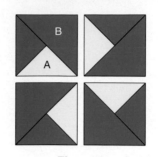

Figure 3
Sew B to each A unit.

Figure 4
Join the A-B units as shown to
complete 1 Large Pinwheel block.

Step 9. Prepare templates for Small Pinwheel blocks using C and D patterns given. Cut as directed on each piece for one block; repeat for two (2) blocks.

Step 10. To piece one block, sew a blue print C to a yellow print C as for Large Pinwheel; repeat for four

units. Sew D to each C unit as for Large Pinwheel; repeat for four units.

Step 11. Join the C-D units as for Large Pinwheel block to complete one Small Pinwheel block; repeat for two (12) blocks. *Note: For twin-size quilt, stop here and refer to instructions given for Twin-Size Quilt after Step 18.*

Step 12. Cut two strips each green solid 4 1/2" x 28 1/2" and 4 1/2" x 36 1/2" and one strip each green print 4 1/2" x 28 1/2", 4 1/2" x 32 1/2", 4 1/2" x 36 1/2" and 4 1/2" x 40 1/2".

Step 13. Sew a 28 1/2" green print and green solid strip with right sides together along length; press seams toward green print. Sew a Large Pinwheel block to the pieced strip referring to Figure 5.

4 1/2" x 28 1/2"

Figure 5
Sew a Large
Pinwheel block to
the pieced strip.

Step 14. Sew a 36 1/2" green print and green solid strip with right sides together along length; press seams toward green print.

Step 15. Sew a Small Pinwheel block to the end of one green solid 28 1/2" and one green solid 36 1/2" strip. Sew the 28 1/2" block/strip to the 32 1/2" green print strip; sew two Large Pinwheel blocks to the end opposite the small block end to make the top strip as shown in Figure 6. Repeat with the 36 1/2" block/strip and the 40 1/2" green print strip to make the bottom border strip as shown in Figure 7.

Step 16. Sew the pieced border strips to the appliquéd center referring to Figure 8.

Step 17. Mark straight vertical lines 1 1/2" apart on center background for quilting referring to the General Instructions.

Step 18. Prepare top for quilting and finish as desired referring to the General Instructions. Bind edges using self-made or purchased binding, again

Good Night Good Earth
Placement Diagram
48" x 52"

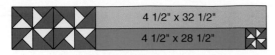

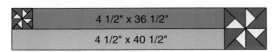

Figure 6
Sew the 28 1/2" block/strip to the 32 1/2" green print strip; sew 2 Large Pinwheel blocks to the end opposite the small block end to make the top strip.

4 1/2" x 36 1/2"
4 1/2" x 40 1/2"

Figure 7
Repeat with the 36 1/2" block/strip and 40 1/2" green print strip to make the bottom border strip.

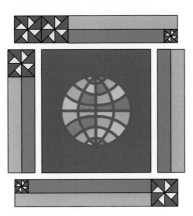

Figure 8
Sew the pieced border strips to the appliquéd center.

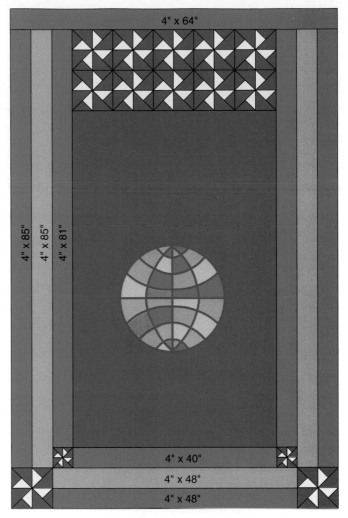

Good Night Good Earth
Placement Diagram
64" x 97"

referring to the General Instructions. *Note: The quilt shown was machine-quilted on marked lines in center background, 2" and 4" from earth shape and in a scallop pattern on border strips using thread to match fabrics.*

Twin-Size Quilt

Step 1. Follow the preceding Steps 1–11.

Step 2. Join five Large Pinwheel blocks to make a row; repeat for two rows. Join rows to make pillow section of quilt; press seams in one direction. Sew the block rows to the top of the appliquéd center.

Step 3. Cut two strips each green solid 4 1/2" x 81 1/2"; sew a strip to opposite long sides of the center section. Press seams toward strips.

Step 4. Cut one strip green solid 4 1/2" x 40 1/2". Sew a Small Pinwheel block to each end of the strip. Sew the block/strip to the bottom of the center section; press seams toward strips.

Step 5. Cut two strips each 4 1/2" x 85 1/2" and 4 1/2" x 48 1/2" green print and green solid. Sew a samelength green solid strip to a green print strip; repeat for two 85 1/2" strip sets and one 48 1/2" strip set. Sew the long strip sets to opposite long sides of the center section; press seams toward strips.

Step 6. Sew a Large Pinwheel block to each end of the 48 1/2" strip set; sew the block/strip set to the bottom of the center section. Press seams toward strips.

Step 7. Cut one strip green solid 4 1/2" x 64 1/2"; sew to the top of the quilt. Press seam toward strip.

Step 8. Prepare top for quilting and finish as desired referring to the General Instructions. Bind edges using self-made or purchased binding, again referring to the General Instructions. ❧

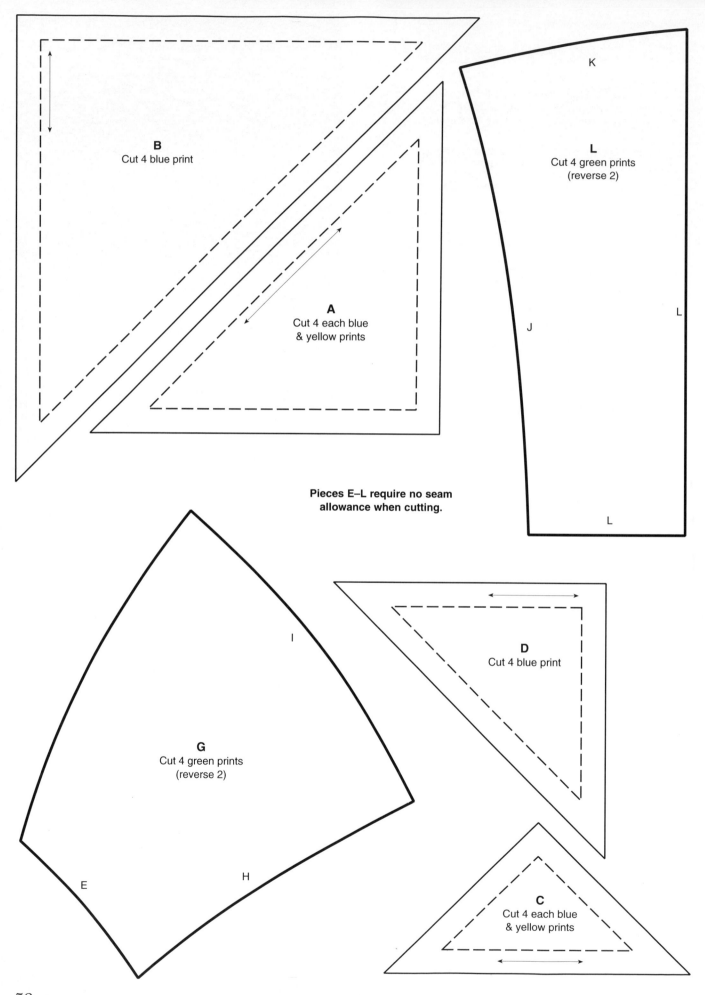

B
Cut 4 blue print

A
Cut 4 each blue
& yellow prints

K

L
Cut 4 green prints
(reverse 2)

J

L

L

Pieces E–L require no seam
allowance when cutting.

I

D
Cut 4 blue print

G
Cut 4 green prints
(reverse 2)

E   H

C
Cut 4 each blue
& yellow prints

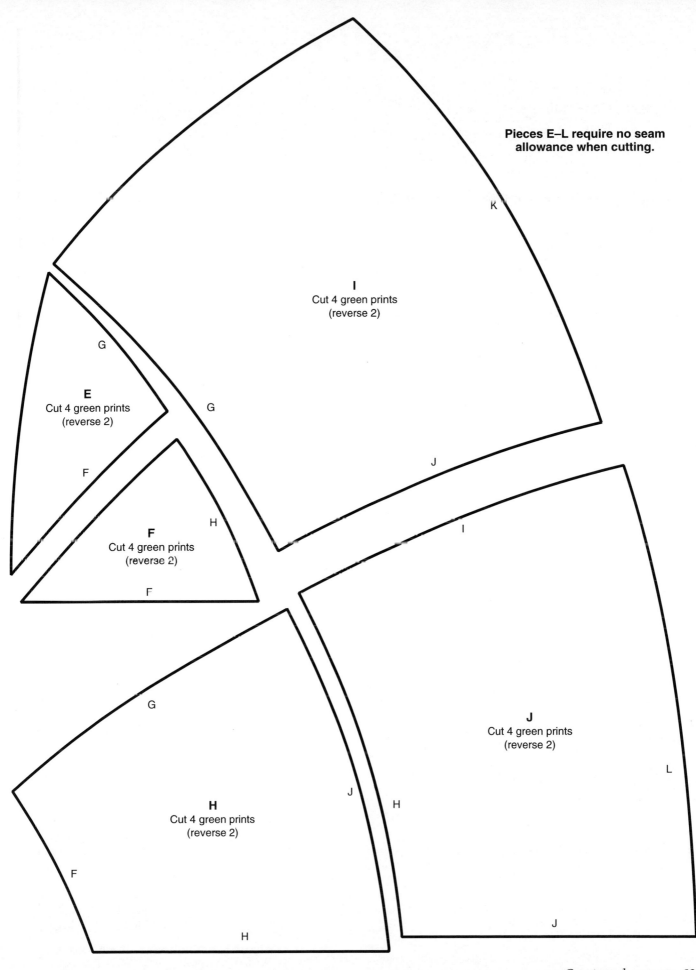

Pieces E–L require no seam
allowance when cutting.

K

I
Cut 4 green prints
(reverse 2)

G

E
Cut 4 green prints
(reverse 2)

G

F

J

H

F
Cut 4 green prints
(reverse 2)

F

I

G

J

J

H

J
Cut 4 green prints
(reverse 2)

L

H
Cut 4 green prints
(reverse 2)

H

F

H

Continued on page 63

Snowball Castles

By Beth Wheeler

This lap-size quilt is just right for a child to snuggle under after an afternoon adventure in a winter wonderland.

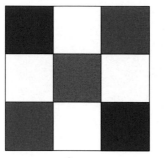

Nine-Patch
4 1/2" x 4 1/2" Block

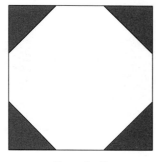

Snowball
4 1/2" x 4 1/2" Block

Quilt Sizes			
	Lap	**Twin**	**Double**
Finished Quilt Size	38 1/2" x 38 1/2"	61" x 88"	79" x 88"
Block Size	4 1/2" x 4 1/2"	9" x 9"	9" x 9"
Number of Blocks	25	40	56

Materials			
Dark red print	1/2 yard	1 yard	1 1/4 yards
Light red print	3/4 yard	2 yards	2 3/8 yards
Medium red print	3/4 yard	1 1/2 yards	1 3/4 yards
White-on-white print	3/4 yard	2 3/4 yards	3 1/2 yards
Backing	42" x 42"	65" x 92"	83" x 92"
Batting	42" x 42"	65" x 92"	83" x 92"
Self-made or purchased binding	4 1/2 yards	9 yards	9 3/4 yards
White all-purpose thread			
Basic sewing supplies and tools			

Instructions

Instructions are given for the size shown in photo, with other sizes in parentheses. When only 1 number is given, it applies to all sizes.

Step 1. Cut the following 2" (3 1/2") (3 1/2") by fabric width strips: two (4) (5) each medium and dark red prints; one (2) (3) light red print; and four (8) (11) white-on-white print.

Step 2. Sew a white-on-white-print strip between dark and medium red print strips to make an A strip set; repeat for two (4) (5) A strip sets. Repeat with the light red print strips between two white-on-white print strips to make one (2) (3) B strip sets. Press seams toward darker fabrics.

Step 3. Cut each strip set into 2" (3 1/2") (3 1/2") segments to make A and B segments as shown in Figure 1.

Step 4. Sew a B segment between two A segments to make a Nine-Patch block as shown in Figure 2; press. Repeat for 13 (20) (28) Nine-Patch blocks.

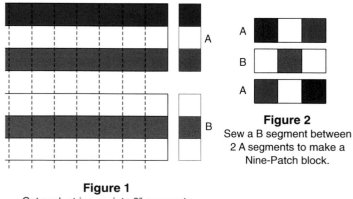

Figure 1
Cut each strip sew into 2" segments to make A and B segments.

Figure 2
Sew a B segment between 2 A segments to make a Nine-Patch block.

Step 5. Cut 12 (20) (28) squares white-on-white print 4 1/2" x 4 1/2" (9 1/2" x 9 1/2") (9 1/2" x 9 1/2") for

C. Cut 48 (80) (112) squares light red print 2" x 2" (3 1/2" x 3 1/2") (3 1/2" x 3 1/2") for D.

Step 6. Place a D square on one corner of C with right sides together. Stitch on the diagonal of D as shown in Figure 3; trim excess seam to 1/4" beyond stitching line as shown in Figure 4. Press C to reveal a triangle on the corner of D as shown in Figure 5. Repeat with D on the remaining three corners as shown in Figure 6 to complete one Snowball block; repeat for 12 (20) (28) blocks.

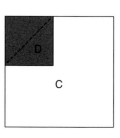

Figure 3
Stitch on the diagonal of D.

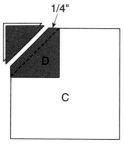

Figure 4
Trim excess seam to 1/4" beyond stitching line as shown.

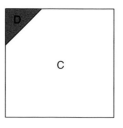

Figure 5
Press C to reveal a triangle on the corner of D.

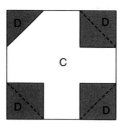

Figure 6
Sew D on the remaining 3 corners.

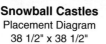

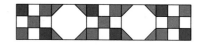

Snowball Castles
Placement Diagram
38 1/2" x 38 1/2"

top and bottom and longer strips to opposite sides; press seams toward strips.

Step 11. Cut two strips each medium red print 2 1/2" x 26" (2 1/2" x 48 1/2") (2 1/2" x 66 1/2") and 2 1/2" x 30" (2 1/2" x 79 1/2") (2 1/2" x 79 1/2"). Sew the shorter strips to the top and bottom and longer strips to opposite sides; press seams toward strips.

Step 12. Cut fabric width strips from all fabrics in a variety of widths ranging from 1 1/2" to 3". Join strips with right sides together along length to make one (2) (2) 20"-wide (24") (24") strip set(s); press seams in one direction.

Step 13. Cut strip set(s) into 5" segments. Join two (4) (4) segments on short ends and trim to make two strips 30" (52 1/2") (70 1/2") long for top and bottom and two strips 39" (88 1/2") (88 1/2") long for opposite sides as shown in Figure 9. Sew strips to pieced center; press seams toward strips.

Step 7. Join three (3) (4) Nine-Patch blocks with two (2) (3) Snowball blocks to make a row as shown in Figure 7; repeat for three (4) (4) rows. Press seams in one direction.

Snowball Castles
Placement Diagram
61" x 88"

Figure 7
Join 3 Nine-Patch blocks with 2
Snowball blocks to make a row.

Step 8. Join three (3) (4) Snowball blocks with two (2) (3) Nine-Patch blocks to make a row as shown in Figure 8; repeat for two (4) (4) rows.

Figure 8
Join 3 Snowball blocks with 2
Nine-Patch blocks to make a row.

Step 9. Join the pieced rows referring to the Placement Diagram for positioning of rows; press seams in one direction.

Step 10. Cut two strips each light red print 2" x 23" (2" x 45 1/2") (2" x 63 1/2") and 2" x 26" (2" x 75 1/2") (2" x 75 1/2"). Sew the shorter strips to the

2" x 66" 1 1/2" x 63"

2" x 79"

1 1/2" x 75"

Snowball Castles
Placement Diagram
79" x 88"

Figure 9
Join segments to make strips as shown.

Step 14. Prepare top for quilting and finish as desired referring to the General Instructions. **Note:** *The quilt shown was machine-quilted 1/4" from seams of all white-on-white print pieces in blocks and in the ditch of border seams using white all-purpose thread in the top of the machine and in the bobbin.* ❧

Good Night Good Earth Quilt
Continued from page 59

K
Cut 4 green prints
(reverse 2)

K

I

**Pieces E–L require no seam
allowance when cutting.**

L

Chapter Three

Traditions With a Twist

Many of the quilts in this chapter are a combination of two or more traditional patterns or an updated version of an old design. You'll also find a few designs you haven't seen before. You'll enjoy stitching these patterns that are both old and new at the same time.

Pinwheels & Garland

By Barbara Clayton

Make this pieced and appliquéd holiday quilt for your bed or to hang on a welcoming wall for all your guests to admire.

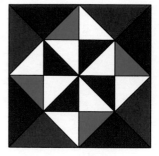

Peace and Plenty
12" x 12" Block

Quilt Sizes

	Lap	Twin	Queen
Finished Quilt Size	60" x 72"	64" x 88"	80" x 92"
Block Size	12" x 12"	12" x 12"	12" x 12"
Number of Blocks	12	15	20

Materials

Red solid	5/8 yard	5/8 yard	5/8 yard
Green solid	1 yard	1 1/8 yards	1 1/8 yards
Green print	1 1/2 yards	1 1/2 yards	2 3/4 yards
Red print	2 yards	2 1/2 yards	2 1/4 yards
White solid	2 yards	2 1/2 yards	2 3/4 yards
Backing	64" x 76"	68" x 92"	84" x 96"
Batting	64" x 76"	68" x 92"	84" x 96"
Self-made or purchased binding	7 3/4 yards	9 yards	10 yards
All-purpose thread to match fabrics			
White and green quilting thread			
Clear nylon monofilament			
Lightweight fusible interfacing	2 yards	2 1/8 yards	2 1/8 yards
Basic sewing supplies and tools, water-erasable marker or pencil and stylet, knitting needle or pencil			

Instructions

Instructions are given for the size shown in photo, with other sizes in parentheses. When only 1 number is given, it applies to all sizes.

Step 1. Cut two strips each 8 1/2" x 32 1/2" (8 1/2" x 32 1/2") (8 1/2" x 44 1/2") and 8 1/2" x 44 1/2" (8 1/2" x 56 1/2") (8 1/2" x 56 1/2") from the length of the white solid. Cut four 10 1/2" x 10 1/2" squares. Set aside for appliqué sections.

Step 2. Cut 24 (30) (40) 5 1/2" x 5 1/2" squares from the remaining white solid. Cut each square on both diagonals to make 96 (120) (160) white solid A triangles.

Step 3. Cut two 7 1/4" by fabric width strips each red and green solids, and red and green prints; subcut into 7 1/4" square segments. Cut each square on both diagonals to make B triangles. You will need 24 (28) (40) each red solid and red print and 24 (32) (40) green solid and green print B triangles.

Step 4. Cut two (3) (3) 5 1/2" by fabric width strips each red and green prints; subcut into 5 1/2" square segments. Cut each square on both diagonals to make A triangles. You will need 48 (60) (80) each red and green print A triangles.

Step 5. Sew a green print A triangle to a white solid A triangle as shown in Figure 1; repeat with all green print A triangles. Repeat with red print and white solid A triangles. Join four A units to make pinwheel units

as shown in Figure 2; repeat to make six (7) (10) red pinwheel and six (8) (10) green pinwheel units as shown in Figure 3.

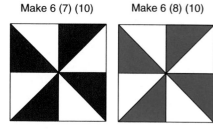

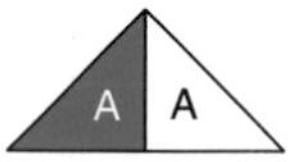

Make 6 (7) (10) Make 6 (8) (10)

Figure 3
Make 6 (7) (10) red pinwheel and 6 (8) (10) green pinwheel units as shown.

Step 6. Sew red/white A units to all sides of each green pinwheel unit as shown in Figure 4. Repeat with green/white A units and red pinwheel units.

Figure 4
Sew red/white A units to all sides of each green pinwheel unit.

Figure 1
Sew a green print A triangle to a white solid A triangle.

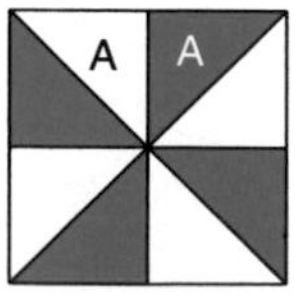

Figure 2
Join the 4 A units to make pinwheel units.

10" x 10"

2" x 60"

2" x 8"

8" x 32"

2" x 36"

2" x 8"

2" x 68"

2" x 48"

8" x 44"

Pinwheels & Garland
Placement Diagram
60" x 72"

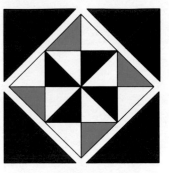

Figure 7
Sew a B unit to each side of a red
pinwheel unit to complete 1 red
Peace and Plenty block.

Step 9. Join two (2) (2) green blocks
with one (1) (2) red block(s) to make a
row as shown in Figure 8; repeat for
two (3) (3) rows.

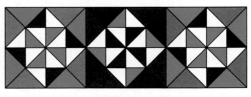

Figure 8
Join 2 green blocks with 1 red block to make a row.

Step 10. Join two (2) (2) red blocks
with one (1) (2) green block(s) to make
a row as shown in Figure 9; repeat for
two (2) (2) rows.

Figure 9
Join 2 red blocks with 1 green block to make a row.

Step 11. Join the rows to complete the pieced center referring to the Placement Diagram for arrangement of rows.

Step 12. Cut and piece two strips red print 2 1/2" x
48 1/2" (2 1/2" x 60 1/2") (2 1/2" x 60 1/2"). Sew a
strip to opposite long sides of the pieced center; press
seams toward strips.

Step 13. Cut eight 2 1/2" x 8 1/2" red print rectangles.
Sew a rectangle to each end of each 8 1/2"-wide white
solid strip cut in Step 1. Sew a 44 1/2"-long (56 1/2")
(56 1/2") strip to opposite long sides of the pieced center.

Step 14. Cut (and piece) two strips red print 2 1/2" x
36 1/2" (2 1/2" x 36 1/2") (2 1/2" x 48 1/2"). Sew a
strip to one long side of the 32 1/2"-long (32 1/2")
(44 1/2") white solid strips. Sew a 10 1/2" x 10 1/2"

Step 7. Sew a green solid B triangle to a green print B
triangle as shown in Figure 5; repeat to make four B
units. Sew a B unit to each side of a green pinwheel unit
to complete one green Peace and Plenty block as shown
in Figure 6; repeat to make six (8) (10) green blocks.

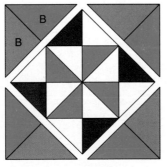

B

B

B

B

Figure 5
Sew a green solid B triangle
to a green print B triangle.

B

B

Figure 6
Sew a B unit to each side of a
green pinwheel unit to complete 1
green Peace and Plenty block.

Step 8. Repeat Step 7 using red print and red solid B triangles and red pinwheel units to make six (7) (10) red
blocks as shown in Figure 7.

Pinwheels & Garland
Placement Diagram
64" x 88"

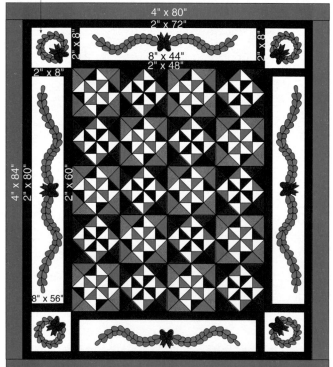

Pinwheels & Garland
Placement Diagram
80" x 92"

white solid square to each end. Sew the resulting pieced strip to the top and bottom of the pieced center.

Step 15. Prepare templates for appliqué pieces using pattern pieces given. Trace shapes onto the smooth side of the lightweight fusible interfacing referring to patterns for number to trace/cut. Cut out shapes, leaving a margin around each one.

Step 16. Pin shapes with fusible side against the right side of appliqué fabrics as directed on each piece for color. Stitch around each shape on traced line; cut out, leaving a 1/8"–1/4" seam allowance all around. Trim points and clip curves.

Step 17. Cut a small slit in the interfacing side of each stitched unit; turn right side out. With a stylet, knitting needle or pencil with broken lead, smooth out edges by running tool around seam on the inside of each piece.

Step 18. Transfer vein lines on each heart using water-erasable marker or pencil. Draw the bow quilting lines on each bow.

Step 19. Arrange 12 wreath heart appliqué shapes on each white corner square to make a circular wreath with a bow at the top and alternating the green solid and green print hearts. Fuse in place referring to manufacturer's instructions. Sew in place close to edge of piece using clear nylon monofilament in the top of the machine and all-purpose thread in the bobbin.

Step 20. Arrange the garlands on the two long white solid side border strips, starting with the bow in the center of each strip. Arrange the garlands in an S shape starting on each side of the bow with a green print heart and alternate with the solid green hearts having six (8) (8) green print and five (7) (7) green solid hearts on each side of the bow. Place an end piece on each end of the garland. Repeat on the opposite side referring to the Placement Diagram. Fuse and stitch in place as in Step 19.

Step 21. Arrange, fuse and stitch the garland on the top and bottom borders as in Steps 19 and 20 using four (4) (6) green solid and four (4) (5) green print hearts and a garland end piece on each end.

Step 22. Cut and piece two strips each 2 1/2" x 60 1/2" (4 1/2" x 64 1/2") (2 1/2" x 72 1/2") red print and 2 1/2" x 68 1/2" (4 1/2" x 80 1/2") (2 1/2" x 80 1/2") red print. Sew the longer strips to opposite long sides and shorter strips to the top and bottom; press seams toward strips. **Note:** *For queen-size quilt, cut two strips each 4 1/2" x 80 1/2" and 4 1/2" x 84 1/2" green print. Sew strips to quilt center as for red print strips.*

Step 23. Prepare top for quilting and finish as desired referring to the General Instructions. **Note:** *The quilt shown was machine-quilted in the ditch of block and border seams using clear nylon monofilament in the top of the* *machine and all-purpose thread in the bobbin, and hand-quilted 1/4" away from appliqué motifs and borders and in 1" diagonal lines in the white sections with green quilting thread, and along the center of the wreath and garland hearts and bow details with white quilting thread.* ❧

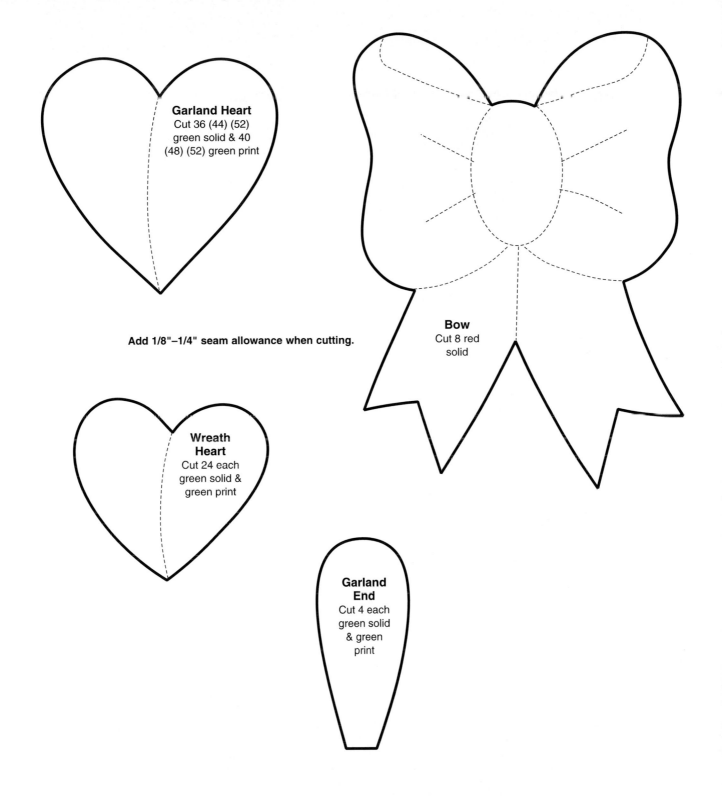

Garland Heart
Cut 36 (44) (52) green solid & 40 (48) (52) green print

Add 1/8"–1/4" seam allowance when cutting.

Wreath Heart
Cut 24 each green solid & green print

Bow
Cut 8 red solid

Garland End
Cut 4 each green solid & green print

Reflections

By Holly Daniels

*Colors of the sea combine to make
this simple and quick-to-stitch quilt
using two old-favorite block designs.*

Nine-Patch Variation
9" x 9" Block
Make 13 (27) (41)

Shoo Fly
9" x 9" Block
Make 12 (27) (40)

	Quilt Sizes		
	Lap	**Twin**	**Queen**
Finished Quilt Size	54" x 54"	63" x 90"	90" x 90"
Block Size	9" x 9"	9" x 9"	9" x 9"
Number of Blocks	25	54	81
Materials			
Lightest blue mottled	1/8 yard	1/4 yard	1/3 yard
Light green mottled	1/3 yard	1/2 yard	3/4 yard
Medium blue mottled	3/8 yard	3/4 yard	1 yard
Dark blue mottled	1/2 yard	3/4 yard	1 yard
Light blue print	1 yard	1 1/4 yards	1 1/2 yards
Medium green mottled	1 yard	1 5/8 yards	2 1/8 yards
White-on-white print	1 1/4 yards	3 yards	4 1/4 yards
Backing	58" x 58"	67" x 94"	94" x 94"
Batting	58" x 58"	67" x 94"	94" x 94"
Self-made or purchased binding	6 1/2 yards	9 yards	10 1/2 yards
Neutral color all-purpose thread			
Clear nylon monofilament			
Basic sewing supplies and tools			

Instructions

Instructions are given for the size shown in photo, with other sizes in parentheses. When only 1 number is given, it applies to all sizes.

Step 1. To make Shoo Fly blocks, cut three (6) (8) strips each dark blue mottled and medium green mottled 3 7/8" by fabric width. Cut strips into 3 7/8" square segments for F. You will need 24 (54) (80) F squares.

Step 2. Layer one square of each color with right sides together. Draw a diagonal line through each set. Sew 1/4" on each side of the line as shown in Figure 1; cut apart on marked line. Press seams toward blue side; repeat for 48 (108) (160) F triangle/squares.

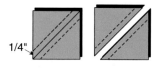

Figure 1
Sew 1/4" on each side of
the line as shown; cut
apart on marked line.

Step 3. Cut four (11) (15) strips white-on-white print and one (3) (4) strip light blue print 3 1/2" by fabric width. Sew the light blue print strip between two white-on-white print strips with right sides together along length to make one (3) (4) strip set. Set aside remaining white-on-white print strips.

Step 4. Cut strip set into 3 1/2" segments as shown in Figure 2 to make 12 (27) (40) E-E units.

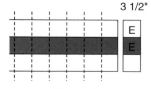

Figure 2
Cut strip set into 3 1/2"
segments for E-E units.

Step 5. Cut the remaining white-on-white print strips into 3 1/2" square segments for E. You will need 24 (54) (80) E squares.

Step 6. Join two F triangle/squares with one E square as shown in Figure 3; repeat for 24 (54) (80) units.

Step 7. Join the pieced units as shown in Figure 4 to complete one Shoo Fly block; repeat for 12 (27) (40) blocks. Set aside.

Figure 3
Join 2 F
triangle/squares
with 1 E square.

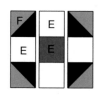

Figure 4
Join the pieced units as shown
to complete 1 Shoo Fly block.

Step 8. To make Nine-Patch Variation blocks, cut five (11) (16) strips each white-on-white print and medium blue mottled 2" by fabric width. Join one strip of each color with right sides together along length to make a strip set; repeat for five (11) (16) strip sets. Press seams

Reflections
Placement Diagram
54" x 54"

toward darker fabric. Cut each strip set into 2" segments to make 104 (216) (328) segments as shown in Figure 5.

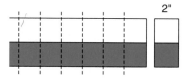

Figure 5
Cut each strip set into 2" segments.

Step 9. Join two segments as shown in Figure 6 to make a Four-Patch unit; repeat for 52 (108) (164) units. Press seams in one direction; set aside.

Figure 6
Join 2 segments as
shown to make a
Four-Patch unit.

Step 10. Cut one (2) (3) 2 5/8" by fabric width strip lightest blue mottled. Cut strip into 13 (27) (41) 2 5/8" square segments for A squares.

Step 11. Cut eight (16) (25) strips white-on-white print 2 3/8" by fabric width; cut strips into 130 (270) (410) 2 3/8" square segments. Cut each square on one diagonal to make 260 (540) (820) B triangles.

Step 12. Sew a B triangle to each side of the lightest blue A squares as shown in Figure 7; press seams away from the square.

Figure 7
Sew a B triangle to
each side of the
lightest blue A squares.

Step 13. Cut two (3) (5) strips each medium and light green mottleds 4 1/4" by fabric width. Cut each strip into 4 1/4" square segments. Cut each square on both diagonals to make 52 (108) (164) C triangles each light and medium green mottleds.

Step 14. Sew a white-on-white print B triangle to each short side of a light green mottled C triangle as shown in Figure 8; press seams toward B. Repeat with medium green C triangles.

Step 15. Join two B-C units as shown in Figure 9; repeat for 52 (108) (164) units.

Figure 8
Sew a white-on-white print B
triangle to each short side of a
light green mottled C triangle.

Figure 9
Join 2 B-C units
as shown.

Step 16. Join two Four-Patch units with a B-C unit to make an A row as shown in Figure 10; repeat for 26 (54) (82) A rows. Join two B-C units with an A-B unit to make a B row as shown in Figure 11; repeat for 13 (27) (41) B rows.

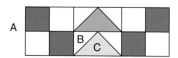

Figure 10
Join 2 Four-Patch units with a
B-C unit to make an A row.

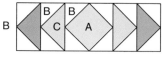

Figure 11
Join 2 B-C units with an
A-B unit to make a B row.

Step 17. Join two A rows with one B row to complete one Nine-Patch Variation block as shown in Figure 12; repeat for 13 (27) (41) blocks.

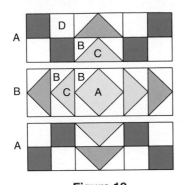

Figure 12
Join 2 A rows with 1 B row to complete
1 Nine-Patch Variation block.

Step 18. Join three (3) (5) Nine-Patch Variation blocks with two (3) (4) Shoo Fly blocks to make a row as shown in Figure 13; repeat for three (5) (5) rows. Press seams in one direction.

Figure 13
Join 3 Nine-Patch Variation blocks with 2 Shoo Fly blocks to make a row.

Step 19. Join three (3) (5) Shoo Fly blocks with two (3) (4) Nine-Patch Variation blocks to make a row as shown in Figure 14; repeat for two (4) (4) rows.

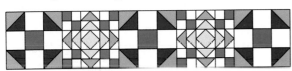

Figure 14
Join 3 Shoo Fly blocks with 2 Nine-Patch Variation blocks to make a row.

Step 20. Join the rows to complete the pieced center referring to the Placement Diagram for arrangement of rows.

Step 21. Cut and piece two strips each 2" x 45 1/2" (2" x 54 1/2") (2" x 81 1/2") and 2" x 48 1/2" (2" x 84 1/2") (2" x 84 1/2") light blue print. Sew the shorter strips to the top and bottom and longer strips to opposite sides; press seams toward strips.

Step 22. Cut and piece two strips each 2" x 48 1/2" (2" x 57 1/2") (2" x 84 1/2") and 2" x 51 1/2" (2" x 87 1/2") (2" x 87 1/2") medium green mottled. Sew the shorter strips to the top and bottom and longer strips to opposite sides; press seams toward strips.

Step 23. Cut and piece two strips each 2" x 51 1/2" (2" x 60 1/2") (2" x 87 1/2") and 2" x 54 1/2" (2" x 90 1/2") (2" x 90 1/2") light blue print. Sew the shorter strips to the top and bottom and longer strips to opposite sides; press seams toward strips.

Step 24. Prepare top for quilting and finish as desired referring to the General Instructions. *Note: The quilt shown was machine-quilted on the diagonal through the centers of each block using clear nylon monofilament in the top of the machine and all-purpose thread in the bobbin.* ❧

Reflections
Placement Diagram
63" x 90"

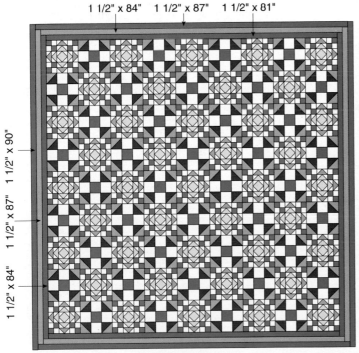

1 1/2" x 84"   1 1/2" x 87"   1 1/2" x 81"

1 1/2" x 90"
1 1/2" x 87"
1 1/2" x 84"

Reflections
Placement Diagram
90" x 90"

Hunter's Star

By Lucy Fazely

Simple squares and triangle/squares combine to make an easy version of the Hunter's Star block. When made in two different color combinations the resulting quilt has a lot of contrast.

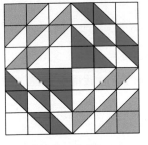

Hunter's Star
15" x 15" Block

Instructions

Instructions are given for the size shown in photo, with other sizes in parentheses. When only 1 number is given, it applies to all sizes.

Step 1. Cut 28 (46) (58) strips natural solid and 14 (23) (29) strips each green and hunter green prints 3" by fabric width; subcut into 3" square segments for A. You will need 384 (640) (800) natural solid A squares and 192 (320) (400) each green and hunter green print A squares.

Step 2. Set aside 48 (80) (100) natural solid and 24 (40) (50) each green and hunter green print A squares.

Step 3. Draw a diagonal line on the wrong side of each of the remaining 336 (560) (700) natural solid A squares. Place each marked square right sides together with the remaining 168 (280) (350) each green and hunter green print A squares.

Step 4. Stitch on the marked diagonal line through each square as shown in Figure 1. Trim seam allowance to 1/4" beyond stitched line as shown in Figure 2.

Figure 1
Stitch on the marked diagonal line through each square.

1/4"

Figure 2
Trim seam allowance to 1/4" beyond stitched line.

Quilt Sizes			
	Lap	**Double**	**Queen**
Finished Quilt Size	57" x 72"	76" x 91"	91" x 91"
Block Size	15" x 15"	15" x 15"	15" x 15"
Number of Blocks	12	20	25

Materials			
Red solid	1/2 yard	3/4 yard	1 yard
Green print	1 1/4 yards	2 yards	2 1/2 yards
Natural solid	2 1/2 yards	4 yards	5 yards
Hunter green print	2 yards	3 1/4 yards	4 yards
Backing	61" x 76"	80" x 95"	95" x 95"
Batting	61" x 76"	80" x 95"	95" x 95"
Self-made or purchased binding	7 1/2 yards	9 3/4 yards	10 1/2 yards
All-purpose thread to match fabrics			
Basic sewing supplies and tools			

4" x 49"

4" x 72"

Hunter's Star
Placement Diagram
57" x 72"

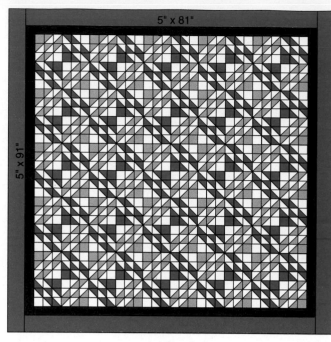

Hunter's Star
Placement Diagram
91" x 91"

Hunter's Star
Placement Diagram
76" x 91"

Step 5. Press seams toward darker fabrics to complete triangle/square units as shown in Figure 3.

Figure 3
Press seams toward
darker fabrics to complete
triangle/square units.

Step 6. Lay out pieced A-A units with A squares in rows referring to Figure 4; join pieces to make rows. Join rows to complete one block; press seams in one direction. Repeat for 12 (20) (25) blocks.

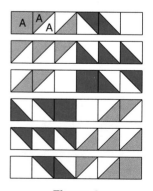

Figure 4
Lay out pieced A-A units with
A squares in rows.

Step 7. Join three (4) (5) blocks to make a row; repeat for four (5) (5) rows. Join the rows to complete the pieced center. Press seams in one direction.

Step 8. Cut and piece two strips each red solid 2 1/2" x 45 1/2" (3 1/2" x 60 1/2") (3 1/2" x 75 1/2") and 2 1/2" x 64 1/2" (3 1/2" x 81 1/2") (3 1/2" x 81 1/2"). Sew the shorter strips to the top and bottom and the longer strips to opposite long sides; press seams toward strips.

Step 9. Cut and piece two strips each hunter green print 4 1/2" x 49 1/2" (5 1/2" x 66 1/2") (5 1/2" x 81 1/2") and 4 1/2" x 72 1/2" (5 1/2" x 91 1/2") (5 1/2" x 91 1/2"). Sew the shorter strips to the top and bottom and the longer strips to opposite long sides; press seams toward strips.

Step 10. Prepare top for quilting and finish as desired referring to the General Instructions. **Note:** *The quilt shown was machine-quilted in a meandering design using thread to match fabrics.* ❧

Sunburst Medallion

By Sue Harvey

This late 1800s quilt was made in an unidentified variation of the Chips & Whetstones pattern. Piecing this block is not for the faint of heart, but the beautiful Sunburst blocks are well worth the effort.

Quilt Sizes			
	Double	**Queen**	**King**
Finished Quilt Size	78" x 90"	84" x 90"	100" x 96"
Block Size	22" x 22"	22" x 22"	22" x 22"
Number of Blocks	9	9	10

Materials			
Green solid	1 yard	1 yard	2 yards
White solid	4 yards	4 1/2 yards	5 1/2 yards
Backing	82" x 94"	88" x 94"	104" x 100"
Batting	82" x 94"	88" x 94"	104" x 100"
Self-made or purchased binding	9 3/4 yard	10 1/2 yards	11 1/2 yards
White all-purpose thread			
Basic sewing supplies and tools			

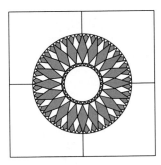

Sunburst
22" x 22" Block

Instructions

Instructions are given for the size shown in photo, with other sizes in parentheses. When only 1 number is given, it applies to all sizes.

Step 1. Cut two strips each from length of white solid 12 1/2" x 66 1/2" (12 1/2" x 66 1/2") (4 1/2" x 88 1/2") and 6 1/2" x 90 1/2" (9 1/2" x 90 1/2") (6 1/2" x 96 1/2"); set aside for borders.

Step 2. Prepare templates using pieces given. Cut as directed on each piece for one block.

Step 3. Sew B and BR to two adjacent sides of A as shown in Figure 1; repeat for 20 A-B units.

Step 4. Sew an A-B unit to two adjacent sides of C as shown in Figure 2; repeat for 20 A-B-C units.

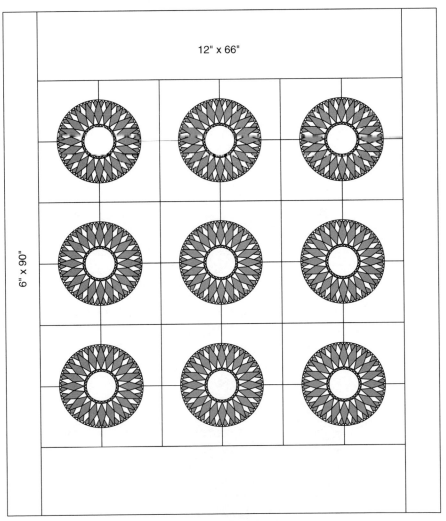

12" x 66"

6" x 90"

Sunburst Medallion
Placement Diagram
78" x 90"

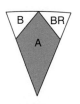

Figure 1
Sew B and BR to adjacent sides of A.

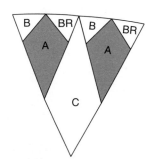

Figure 2
Sew an A-B unit to 2 adjacent sides of C.

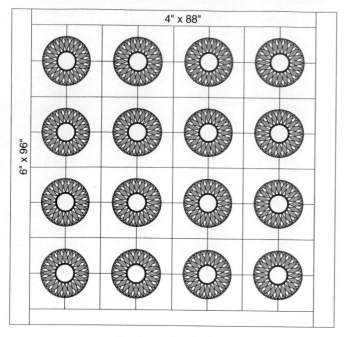

Sunburst Medallion
Placement Diagram
100" x 96"

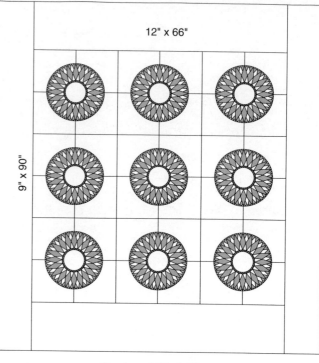

Sunburst Medallion
Placement Diagram
84" x 90"

Step 5. Sew an A-B-C unit to one side of D as shown in Figure 3; repeat for 20 units. Add E to the opposite side of D again referring to Figure 3; repeat for 20 units.

Step 6. Join five pieced units to make a quarter circle as shown in Figure 4; repeat for four quarter circles. Join quarter circles to form outer ring as shown in Figure 5.

Step 7. Sew a white solid G to a green solid F as shown in Figure 6; repeat for 30 F-G units. Join F-G units as shown in Figure 7 to form inner ring.

Step 8. Place the inner ring right sides together with H as shown in Figure 8, pinning in several places to hold evenly together. Stitch around; press seams toward H.

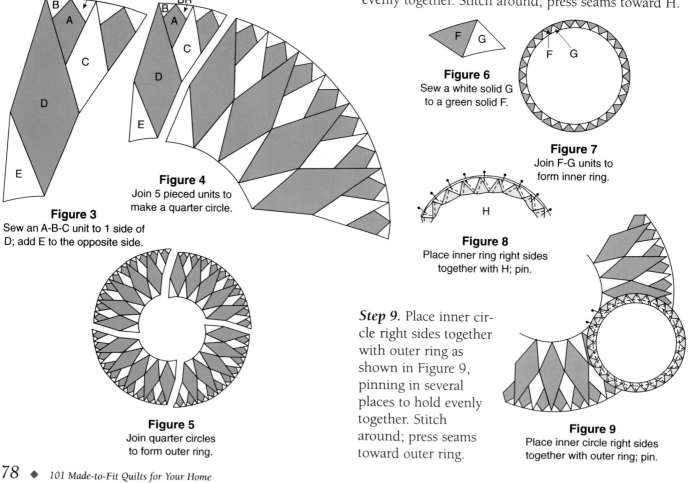

Figure 3
Sew an A-B-C unit to 1 side of
D; add E to the opposite side.

Figure 4
Join 5 pieced units to
make a quarter circle.

Figure 5
Join quarter circles
to form outer ring.

Figure 6
Sew a white solid G
to a green solid F.

Figure 7
Join F-G units to
form inner ring.

Figure 8
Place inner ring right sides
together with H; pin.

Step 9. Place inner circle right sides together with outer ring as shown in Figure 9, pinning in several places to hold evenly together. Stitch around; press seams toward outer ring.

Figure 9
Place inner circle right sides
together with outer ring; pin.

Step 10. Sew I to I as shown in Figure 10; repeat. Join I-I units to complete the block frame; press.

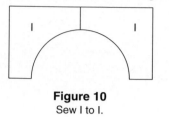

Figure 10
Sew I to I.

Step 11. Place the pieced circle right sides together with the block frame as shown in Figure 11, pinning in several places to hold evenly together. Stitch around; press seam toward block frame to complete one Sunburst block. Repeat for nine (9) (16) blocks.

Step 12. Join blocks in three (3) (4) rows of three (3) (4) blocks each. Join rows to complete pieced center.

Step 13. Sew the 12 1/2"-wide (12 1/2") (4 1/2") border strips to opposite sides of the pieced center; press seams toward strips. Sew the 6 1/2"-wide (9 1/2") (6 1/2") border strips to remaining opposite sides; press seams toward strips.

Step 14. Prepare top for quilting and finish as desired referring to the General Instructions. *Note: The quilt shown was hand-quilted with two feathered circles in the block frame pieces and in lines spaced 1/2" apart over remaining top using white quilting thread.* ❧

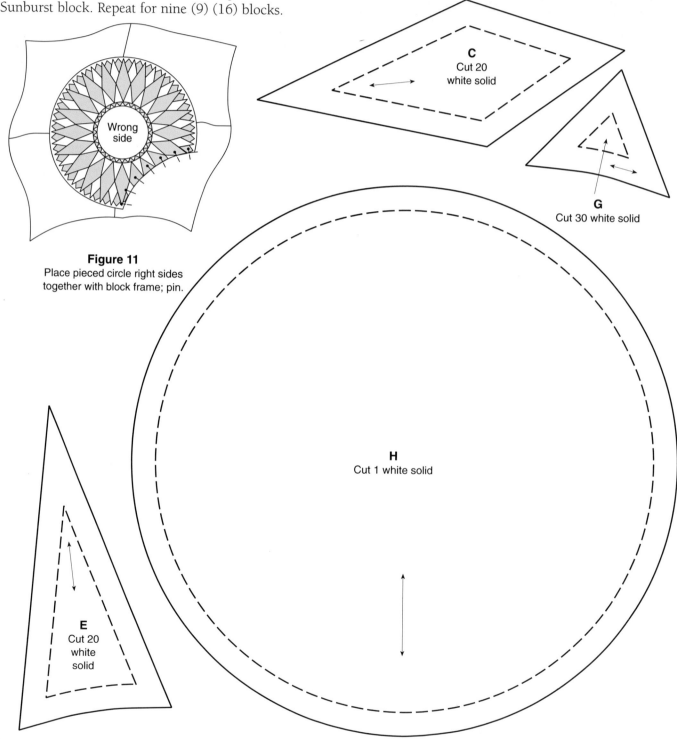

Figure 11
Place pieced circle right sides together with block frame; pin.

C
Cut 20
white solid

G
Cut 30 white solid

H
Cut 1 white solid

E
Cut 20
white
solid

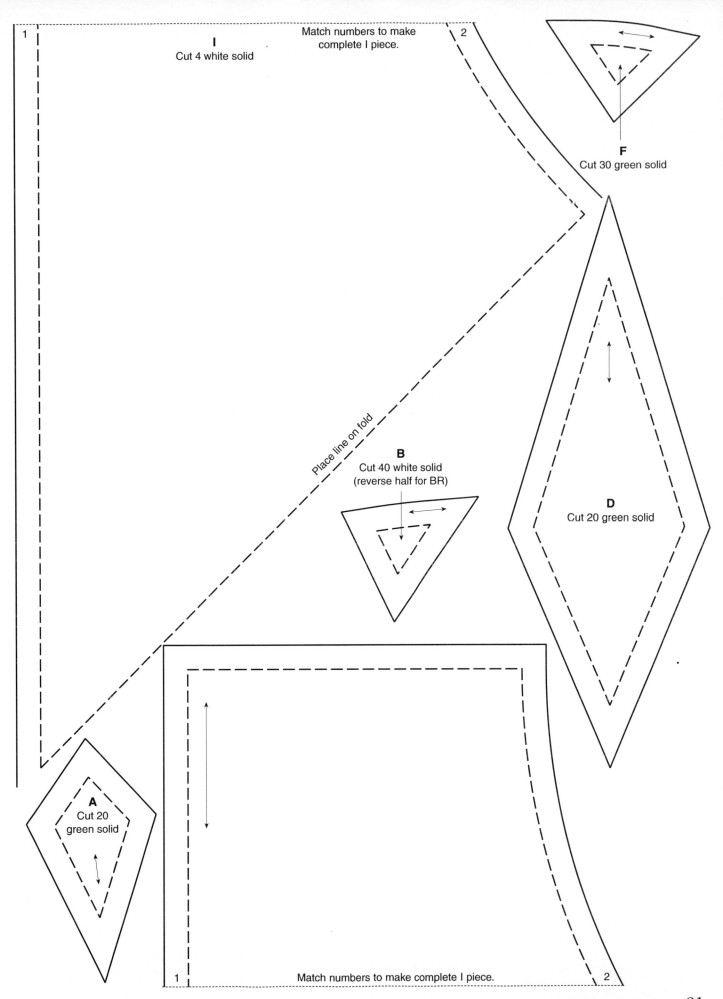

I
Cut 4 white solid

Match numbers to make complete I piece.

F
Cut 30 green solid

Place line on fold

B
Cut 40 white solid
(reverse half for BR)

D
Cut 20 green solid

A
Cut 20
green solid

Match numbers to make complete I piece.

Scrappy Pieced Puzzle

By Patsy Moreland

This pattern was used by stone masons around the 12th century in Florence, Italy. It is a combination of two traditional patterns which, when set together, appear to create a puzzle.

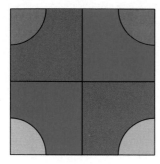

Drunkard's Path Variation
10" x 10" Block

Instructions

Instructions are given for the size shown in photo, with other sizes in parentheses. When only 1 number is given, it applies to all sizes.

Step 1. Prepare templates using pattern pieces given. Cut as directed on each piece for one Drunkard's Path Variation block; repeat for seven (17) (28) blocks.

Step 2. Sew an orange print A to a blue print B, matching centers and clipping curves as shown in Figure 1; repeat with purple print A and blue print B. Repeat with purple print A and green print B and orange print A and green print B pieces to make two units. Join the A-B units to complete one Drunkard's Path Variation block as shown in Figure 2; repeat for seven (17) (28) blocks. Set aside.

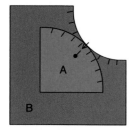

Figure 1
Sew an orange print A to a blue print B, matching centers and clipping curves.

Figure 2
Join the A-B units to complete 1 Drunkard's Path Variation block.

Step 3. Cut two (5) (7) strips each 3 1/2" by fabric width orange, tan, yellow and purple prints. Join strips along length with right sides together in the order listed and referring to Figure 3; press seams open. Repeat for two (5) (7) strip sets.

Step 4. Cut strip sets into 10 1/2" segments as shown in Figure 4; repeat for eight (18) (28) segments.

Quilt Sizes

	Lap	Twin	Queen
Finished Quilt Size	46" x 66"	66" x 86"	86" x 96"
Block Size	10" x 10"	10" x 10"	10" x 10"
Number of Blocks	7	17	28

Materials

	Lap	Twin	Queen
Tan print	1/4 yard	5/8 yard	3/4 yard
Orange and purple prints	3/8 yard each	1 yard each	1 1/8 yards each
Green print	3/8 yard	1 yard	1 1/3 yards
Cream-on-tan print	1/3 yard	3/8 yard	1/2 yard
Tan pin dot	5/8 yard	3/4 yard	1 yard
Blue print	5/8 yard	1 yard	1 1/2 yards
Multicolored print	3/4 yard	1 1/8 yards	1 1/4 yards
Backing	50" x 70"	70" x 90"	90" x 100"
Batting	50" x 70"	70" x 90"	90" x 100"
Self-made or purchased binding	6 1/2 yards	8 3/4 yards	10 1/2 yards
All-purpose thread to match fabrics			
Basic sewing supplies and tools			

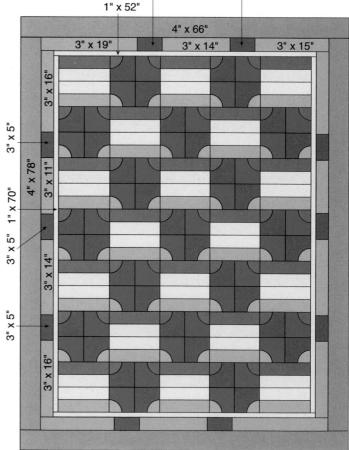

Scrappy Pieced Puzzle
Placement Diagram
66" x 86"

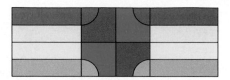

Figure 5
Join 2 segments and 1 Drunkard's
Path Variation block to make a row.

Step 6. Join one (2) (3) segment and two (3) (4) Drunkard's Path Variation blocks to make a row as shown in Figure 6; repeat for two (3) (4) rows. Press seams in one direction.

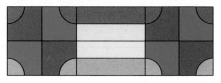

Figure 6
Join 1 segment and 2 Drunkard's
Path Variation blocks to make a row.

Step 7. Join the rows to complete the pieced center referring to the Placement Diagram; press seams in one direction.

Step 8. Cut and piece two strips each 1 1/2" x 50 1/2" (1 1/2" x 70 1/2") (1 1/2" x 80 1/2") and 1 1/2" x 32 1/2" (1 1/2" x 52 1/2") (1 1/2" x 72 1/2") cream-on-tan print. Sew the longer strips to opposite long sides and shorter strips to the top and bottom; press seams toward strips.

Step 9. Cut the following 3 1/2"-wide strips tan pin dot: two (2) (0) 11 1/2"; two (4) (4) 14 1/2"; two (2) (6) 15 1/2"; two (4) (0) 16 1/2"; and two (2) (6) 19 1/2". Cut six (10) (12) strips 3 1/2" x 5 1/2" blue print.

Step 10. Join the tan pin-dot strips with the blue print strips to make border strips as shown in Figure 7. Make two strips in each size. *Note: Refer to the Placement Diagram to piece the tan pin-dot border strips for twin and queen sizes.*

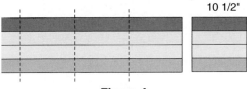

3 1/2" x 5 1 2"   Make 2 strips

| 3 1/2" x 14 1/2" | | 3 1/2" x 19 1/2" |

3 1/2" x 5 1 2"   Make 2 strips   3 1/2" x 5 1 2"

| 3 1/2" x 16 1/2" | | 3 1/2" x 15 1/2" | | 3 1/2" x 11 1/2" |

Figure 7
Join the tan pin-dot strips with the blue print strips to make border strips as shown.

Step 11. Sew the longer pieced strips to opposite long sides and shorter pieced strips to the top and bottom of the pieced center; press seams toward strips.

Step 12. Cut and piece two strips each 4 1/2" x 58 1/2" (4 1/2" x 78 1/2") (4 1/2" x 88 1/2") and 4 1/2" x 46 1/2"

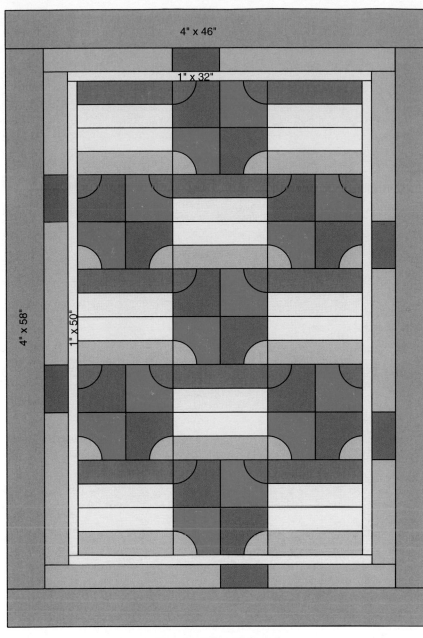

4" x 46"

1" x 32"

4" x 58"

1" x 50"

Scrappy Pieced Puzzle
Placement Diagram
46" x 66"

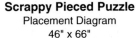

Figure 3
Join strips along length in the color order shown.

10 1/2"

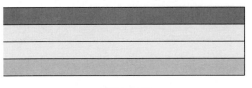

Figure 4
Cut strip sets into 10 1/2" segments.

Step 5. Join two (3) (4) segments and one (2) (3) Drunkard's Path Variation block to make a row as shown in Figure 5; repeat for three (4) (4) rows. Press seams in one direction.

Curved Piecing

Curved piecing requires a little practice and some special techniques.

It helps to mark the sewing line on each curved piece on the wrong side of the fabric. Clip the seam allowance in the center of each curve. To find the center, fold the piece in half and crease with fingers. Concave pieces require more clips than convex pieces as shown in Figure 8.

Pin the concave piece to the convex piece matching centers as shown in Figure 9. Pin ends of pieces and then ease remaining area between centers and ends; pin.

Stitch on marked seam line by hand or machine, removing pins as you stitch. Press seam allowance toward the darker fabric. It should lie flat on either side of the seam.

Figure 8
Clip curves as shown.

Figure 9
Remove pins as you stitch on the marked seam line.

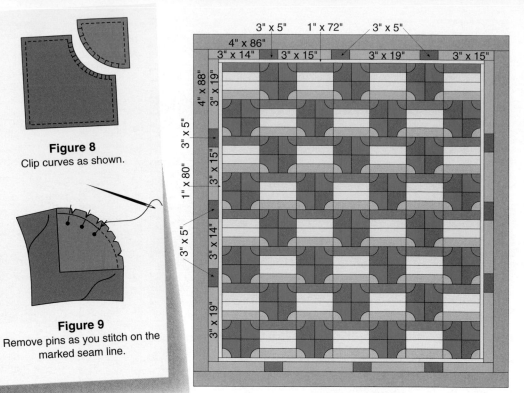

Scrappy Pieced Puzzle
Placement Diagram
86" x 96"

(4 1/2" x 66 1/2") (4 1/2" x 86 1/2") multicolored print. Sew the longer strips to opposite long sides and shorter strips to the top and bottom; press seams toward strips.

Step 13. Prepare top for quilting and finish as desired referring to the General Instructions. *Note: The quilt shown was machine-quilted in a meandering design using white thread.* ❥

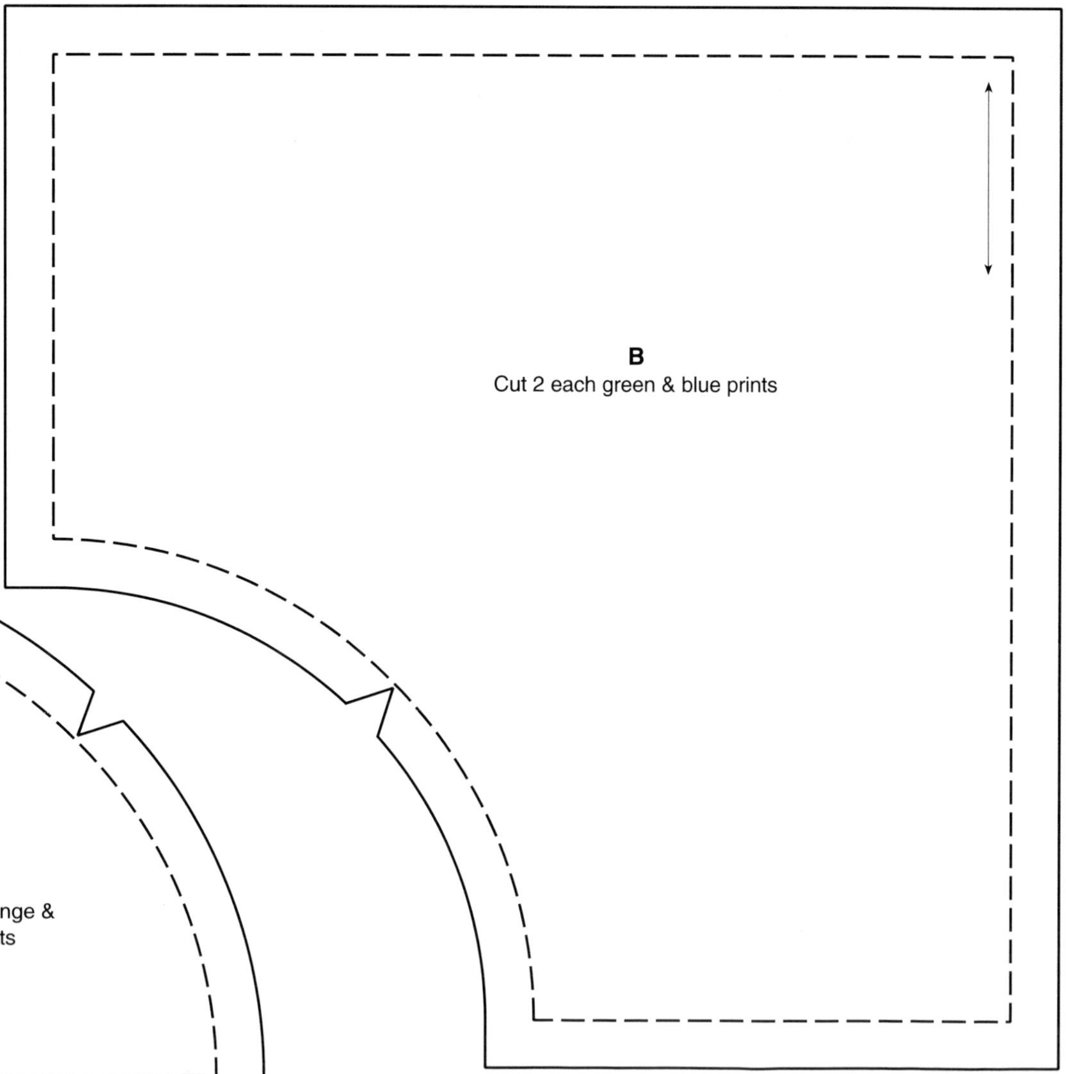

A
Cut 2 each orange & purple prints

B
Cut 2 each green & blue prints

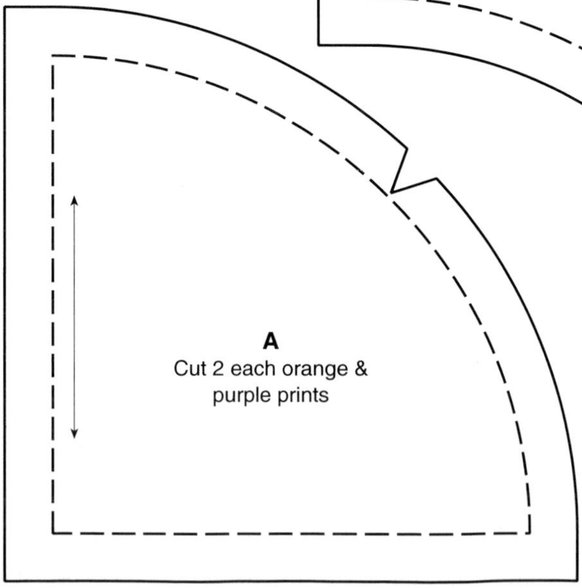

Peppermint Twist

By Jill Reber

Triangles combine to make two different blocks. When these blocks are joined together the results are a spectacular, but simple design.

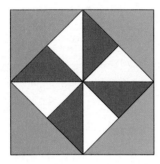

Peppermint Twist
8" x 8" Block

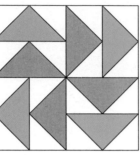

Wild Goose Chase
8" x 8" Block

Quilt Sizes			
	Lap	**Twin**	**Queen**
Finished Quilt Size	56" x 72"	64" x 88"	80" x 88"
Block Size	8" x 8"	8" x 8"	8" x 8"
Number of Blocks	35	54	72

Materials			
Floral print	1 1/4 yards	1 1/2 yards	1 1/2 yards
Pink prints	1 1/4 yards total	1 1/2 yards total	2 yards total
Green prints	1 1/2 yards total	2 yards total	2 1/2 yards total
Tan mottled	1 3/4 yards	2 1/2 yards	3 1/4 yards
Backing	60" x 76"	68" x 92"	84" x 92"
Batting	60" x 76"	68" x 92"	84" x 92"
Self-made or purchased binding	7 1/2 yards	9 yards	10 1/4 yards
All-purpose thread to match fabrics			
Basic sewing supplies and tools			

Instructions

Instructions are given for the size shown in photo, with other sizes in parentheses. When only 1 number is given, it applies to all sizes.

Step 1. From pink prints, cut five (7) (9) strips 5 1/4" by fabric width. Subcut each strip into 5 1/4" segments; cut each segment on both diagonals to make 140 (216) (288) A triangles.

Step 2. From green prints, cut three (4) (5) strips 5 1/4" by fabric width. Subcut each strip into 5 1/4" segments; cut each segment on both diagonals to make 68 (108) (144) A triangles. Cut five (7) (9) strips 4 7/8" by fabric width; subcut into 4 7/8" segments; cut each segment on one diagonal to make 72 (108) (144) B triangles.

Step 3. From tan mottled, cut three (4) (5) strips 5 1/4" by fabric width. Subcut each strip into 5 1/4" segments; cut each segment on both diagonals to make 72 (108) (144) A triangles. Cut 10 (16) (21) strips 2 7/8" by fabric width. Subcut into 2 7/8" segments; cut each segment on one diagonal to make 272 (432) (576) C triangles.

Step 4. To piece one Peppermint Twist block, sew a tan mottled A triangle to a pink print A triangle as shown in Figure 1; repeat for four units.

Step 5. Sew an A unit to B as shown in Figure 2; repeat for four units.

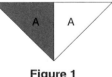

Figure 1
Sew a tan mottled A triangle to a pink print A triangle.

Figure 2
Sew an A unit to B.

Peppermint Twist
Placement Diagram
56" x 72"

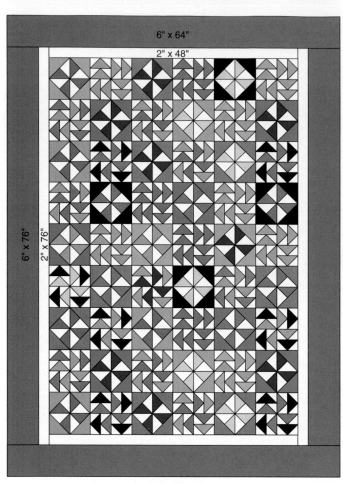

6" x 64"
2" x 48"
6" x 76"
2" x 76"

Peppermint Twist
Placement Diagram
64" x 88"

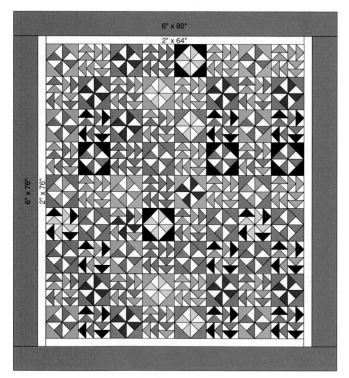

6" x 80"
2" x 64"
6" x 76"
2" x 76"

Peppermint Twist
Placement Diagram
80" x 88"

Step 6. Join the A-B units to complete one Peppermint Twist block as shown in Figure 3. Repeat for 18 (27) (36) blocks.

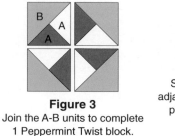

Figure 3
Join the A-B units to complete
1 Peppermint Twist block.

Figure 4
Sew a C triangle to
adjacent short sides of a
pink print A triangle.

Step 7. To piece one Wild Goose Chase block, sew a C triangle to adjacent short sides of a pink print A triangle as shown in Figure 4; repeat for four pink print and four green print A-C units.

Step 8. Join a green print and a pink print A-C unit as shown in Figure 5; repeat for four units.

Step 9. Join the A-C units to complete one Wild Goose Chase block as shown in Figure 6; repeat for 17 (27) (36) blocks.

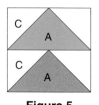

Figure 5
Join a green print and a
pink print A-C unit.

Figure 6
Join the A-C units to
complete 1 Wild Goose
Chase block.

Step 10. Join three (3) (4) Peppermint Twist blocks with two (3) (4) Wild Goose Chase blocks to make a row as shown in Figure 7; repeat for four (5) (5) rows. Press seams in one direction.

Step 11. Join three (3) (4) Wild Goose Chase blocks with two (3) (4) Peppermint Twist blocks to make a row as shown in Figure 8; repeat for three (4) (4) rows. Press seams in one direction.

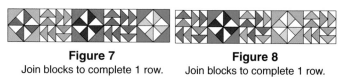

Figure 7
Join blocks to complete 1 row.

Figure 8
Join blocks to complete 1 row.

Step 12. Join rows referring to the Placement Diagram to complete pieced center; press seams in one direction.

Step 13. Cut and piece two strips each 2 1/2" x 40 1/2" (2 1/2" x 48 1/2") (2 1/2" x 64 1/2") and 2 1/2" x 60 1/2" (2 1/2" x 76 1/2") (2 1/2" x 76 1/2") tan mottled. Sew the shorter strips to the top and bottom and longer strips to opposite long sides; press seams toward strips.

Step 14. Cut and piece two strips each 6 1/2" x 60 1/2" (6 1/2" x 76 1/2") (6 1/2" x 76 1/2") floral print; sew

Continued on page 95

Desert Courtyard

By Carla Schwab

Solid fabrics in desert colors combine to make Courthouse Steps blocks in two color variations in this simple, but decorative quilt.

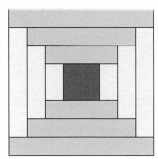

Courthouse Steps
8" x 8" Block
Make 10 (24) (40)

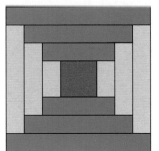

Courthouse Steps
8" x 8" Block
Make 16 (50) (54)

Instructions

Instructions are given for the size shown in photo, with other sizes in parentheses. When only 1 number is given, it applies to all sizes.

Step 1. Cut two (5) (6) strips 2 1/2" by fabric width rose solid. Subcut each strip into 2 1/2" square segments for block centers. You will need 26 (74) (94) center squares.

Step 2. Cut 10 (24) (40) strips 1 1/2" by fabric width light green solid.

Step 3. Cut seven (16) (27) strips 1 1/2" by fabric width cream solid.

Step 4. Cut 16 (50) (54) strips 1 1/2" by fabric width teal solid.

Step 5. Cut 11 (34) (36) strips 1 1/2" by fabric width peach solid.

Step 6. To make green/cream Courthouse Steps blocks, sew 10 (24) (40) rose solid center squares to a 1 1/2"-wide cream solid strip as shown in Figure 1. Press seams toward squares; trim strips even with squares as shown in Figure 2.

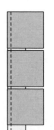

Figure 1
Sew rose solid center squares to a 1 1/2"-wide cream solid strip.

Figure 2
Trim strips even with squares as shown.

Quilt Sizes			
	Crib	**Twin**	**Queen**
Finished Quilt Size	46" x 54"	78" x 86"	86" x 94"
Block Size	8" x 8"	8" x 8"	8" x 8"
Number of Blocks	26	74	94

Materials			
Rose solid	1/4 yard	1/2 yard	1/2 yard
Peach solid	5/8 yard	1 5/8 yards	1 2/3 yards
Light green solid	1 yard	1 3/4 yards	2 1/4 yards
Cream solid	1 yard	1 3/4 yards	2 1/4 yards
Teal solid	1 1/8 yards	2 3/4 yards	3 yards
Backing	50" x 58"	82" x 90"	90" x 98"
Batting	50" x 58"	82" x 90"	90" x 98"
Neutral color all-purpose thread			
Cream quilting thread			
Basic sewing supplies and tools			

Step 7. Sew opposite side of center square to another cream solid strip as shown in Figure 3. Press and trim as in Step 6, referring to Figure 4.

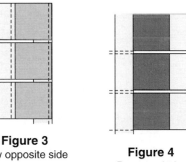

Figure 3
Sew opposite side of center square to another cream solid strip.

Figure 4
Press and trim as shown.

Step 8. Continue sewing pieced segments to strips, alternating colors to complete 10 (24) (40) green/cream Courthouse Steps blocks.

Step 9. Sew the remaining 16 (50) (54) rose solid center squares to peach and teal solid strips referring to Steps 6–8 for method to complete 16 (50) (54) peach/teal Courthouse Steps blocks.

Step 10. Cut two (8) (8) 8 7/8" x 8 7/8" squares each cream and teal solids. Cut each square in half on one diagonal to make triangles; join a cream and teal triangle to make a triangle/square. Repeat for four (16) (16) triangle/squares.

Step 11. Arrange the peach/teal and cream/green Courthouse Steps blocks with the triangle/squares in rows referring to the Placement Diagram for positioning

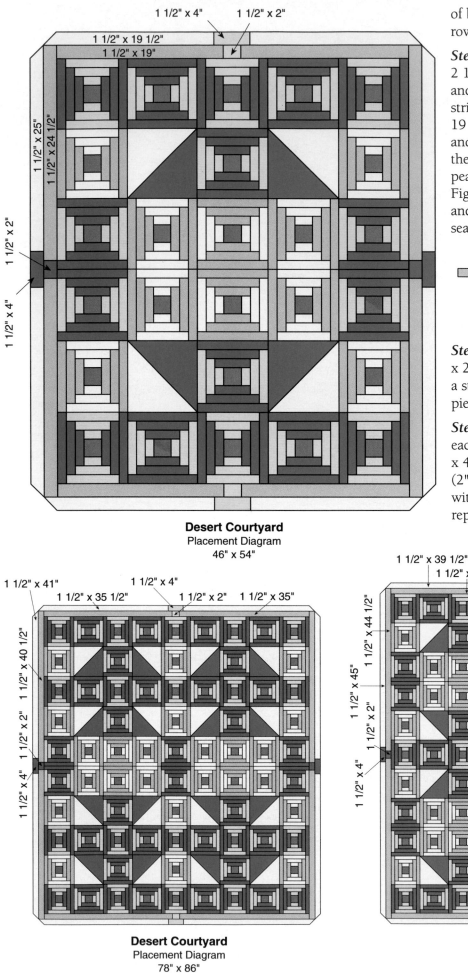

Desert Courtyard
Placement Diagram
46" x 54"

of blocks. Join blocks in rows; join rows to complete the pieced center.

Step 12. Cut two rectangles each 2" x 2 1/2" and 2" x 4 1/2" from both peach and teal solids. Cut (and piece) four strips each light green solid 2" x 19 1/2" (2" x 35 1/2") (2" x 39 1/2") and 2" x 25" (2" x 41") (2" x 45"). Join the two shorter strips with a 2" x 2 1/2" peach solid rectangle as shown in Figure 5; repeat. Sew a strip to the top and bottom of the pieced center; press seams toward strips.

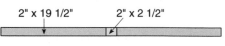

Figure 5
Join the 2 shorter strips with a 2" x 2 1/2" peach solid rectangle.

Step 13. Join two longer strips with a 2" x 2 1/2" teal solid rectangle; repeat. Sew a strip to opposite long sides of the pieced center; press seams toward strips.

Step 14. Cut (and piece) four strips each cream solid 2" x 20" (2" x 36") (2" x 40") and 2" x 25 1/2" (2" x 41 1/2") (2" x 45 1/2"). Join two shorter strips with a 2" x 4 1/2" peach solid rectangle; repeat. Sew a strip to the top and

Continued on page 99

Desert Courtyard
Placement Diagram
78" x 86"

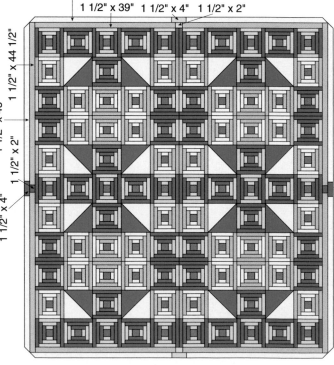

Desert Courtyard
Placement Diagram
86" x 94"

Rainbow of Tumbling Blocks

By Jill Reber

Combine black with bright fabrics to create this large Tumbling Block. Continue the burst of color in the borders to make this pretty scrap quilt.

Tumbling Blocks
28" x 32 1/2"

Project Notes

Scraps of a variety of light, medium and dark values of the same color fabrics may be used instead of purchased coordinating fabrics. The colored units may be made in a variety of colors and arranged as desired to create a quilt with similar qualities, but a different look. The instructions are given to recreate the block as it is shown in the sample quilt.

Instructions

Instructions are given for the size shown in photo, with other sizes in parentheses. When only 1 number is given, it applies to all sizes.

Step 1. From each of the gold, pink and teal prints, cut two (6) (8) strips 2 1/2" by fabric width. From each of the purple prints, cut two (5) (7) strips 2 1/2" by fabric width.

Step 2. Prepare templates for A and B using pattern pieces given.

Step 3. Place the A piece on the strips as shown in Figure 1; cut as directed on pattern for number and color.

Step 4. Sew a gold print A to a gold print A as shown in Figure 2; set in a gold print A, again referring to Figure 2. Repeat to make nine (54) (81) gold A units. *Note: Each unit is made with three different values of the same color fabric. In this case, three gold fabrics are used in each A unit.*

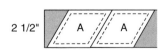
2 1/2"

Figure 1
Place the A piece on
the strips as shown.

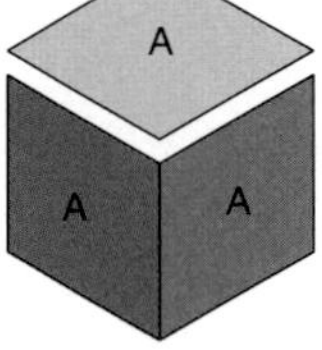

Figure 2
Sew a gold print A to a gold
print A; set in a gold print A.

Step 5. Repeat Step 4 to make 10 (60) (90) pink, eight (48) (72) purple and 10 (60) (90) teal A units. Set aside remaining A pieces for borders.

	Quilt Sizes		
	Lap	**Twin**	**King**
Approximate Finished Quilt Size	36" x 36 1/2"	64" x 101"	92" x 101"
Block Size	28" x 32 1/2"	28" x 32 1/2"	28" x 32 1/2"
Number of Blocks	1	6	9

Materials			
Dark, medium and light gold prints	1/4 yard each	1/2 yard each	5/8 yard each
Dark, medium and light teal prints	1/4 yard each	1/2 yard each	5/8 yard each
Dark, medium and light pink prints	1/4 yard each	1/2 yard each	5/8 yard each
Dark, medium and light purple prints	1/4 yard each	1/2 yard each	5/8 yard each
Black solid	3/4 yard	3 1/8 yards	4 3/4 yards
Backing	40" x 40"	68" x 105"	96" x 105"
Batting	40" x 40"	68" x 105"	96" x 105"
Self-made or purchased binding	4 1/2 yards	9 3/4 yards	11 1/4 yards
Black all-purpose thread			
Basic sewing supplies and tools			

Step 6. Cut three (18) (27) strips black solid 2 3/4" by fabric width. Place the B template on strips as shown in Figure 3 referring to the template for number to cut.

Step 7. To piece one unit, sew B to the top and bottom of a gold A unit as shown in Figure 4; repeat to make eight gold, five purple, six pink and 10 teal block units.

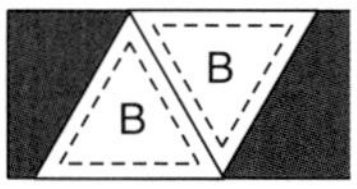

Figure 3
Place the B
template on strips.

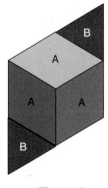

Figure 4
To piece 1 unit, sew B to the
top and bottom of a gold A unit.

Step 8. Sew B to the bottom only of a gold A unit as shown in Figure 5; repeat to make one gold and three purple top units.

Step 9. Sew B to the top only of a pink A unit as shown in Figure 6; repeat to make four pink bottom units.

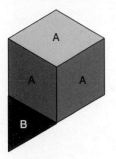

Figure 5
Sew B to the bottom
only of a gold A unit.

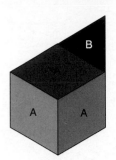

Figure 6
Sew B to the top only
of a pink A unit.

Step 10. Arrange block units with top
and bottom units in seven diagonal rows
as shown in Figure 7; join rows. Set in B
pieces as shown in Figure 8.

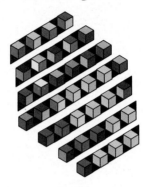

Figure 7
Arrange block units with top and
bottom units in 7 diagonal rows.

Step 11. Cut two rectangles
black solid 9" x 15 1/4"; cut
each rectangle in half on one
diagonal as shown in Figure 9.
Sew a triangle to each angled
edge of the pieced unit to complete one Tumbling Blocks
block as shown in Figure 10.
Trim rectangle even with edge
of pieced section, if necessary.
Note: *For twin and king sizes,
repeat Steps 7–11 to make (6) (9) blocks.*

Step 12. Cut (and piece) two strips black solid 2 1/2" x
33" (2 1/2" x 98") (2 1/2" x 98"). Sew a strip to opposite long sides of the pieced center; trim if necessary.

Step 13. To piece border strips, join eight (9) (7) same-
color A pieces varying values as shown in Figure 11;
repeat for two (4) (6) strips of each color. Join strips to
make two border strips each 32 1/2"-long (60 1/2")
(88 1/2") and 37"-long (102") (102"). Center and sew the
shorter strips to the top and bottom and longer strips to
opposite sides. Trim excess at ends as necessary. Press
seams away from pieced strips.

Step 14. Prepare top for quilting and finish as desired
referring to the General Instructions. ***Note:*** *The quilt*

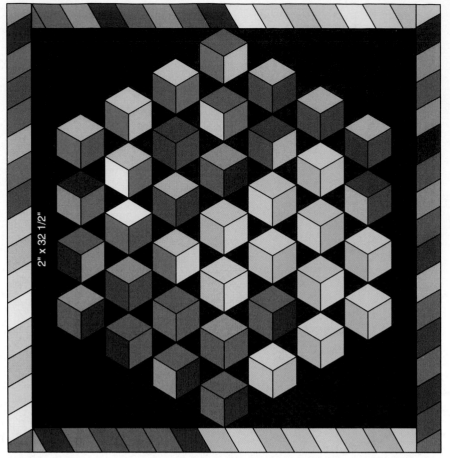

Rainbow of Tumbling Blocks
Placement Diagram
Approximately 36" x 36 1/2"

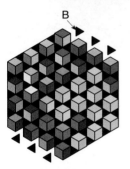

Figure 8
Set in B pieces as shown.

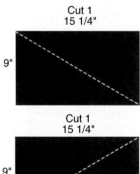

Cut 1
15 1/4"

9"

Cut 1
15 1/4"

9"

Figure 9
Cut 2 rectangles black solid
9" x 15 1/4"; cut each rectangle
in half on 1 diagonal as shown.

Figure 10
Sew a triangle to each angled edge
of the pieced unit to complete 1
Tumbling Blocks block.

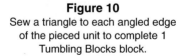

Figure 11
Join 8 same-color A pieces of varying values to make a border strip.

*shown was machine-quilted using black all-purpose thread
in the ditch of border pieces, around each block unit and in
lines 1" apart in black solid corners.* ❧

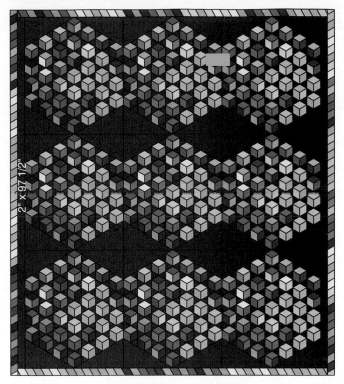

Rainbow of Tumbling Blocks
Placement Diagram
Approximately 92" x 101"

Rainbow of Tumbling Blocks
Placement Diagram
Approximately 64" x 101"

A
Cut 16 (72) (104) each light,
medium & dark pink & teal prints
Cut 14 (60) (86) each light,
medium & dark purple prints
Cut 15 (66) (95) each light,
medium & dark gold prints

B
Cut 72 (432)(648) black solid

Peppermint Twist
Continued from page 88

strips to opposite long sides. Cut and piece two strips each 6 1/2" x 56 1/2" (6 1/2" x 64 1/2") (6 1/2" x 80 1/2") floral print; sew to top and bottom. Press seams toward strips.

Step 15. Prepare top for quilting and finish as desired referring to the General Instructions. ***Note:*** *The quilt shown was machine-quilted in a meandering design using thread to match fabrics.* ❧

Crossroads

By Johanna Wilson

Give a traditional block an updated twist using a good variety of fabrics with contrast to give your finished quilt sparkle.

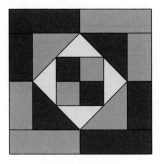

Crossroads
9" x 9" Block

Instructions

Instructions are given for the size shown in photo, with other sizes in parentheses. When only 1 number is given, it applies to all sizes.

Step 1. Cut six (7) (9) strips 2" by fabric width each green and paisley prints. Sew a green print strip to a paisley print strip with right sides together along length; press seams toward darker fabric. Repeat for six (7) (9) strip sets. Cut each strip set into 2" segments as shown in Figure 1; you will need 126 (144) (180) segments.

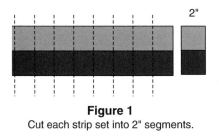

Figure 1
Cut each strip set into 2" segments.

Step 2. Join two segments to make a Four-Patch unit as shown in Figure 2; repeat for 63 (72) (90) units.

Figure 2
Join 2 segments to
make a Four-Patch unit.

Step 3. Cut nine (11) (13) strips tan print 3" by fabric width. Subcut strips into 3" square segments. You will need 126 (144) (180) squares. Cut each square in half on one diagonal to make 252 (288) (360) triangles.

Step 4. Finger-press each triangle to find the center of the diagonal. Center a triangle on opposite sides of a

Quilt Sizes			
	Double	**Queen**	**King**
Finished Quilt Size	77" x 95"	86" x 95"	104" x 95"
Block Size	9" x 9"	9" x 9"	9" x 9"
Number of Blocks	63	72	90

Materials			
Red print	1/2 yard	1/2 yard	1/2 yard
Tan print	1 1/2 yards	1 3/4 yards	2 yards
Green print	2 3/4 yards	3 yards	3 3/4 yards
Paisley print	4 yards	4 1/4 yards	5 1/4 yards
Backing	81" x 99"	90" x 99"	108" x 99"
Batting	81" x 99"	90" x 99"	108" x 99"
Self-made or purchased binding	10 yards	10 1/2 yards	11 1/2 yards
Neutral color all-purpose thread			
Tan quilting thread			
Basic sewing supplies and tools			

Four-Patch unit as shown in Figure 3; stitch and press seams away from center.

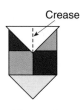

Figure 3
Center a triangle on opposite
sides of a Four-Patch unit.

Step 5. Repeat with two more triangles on the remaining two sides of the Four-Patch unit to complete the block center as shown in Figure 4; repeat for all Four-Patch units.

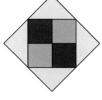

Figure 4
Sew 2 more triangles on the
remaining 2 sides of the Four-Patch
unit to complete the block center.

Step 6. Cut seven (8) (9) strips 3 7/8" by fabric width each green and paisley prints. Cut each strip into 3 7/8" square segments. You will need 63 (72) (90)

squares. Cut each square in half on one diagonal to make 126 (144) (180) triangles. Fold to find centers of each triangle. Sew two matching triangles to opposite sides of the pieced Four-Patch center units referring to Figure 5; repeat on all Four-Patch units. Press seams toward larger triangles.

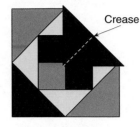

Figure 5
Sew 2 matching triangles to
opposite sides of the pieced
Four-Patch center units.

Step 7. Cut six (7) (9) strips each 3 1/2" by fabric width green and paisley prints. Sew a green print strip to a paisley print strip with right sides together along length; press seams toward darker fabric. Repeat with all strips. Cut strip sets into 2" segments as shown in Figure 6; you will need 126 (144) (180) segments. Sew a segment to opposite sides of a pieced unit as shown in Figure 7; repeat for all pieced units. Press seams toward segments.

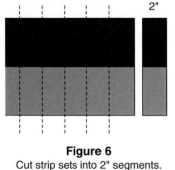

Figure 6
Cut strip sets into 2" segments.

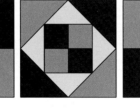

Figure 7
Sew a segment to opposite
sides of a pieced unit.

Step 8. Cut six (7) (9) strips each 5" by fabric width green and paisley prints. Sew a green print strip to a paisley print strip with right sides together along length; press seams toward darker fabric. Repeat with all strips. Cut strip sets into 2" segments as shown in Figure 6; you will need 126 (144) (180)) segments. Sew a segment to each remaining side of the pieced Four-Patch units to complete one block as shown in Figure 8. Repeat for 63 (72) (90) blocks.

Step 9. Join seven (8) (10) blocks to make a row; repeat for nine (9) (9) rows. Press seams in one

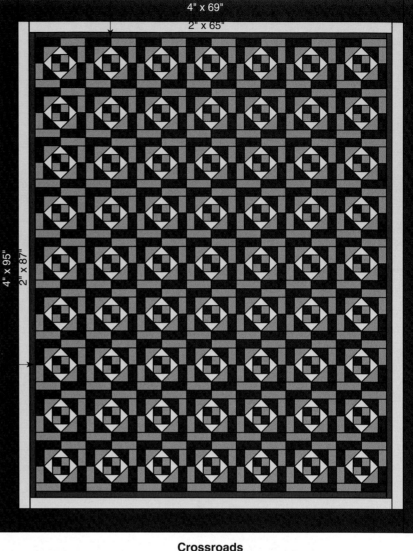

Crossroads
Placement Diagram
77" x 95"

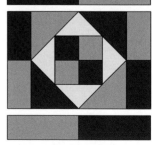

Figure 8
Sew a segment to each remaining
side of the pieced Four-Patch units
to complete 1 block.

direction. Join rows to complete pieced center; press seams in one direction.

Step 10. Cut and piece two strips 1 1/2" x 63 1/2" (1 1/2" x 72 1/2") (1 1/2" x 90 1/2") red print. Sew to top and bottom of pieced center; press seams toward strips. Cut and piece two strips 1 1/2" x 83 1/2"

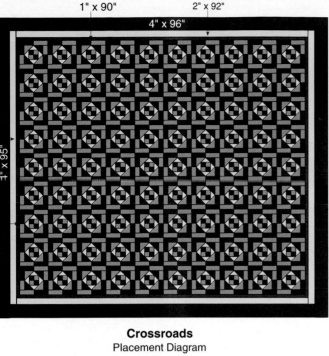

Crossroads
Placement Diagram
104" x 95"

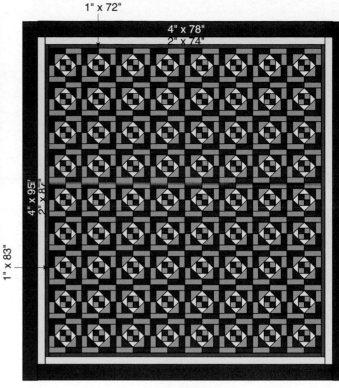

Crossroads
Placement Diagram
86" x 95"

(1 1/2" x 83 1/2") (1 1/2" 83 1/2") red print. Sew to opposite sides of the pieced center; press seams toward strips.

Step 11. Cut and piece two strips 2 1/2" x 65 1/2" (2 1/2" x 74 1/2") (2 1/2" x 92 1/2") tan print. Sew to the top and bottom of the pieced center; press seams toward strips. Cut and piece two strips 2 1/2" x 87 1/2" (2 1/2" x 87 1/2") (2 1/2" x 87 1/2") tan print. Sew to opposite sides of the pieced center; press seams toward strips.

Step 12. Cut and piece two strips 4 1/2" x 69 1/2" (4 1/2" x 78 1/2") (4 1/2" x 96 1/2") paisley print. Sew to the top and bottom of the pieced center; press seams toward strips. Cut and piece two strips 4 1/2" x 95 1/2" (4 1/2" x 95 1/2") (4 1/2" x 95 1/2") paisley print. Sew to opposite sides of the pieced center; press seams toward strips.

Step 13. Prepare top for quilting and finish as desired referring to the General Instructions. **Note:** *The quilt shown was hand-quilted in an X through Four-Patch units and in the ditch of border seams using tan quilting thread.* ❧

Desert Courtyard
Continued from page 90

bottom of the pieced center; press seams toward strips.

Step 15. Join two longer strips with a 2" x 4 1/2" teal solid rectangle; repeat. Sew a strip to opposite long sides of the pieced center; press seams toward strips.

Step 16. Prepare top for quilting referring to the General Instructions. Quilt as desired by hand or machine. **Note:** *The quilt shown was hand-quilted in the ditch of seams and with a deer design in the triangle/squares using cream quilting thread.*

Step 17. When quilting is complete, trim edges even. Trim quilt corners diagonally from corner of light green border strips as shown in Figure 6.

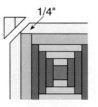

Figure 6
Trim quilt corners diagonally
from corner of light green
border strips as shown.

Step 18. Trim batting 1/4" smaller than quilt top and backing all around. Turn edges of backing and quilt top in 1/4"; slipstitch in place around edges to finish. ❧

Chapter Four

Patchwork Garden

You'll find a garden full of beautiful
blooms to appliqué and piece in this
chapter. Of course, no garden is
complete without a few bugs and
butterflies, so you'll find quilts featuring
those as well. Begin now to grow a
garden of patchwork quilts.

Nine-Patch Posies

By Leslie Beck

Use reproduction prints with a 1930s flavor, and turn the traditional Nine-Patch block into a Flower block.

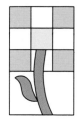 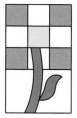

Nine-Patch Posy Reversed
4 1/2" x 7 1/2" Block

Nine-Patch Posy
4 1/2" x 7 1/2" Block

Quilt Sizes

	Twin	Crib	Queen
Finished Quilt Size	61 1/2" x 93 1/2"	34" x 56"	83 1/2" x 93 1/2"
Block Size	4 1/2" x 7 1/2"	4 1/2" x 7 1/2"	4 1/2" x 7 1/2"
Number of Blocks	132	42	180

Materials

Seven different prints	1/3 yard each	1/6 yard each	3/8 yard each
Yellow solid	1/2 yard	1/6 yard	5/8 yard
Green solid	3/4 yard	1/3 yard	1 yard
Cream print	5 yards	2 yards	6 5/8 yards
Backing	66" x 98"	38" x 60"	88" x 98"
Batting	66" x 98"	38" x 60"	88" x 98"
Self-made or purchased binding	9 1/4 yards	5 1/2 yards	10 1/2 yards
Green and off-white all-purpose thread			
Fusible transfer web	2 yards	1 yard	2 1/2 yards
Tear-off fabric stabilizer	3 yards	1 yard	4 yards
Basic sewing supplies and tools			

Instructions

Instructions are given for the size shown in photo, with other sizes in parentheses. When only 1 number is given, it applies to all sizes.

Step 1. From each of the seven prints, cut four (0) (4) strips 2" by fabric width. Cut 0 (4) (4) strips each print 2" x 21".

Step 2. Cut seven (2) (9) strips 2" by fabric width yellow solid.

Step 3. Cut 28 (4) (32) strips 2" by fabric width cream print. Cut 0 (14) (14) strips 2" x 21".

Step 4. Sew a cream print strip between two same-length same-print strips. Repeat with all print strips to make 14 (0) (14) fabric width strip sets and 0 (14) (14) 21" strip sets. Cut each strip set into 2" segments as shown in Figure 1. You will need 38 (12) (52) segments of each print.

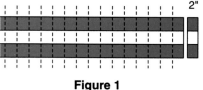

Figure 1
Cut each strip set into 2" segments.

Step 5. Sew a yellow solid strip between two cream print strips; repeat for seven (2) (9) strip sets. Cut each strip set into 2" segments as shown in Figure 2. You will need 132 (42) (180) cream/yellow segments.

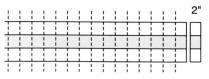

Figure 2
Cut each strip set into 2" segments.

Step 6. Sew a cream/yellow segment between two same-print segments to complete one Nine-Patch unit as shown in Figure 3; repeat to make 132 (42) (180)

Nine-Patch units. **Note:** *You will have two (0) (4) segments left of each print. Set aside for another project.*

Step 7. Cut 14 (5) (19) strips 5" by fabric width cream print. Subcut into 11 (6) (15) 2" x 5" segments and 132 (42) (180) 3 1/2" x 5" segments.

Step 8. Sew a 3 1/2" x 5" segment to each Nine-Patch unit as shown in Figure 4.

Figure 3
Sew a cream/yellow segment between 2 same-print segments to complete 1 Nine-Patch unit.

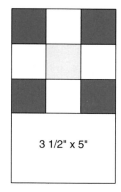

3 1/2" x 5"

Figure 4
Sew a 3 1/2" x 5" segment to each Nine-Patch unit.

Step 9. Prepare templates for stem and leaf. Bond fusible transfer web to the wrong side of the green solid. Trace stem and leaf pieces on the paper side of the fusible transfer web referring to patterns for number to cut. Cut out shapes on traced lines; remove paper backing.

Step 10. Fuse leaf and stem pieces in place on Nine-Patch units making 66 (21) (90) each Nine-Patch Posy and Nine-Patch Posy Reversed blocks referring to the block drawings for positioning of appliqué pieces. *Note: To make reverse blocks, turn stem and leaf pieces from top to bottom and place leaf on opposite side of stem referring to the block drawings.*

Step 11. Place tear-off fabric stabilizer behind each stem and leaf area. Machine satin-stitch or buttonhole-stitch in place using green all-purpose thread. Tear off fabric stabilizer.

Step 12. Arrange 12 (7) (12) blocks in 11 (6) (15) vertical rows, alternating blocks with reversed blocks and placing a 2" x 5" cream print segment on the top of five (3) (7) rows and at the bottom of six (3) (8) rows referring to Figure 5. Press seams in one direction.

1" x 91 1/2"   1" x 61 1/2"

Nine-Patch Posies
Placement Diagram
61 1/2" x 93 1/2"

Make 6   Make 5

2" x 5"

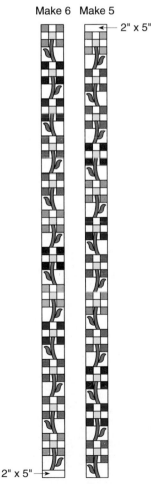

2" x 5"

Figure 5
Join blocks to make rows
and add 2" x 5" cream
print rectangles to top or
bottom as shown.

Step 13. Cut and piece 12 (7) (16) strips each 1 1/2" x 92" (1 1/2" x 54 1/2") (1 1/2" x 92") cream print. Join strips with rows beginning and ending with a strip; press seams toward strips.

Step 14. Cut and piece two strips each 1 1/2" x 62" (1 1/2" x 34 1/2") (1 1/2" x 84") cream print. Sew a strip to the top and bottom; press seams toward strips.

Step 15. Prepare top for quilting and finish as desired referring to the General Instructions. *Note: The quilt shown was machine-quilted in the ditch of border and sashing strip seams using off-white all-purpose thread.* ❧

1" x 54"　　　　　1" x 34"

Nine-Patch Posies
Placement Diagram
34" x 56"

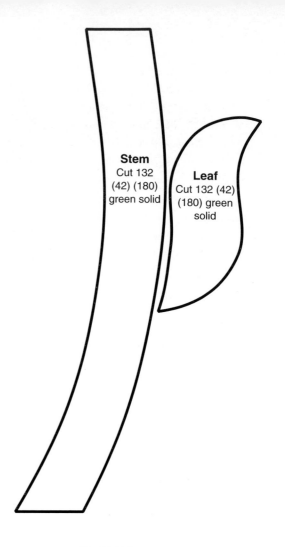

Stem
Cut 132
(42) (180)
green solid

Leaf
Cut 132 (42)
(180) green
solid

1" x 91 1/2"　　　　1" x 83 1/2"

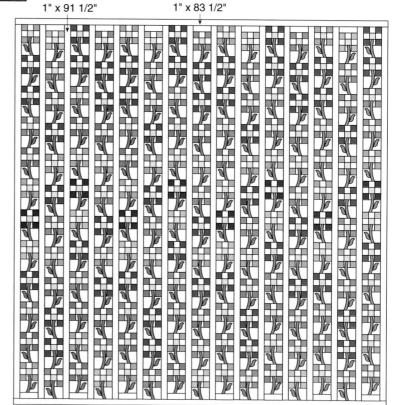

Nine-Patch Posies
Placement Diagram
83 1/2" x 93 1/2"

Pinwheels in the Breeze

By Leslie Beck

Monochromatic quilts make a wonderful statement about value. The traditional Pinwheel block is made in several shades of blue to create the movement in this energetic quilt.

Make 46 (30) (75)

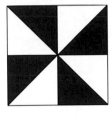

Make 62 (40) (109)

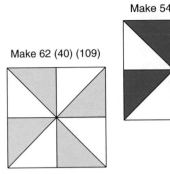

Make 54 (22) (104)

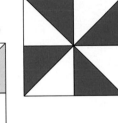

Pinwheel
4" x 4" Block

Quilt Sizes			
	Youth	**Crib**	**Twin**
Finished Quilt Size	52" x 64"	36" x 56"	64" x 88"
Block Size	4" x 4"	4" x 4"	4" x 4"
Number of Blocks	162	92	288

Materials			
Dark blue print	3/4 yard	1/2 yard	1 yard
Medium blue print	3/4 yard	1/2 yard	1 3/8 yards
Light blue print	7/8 yard	5/8 yard	1 3/8 yards
Off-white print	2 3/4 yards	1 3/4 yards	4 3/8 yards
Backing	56" x 68"	40" x 60"	68" x 92"
Batting	56" x 68"	40" x 60"	68" x 92"
Self-made or purchased binding	7 yards	5 1/2 yards	9 yards
Off-white all-purpose thread			
Basic sewing supplies and tools			

Instructions

Instructions are given for the size shown in photo, with other sizes in parentheses. When only 1 number is given, it applies to all sizes.

Step 1. Cut seven (5) (11) strips dark blue print, eight (4) (15) strips medium blue print, nine (6) (16) strips light blue print and 24 (14)(42) strips off-white print 2 7/8" by fabric width.

Step 2. Cut all strips into 2 7/8" square segments. You will need 92 (60) (150) dark blue, 108 (44) (208) medium blue, 124 (80) (218) light blue and 324 (184) (576) off-white squares.

Step 3. Draw a diagonal line on each of the off-white squares. Place a colored square right sides together with an off-white square. Sew 1/4" from both sides of the diagonal line; cut apart on diagonal to make two triangle/squares as shown in Figure 1. Repeat with all off-white squares.

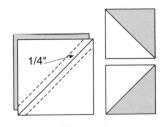

Figure 1
Sew 1/4" from both sides of the
diagonal line cut apart on diagonal
to make 2 triangle/squares.

Pinwheels in the Breeze
Placement Diagram
52" x 64"

Pinwheels in the Breeze
Placement Diagram
64" x 88"

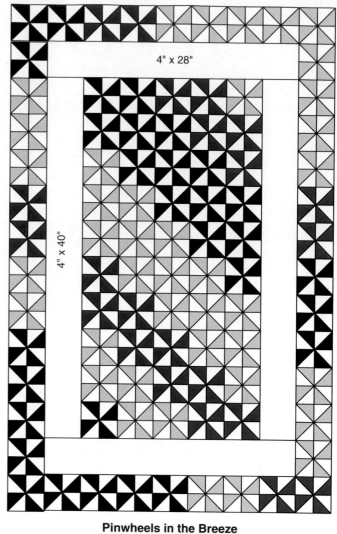

Pinwheels in the Breeze
Placement Diagram
36" x 56"

Step 4. Join two same-color triangle/squares as shown in Figure 2; repeat. Join two units to complete one Pinwheel block as shown in Figure 3. Repeat for 46 (30) (75) dark blue, 54 (22) (104) medium blue and 62 (40) (109) light blue Pinwheel blocks.

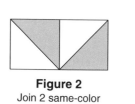

Figure 2
Join 2 same-color
triangle/squares.

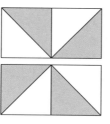

Figure 3
Join 2 units to complete
1 Pinwheel block.

Step 5. Arrange blocks in 12 (10) (18) rows of nine (5) (12) blocks each referring to the Placement Diagram for color arrangement. Join blocks in rows; join rows to complete pieced center. Press seams in one direction.

Step 6. Cut and piece, if necessary, two strips each 4 1/2" x 44 1/2" (4 1/2" x 28 1/2") (4 1/2" x 56 1/2") off-white print and two strips each 4 1/2" x 48 1/2"

(4 1/2" x 40 1/2") (4 1/2" x 72 1/2"). Sew longer strips to opposite sides and shorter strips to the top and bottom; press seams toward strips.

Step 7. Join 14 (12) (20) blocks to make a side border strip referring to the Placement Diagram for positioning of blocks. Repeat for two border strips. Sew a strip to opposite long sides of the pieced center; press seams away from block strips.

Step 8. Join 13 (9) (16) blocks to make the top border strip referring to the Placement Diagram(s) for positioning of blocks. Repeat for bottom border strip. Sew strips to the top and bottom of the pieced center; press seams away from block strips.

Step 9. Prepare top for quilting and finish as desired referring to the General Instructions. **Note:** *The quilt shown was machine-quilted in a spiral design in blocks and a diamond design in borders using off-white all-purpose thread.* ❧

Spring Bouquet

By Michele Crawford

Pieced flower blocks combine with a pretty floral print to make this colorful quilt.

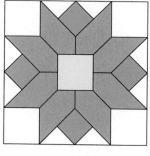

Diamond Star
12" x 12" Block

Instructions

Instructions are given for the size shown in photo, with other sizes in parentheses. When only 1 number is given, it applies to all sizes.

Step 1. Prepare template for piece E using pattern given; cut fabric patches as directed on the piece.

Step 2. Cut four (12) (18) pink print and five (12) (18) yellow print 3 1/2" x 3 1/2" squares for A.

Step 3. Cut three (8) (12) 3 1/2" by fabric width strips white-on-white print; subcut each strip into 3 1/2" squares for B. You will need 36 (96) (144) B squares.

Step 4. Cut two (6) (8) 4 1/4" by fabric width strips white-on-white print; subcut each strip into 4 1/4" segments. Cut each segment on both diagonals to make D triangles. You will need 72 (192) (288) D triangles.

Step 5. Cut three (6) (9) 2 5/8" by fabric width strips green solid; subcut each strip into 2 5/8" squares for C. You will need 36 (96) (144) C squares.

Step 6. To make one pink Diamond Star block, sew pink print E to ER as shown in Figure 1; repeat for four E units. Join E units as shown in Figure 2.

Quilt Sizes			
	Lap	**Twin**	**Queen**
Finished Quilt Size	47" x 47"	62" x 88"	88" x 88"
Block Size	12" x 12"	12" x 12"	12" x 12"
Number of Blocks	9	24	36

Materials			
Yellow print	1/2 yard	1 yard	1 2/3 yards
Floral print	5/8 yard	1 1/8 yards	1 1/3 yards
White-on-white print	2/3 yard	1 2/3 yards	2 1/4 yards
Green solid	2/3 yard	1 1/2 yards	2 yards
Pink print	3/4 yard	1 1/4 yards	1 3/4 yards
Backing	51" x 51"	66" x 92"	92" x 92"
Batting	51" x 51"	66" x 92"	92" x 92"
Self-made or purchased binding	5 3/4 yards	8 3/4 yards	10 1/4 yards
All-purpose thread to match fabrics			
Basic sewing supplies and tools			

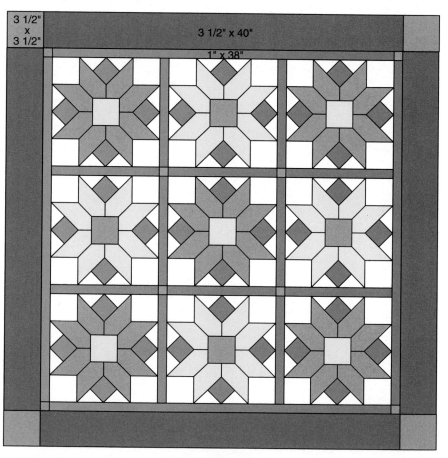

Spring Bouquet
Placement Diagram
47" x 47"

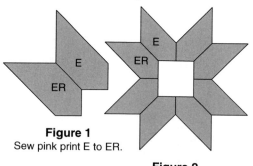

Figure 1
Sew pink print E to ER.

Figure 2
Join E units as shown.

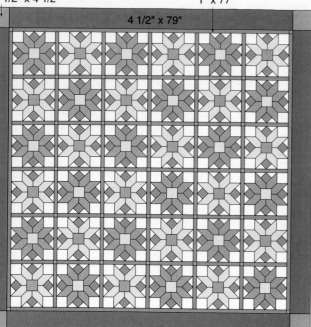

4 1/2" x 4 1/2"   1" x 77"

4 1/2" x 79"

Spring Bouquet
Placement Diagram
88" x 88"

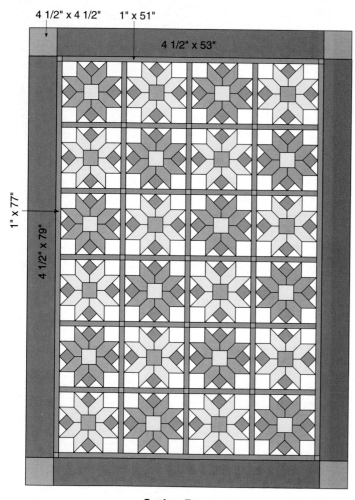

4 1/2" x 4 1/2"   1" x 51"

4 1/2" x 53"

1" x 77"

4 1/2" x 79"

Spring Bouquet
Placement Diagram
62" x 88"

Step 7. Sew D to two adjacent sides of C as shown in Figure 3; repeat for four C-D units.

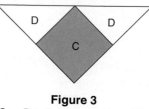

Figure 3
Sew D to 2 adjacent sides of C.

Step 8. Set the C-D units, B squares and yellow print A into the E unit as shown in Figure 4 to complete one block. Repeat for five (12) (18) pink Diamond Star blocks.

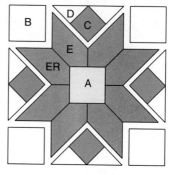

Figure 4
Set the C-D units, B squares and
yellow print A into the E unit as shown
to complete 1 pink block.

Step 9. To make one yellow Diamond Star block, repeat Steps 6–8 except use yellow print E and ER and pink print A as shown in Figure 5. Repeat for four (12) (18) yellow Diamond Star blocks.

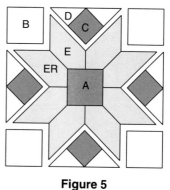

Figure 5
Complete 1 yellow block as shown.

Step 10. Cut four (13) (20) strips 1 1/2" by fabric width green solid; subcut into 12 1/2" x 12 1/2" segments. You will need 12 (38) (60) sashing strips.

Step 11. Cut eight (19) (29) 1 1/2" x 1 1/2" squares pink print for sashing squares.

Step 12. Join two (2) (3) pink blocks and one (2) (3) yellow block with two (3) (5) sashing strips to make a row; repeat for two (3) (3) rows. Press seams toward sashing strips.

Step 13. Join two (2) (3) yellow blocks and one (2) (3) pink block with two (3) (5) sashing strips to make a row; repeat for (3) (3) rows for larger sizes. Press seams toward sashing strips.

Step 14. Join two (3) (5) sashing squares with three (4) (6) sashing strips to make a row as shown in Figure 6; repeat for two (5) (5) rows. Press seams toward sashing squares.

1 1/2" x 12 1/2"   1 1/2" x 1 1/2"

Figure 6
Join 2 sashing squares with 3 sashing strips to make a row.

Step 15. Join the block rows with the sashing rows to complete the pieced center referring to the Placement Diagram for positioning of rows. Press seams toward sashing rows.

Step 16. Cut (and piece) two strips each 1 1/2" x 38 1/2" (1 1/2" x 51 1/2") (1 1/2" x 77 1/2") and two each 1 1/2" x 38 1/2" (1 1/2" x 77 1/2") (1 1/2" x 77 1/2") green solid.

Step 17. Sew a strip to the top and bottom of the pieced center; press seams toward strips. Sew a sashing square to each end of the two remaining strips; press seams toward sashing squares. Sew strips to remaining sides of the pieced center; press seams toward strips.

Step 18. Cut four 4" x 4" (5" x 5") (5" x 5") squares pink print for corner squares. Cut (and piece) two strips each 4" x 40 1/2" (5" x 53 1/2") (5" x 79 1/2") and two each 4" x 40 1/2" (5" x 79 1/2") (5" x 79 1/2") floral print.

Step 19. Sew a strip to the top and bottom of the pieced center; press seams toward strips. Sew a corner square to each end of the two remaining strips; press seams toward corner squares. Sew strips to remaining sides of the pieced center; press seams toward strips.

Step 20. Prepare top for quilting and finish as desired referring to the General Instructions. *Note: The quilt shown was machine-quilted in the ditch of seams, in a meandering design within the blocks and in a vine pattern in the border using thread to match fabrics.* ❧

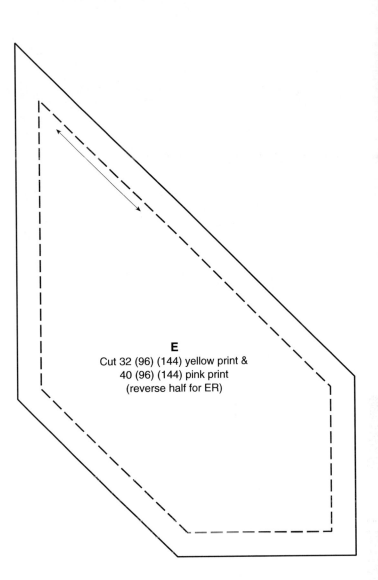

E
Cut 32 (96) (144) yellow print &
40 (96) (144) pink print
(reverse half for ER)

Bluebell Medallion

By Holly Daniels

Bring the look of summer indoors with this lovely medallion quilt.

Instructions

Instructions are given for the size shown in photo, with other sizes in parentheses. When only 1 number is given, it applies to all sizes.

Step 1. Cut a 30 1/2" x 30 1/2" square white solid for center background. Fold and crease to mark centers (diagonal, vertical and horizontal).

Step 2. Prepare templates for appliqué pieces using pattern pieces given. Trace shapes onto paper side of fusible transfer web referring to patterns for number to cut. Cut out each shape leaving a margin around each one.

Step 3. Fuse shapes to the wrong side of the fabrics as directed on each piece for color. Cut out shapes on traced lines; remove paper backing.

Step 4. Arrange center motif (flower, four leaves, flower center) on the center background in numerical order using crease marks as guides for placement as shown in Figure 1. Fuse shapes in place.

Step 5. Using thread to match fabrics, machine-appliqué each shape in place with a narrow zigzag stitch.

Step 6. Arrange and layer heart shapes around center shape, again using crease marks as guides for placement referring to Figure 2; fuse shapes in place and appliqué as in Step 5.

	Quilt Sizes		
	Queen	**Twin**	**Double**
Finished Quilt Size	88 1/2" x 88 1/2"	67 1/4" x 88 1/2"	78 1/2" x 88 1/2"
Materials			
Blue solid	1/8 yard	1/8 yard	1/8 yard
Pink solid	1/8 yard	1/8 yard	1/8 yard
Yellow print	1/8 yard	1/8 yard	1/8 yard
Blue print	1/4 yard	1/4 yard	1/4 yard
Green print	1 1/2 yards	1 1/4 yards	1 1/2 yards
White solid	1 7/8 yards	1 1/2 yards	1 7/8 yards
Pink print	2 1/8 yards	1 1/2 yards	2 1/8 yards
Floral print	2 5/8 yards	2 yards	2 1/4 yards
Backing	93" x 93"	72" x 93"	83" x 93"
Batting	93" x 93"	72" x 93"	83" x 93"
Self-made or purchased binding	10 1/2 yards	9 1/4 yards	9 3/4 yards
All-purpose thread to match fabrics			
Fusible transfer web	1 3/4 yards	1 3/4 yard	1 3/4 yards
Tear-off fabric stabilizer	1 3/4 yards	1 3/4 yard	1 3/4 yards
Basic sewing supplies and tools			

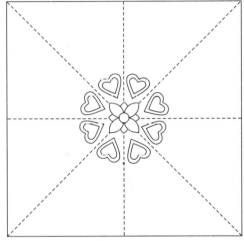

Figure 2
Arrange and layer heart shapes around center shape, again using crease marks as guides for placement.

Step 7. Arrange stems and irises, bluebells and leaves around the center motif referring to the Placement Diagram(s) for positioning. Fuse shapes in place and appliqué as in Step 5.

Step 8. Cut two strips each 2" x 30 1/2" and 2" x 33 1/2" pink print. Sew shorter strips to opposite sides and longer strips to top and bottom of the appliquéd center; press seams toward strips.

Step 9. Prepare templates for pieces A and B using pattern pieces given; cut as directed on each piece.

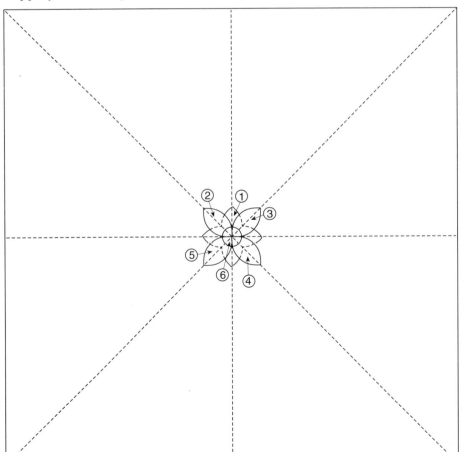

Figure 1
Place center motif on background in numerical order using crease marks as guides as shown.

Step 10. Join six green print A triangles with five white solid A triangles; add B and BR to each end as shown in Figure 3. Repeat for four strips; press each strip.

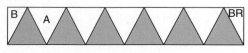

Figure 3
Join 6 green print A triangles with 5 white solid A triangles; add B and BR to each end.

Step 11. Sew a pieced strip to two opposite sides of the appliquéd center. Cut four 5 3/4" x 5 3/4" squares white solid; sew a square to each end of the remaining pieced strips. Sew strips to the top and bottom of the appliquéd center; press seams toward strips.

Step 12. Cut and piece two strips each 2 3/8" x 44" and 2 3/8" x 47 3/4" pink print. Sew shorter strips to opposite sides and longer strips to the top and bottom of bordered center; press seams toward strips.

Step 13. Cut 12 (7) (12) strips 2 1/4" by fabric width and one (0) (1) strip 2 1/4" x 21" pink print. Cut 1 (5) (11) strip 2 1/4" by fabric width and one (2) (1) strip 2 1/4" x 21" white solid. Cut 12 (5) (12) strips 2 1/4" by fabric width and two (3) (2) strips 2 1/4" x 21" green print.

Step 14. Sew a fabric-width pink print strip to a same-length green print strip with right sides together along length; repeat with 21"-long strips. *Note: For twin size make only the fabric-width strips set.* Cut strip sets into 2 1/4" segments as shown in Figure 4; you will need 24 (12) (24) pink/green segments.

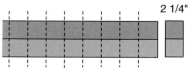

Figure 4
Cut strip sets into 2 1/4" segments.

Step 15. Sew a fabric-width pink print strip between two same-length green print strips with right sides together along length; repeat for three (2) (3) strip sets. Cut strip sets into 2 1/4" segments as shown in Figure 5. You will need 52 (26) (52) green/pink/green segments.

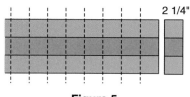

Figure 5
Cut strip sets into 2 1/4" segments.

Step 16. Sew a fabric-width white solid strip between two same-length green print strips with right sides together

Bluebell Medallion
Placement Diagram
88 1/2" x 88 1/2"

along length. *Note: For twin size, use 21"-long strips.* Cut strip set into 2 1/4" segments as shown in Figure 6. You will need 12 (6) (12) green/white/green segments.

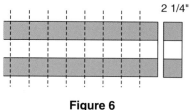

Figure 6
Cut strip sets into 2 1/4" segments.

Step 17. Sew a 21" white solid strip to a same-length green print strip with right sides together along length. Cut strip set into 2 1/4" segments; you will need eight (2) (8) white/green segments.

Step 18. Cut two (1) (2) fabric-width pink print strips into 4" segments. You will need 20 (10) (20) 4" pink segments. Cut six (3) (6) fabric-width pink print strips into 5 3/4" segments. You will need 36 (18) (36) 5 3/4" pink segments.

Step 19. Cut three (2) (3) fabric-width white solid strips into 4" segments. You will need 24 (12) (24) 4" white segments. Cut five (3) (5) strips into 5 3/4" segments. You will need 32 (16) (32) 5 3/4" white segments.

Step 20. Arrange and join segments as shown in Figure 7 for one A border unit; repeat to make eight (4) (8) A border units. Press seams in one direction.

Bluebell Medallion
Placement Diagram
67 1/4" x 88 1/2"

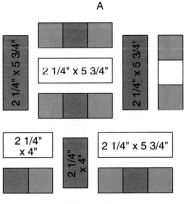

Figure 7
Arrange and join segments
as shown for 1 A border unit.

Step 21. Arrange and join segments as shown in Figure 8 for one B border unit; repeat to make eight (4) (8) B border units. Press seams in one direction.

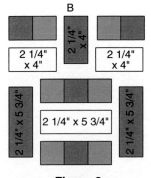

Figure 8
Arrange and join segments
as shown for 1 B border unit.

Bluebell Medallion
Placement Diagram
78 1/2" x 88 1/2"

Step 22. Arrange and join segments as shown in Figure 9 for one C border unit; repeat to make four (2) (4) C border units. Press seams in one direction.

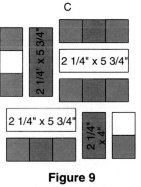

Figure 9
Arrange and join
segments as shown
for 1 C border unit.

Step 23. To piece one corner unit, sew a white solid strip to a white/green segment; trim strip even with segment as shown in Figure 10. Sew a green print strip to the adjacent side of the pieced unit; press and trim strip even with unit as shown in Figure 11. Repeat with green print strip on adjacent side; trim.

Figure 10
Sew a white solid
strip to a white/green
segment; trim strip
even with segment.

Figure 11
Sew a green print strip to
the adjacent side of the
pieced unit; trim strip
even with unit as shown.

Step 24. Continue to sew strips to the pieced unit adding another white set and another green set to complete one corner unit as shown in Figure 12. Repeat for four (0) (4) corner units; press.

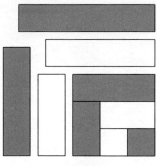

Figure 12
Continue to sew strips to the pieced unit adding another white set and another green set to complete 1 corner unit.

Step 25. Arrange and join two A, two B and one C border unit to make a border strip as shown in Figure 13; repeat to make four (2) (4) strips. Press seams in one direction. Sew a strip to top and bottom; press seams toward strips.

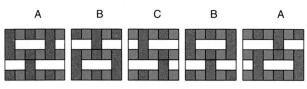

A   B   C   B   A

Figure 13
Arrange and join 2 A, 2 B and 1 C border unit to make a border strip.

Step 26. Sew a corner unit to each end of one remaining border strip as shown in Figure 14; repeat for two strips. Sew a strip to remaining sides. *Note: For twin size, border strips are added to the top and bottom only.* Press seams toward strips.

Figure 14
Sew a corner unit to each end of 1 remaining border strip.

Step 27. Cut and piece two strips each 2 3/8" x 65 1/4" pink print for queen and double sizes; sew to opposite sides. Press seams toward strips. Cut and piece two strips each 2 3/8" x 69" (2 3/8" x 47 3/4") (2 3/8" x 69") pink print; sew a strip to the top and bottom. Press seams toward strips.

Step 28. Cut two strips each 10 1/2" x 69" (10 1/2" x 69") (5 1/2" x 69") and 10 1/2" x 89" (10 1/2" x 67 3/4") (10 1/2" x 79") from length of floral print. Sew strips to quilt sides referring to Placement Diagram; press seams toward strips.

Step 29. Prepare top for quilting and finish as desired referring to the General Instructions. *Note: The quilt shown was machine-quilted in a meandering design using white all-purpose thread.* ❧

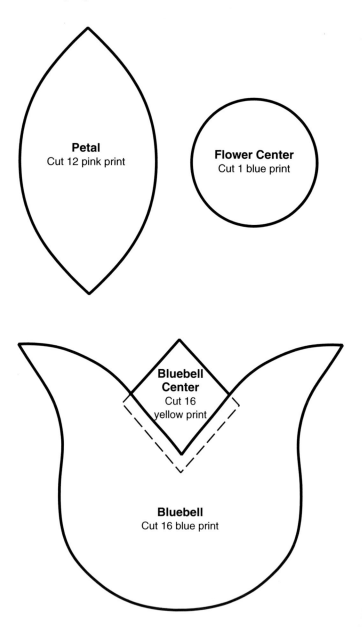

Petal
Cut 12 pink print

Flower Center
Cut 1 blue print

Bluebell Center
Cut 16 yellow print

Bluebell
Cut 16 blue print

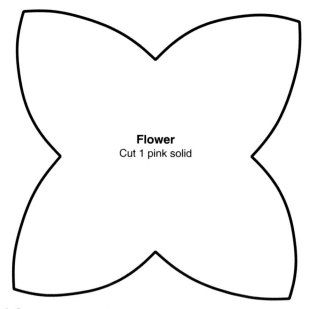

Flower
Cut 1 pink solid

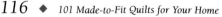

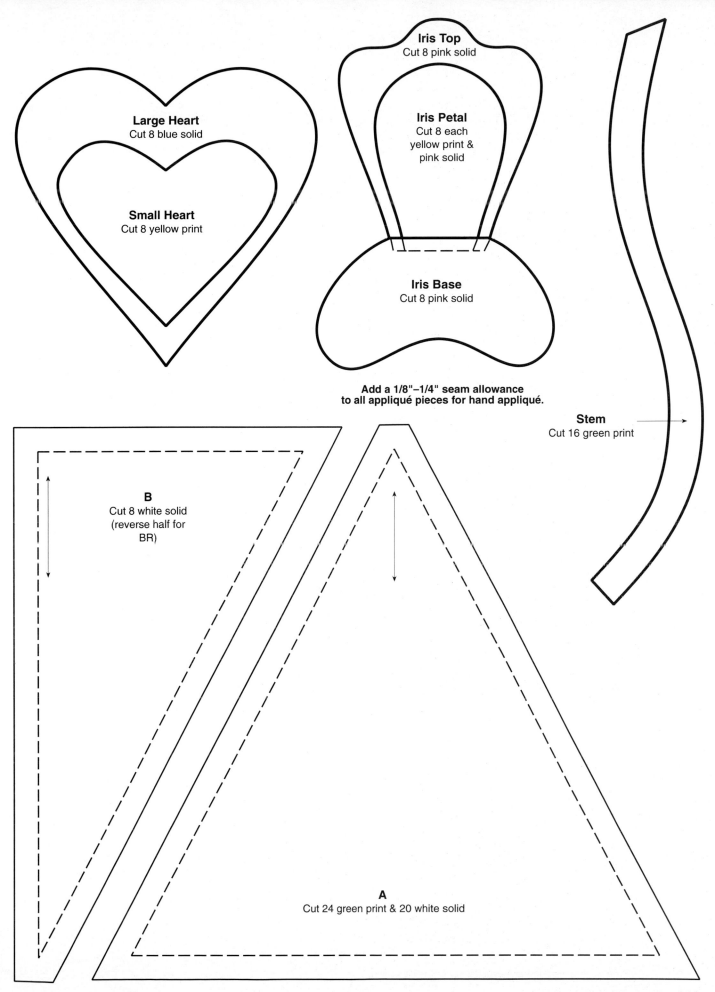

Large Heart
Cut 8 blue solid

Small Heart
Cut 8 yellow print

Iris Top
Cut 8 pink solid

Iris Petal
Cut 8 each
yellow print &
pink solid

Iris Base
Cut 8 pink solid

**Add a 1/8"–1/4" seam allowance
to all appliqué pieces for hand appliqué.**

Stem
Cut 16 green print

B
Cut 8 white solid
(reverse half for
BR)

A
Cut 24 green print & 20 white solid

Something's Been Bugging Me

By Connie Rand

I've had a small stash of fabrics with insect and spider motifs sitting on my shelf for quite awhile. I finally decided to use them all together in this design.

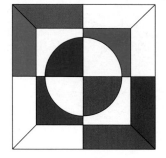

Something's Been Bugging Me
12" x 12" Block

Instructions

Instructions are given for the size shown in photo, with other sizes in parentheses. When only 1 number is given, it applies to all sizes.

Step 1. Cut and piece two strips each 4 1/2" x 56 1/2" (4 1/2" x 68 1/2) (4 1/2" x 80 1/2") and 4 1/2" x 72 1/2" (4 1/2" x 84 1/2") (4 1/2" x 84 1/2") butterfly print for borders; set aside.

Step 2. Prepare templates using pattern pieces given. Cut as directed on each piece for one block; repeat for 24 (35) (42) blocks.

Step 3. Sew a light A to a dark B and a dark A to a light B as shown in Figure 1; repeat. ***Note:*** *For piecing help, refer to sidebar on page 85 for curved piecing.*

Figure 1
Sew a light A to a dark B
and a dark A to a light B.

Step 4. Sew C to the A-B units; set in CR as shown in Figure 2. Repeat for four A-B-C units.

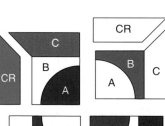

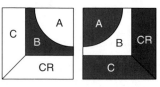

Figure 2
Sew C to the A-B units; set in CR as shown.

Quilt Sizes

	Lap	Twin	Queen
Finished Quilt Size	56" x 80"	68" x 92"	80" x 92"
Block Size	12" x 12"	12" x 12"	12" x 12"
Number of Blocks	24	35	42

Materials

	Lap	Twin	Queen
Butterfly print	1 yard	1 1/8 yards	1 1/8 yards
Dark insect print scraps	2 1/2 yards total	4 yards total	4 1/2 yards total
Light insect print scraps	2 1/2 yards total	4 yards total	4 1/2 yards total
Backing	60" x 84"	72" x 96"	84" x 96"
Batting	60" x 84"	72" x 96"	84" x 96"
Self-made or purchased binding	8 yards	9 1/2 yards	10 yards
All-purpose thread to match fabrics			
Basic sewing supplies and tools			

Step 5. Sew units together as shown in Figure 3 to complete one block. Repeat for 24 (35) (42) blocks.

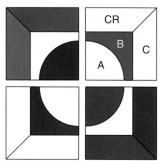

Figure 3
Join A-B-C units
to complete 1 block.

Step 6. Arrange four (5) (6) blocks to make six (7) (7) rows as shown in Figure 4 (on page 122) and referring to the Placement Diagram. Join blocks in rows; join rows to complete the pieced center. Press seams in one direction.

Step 7. Sew the longer border strips cut in Step 1 to opposite long sides of the pieced center; press seams toward strips. Sew the remaining border strips to top and bottom; press seams toward strips.

Step 8. Prepare top for quilting and finish as desired referring to the General Instructions. ***Note:*** *The quilt shown was machine-quilted in the ditch of seams using white all-purpose thread.* ❧

Figure 4
Arrange blocks in rows as shown.

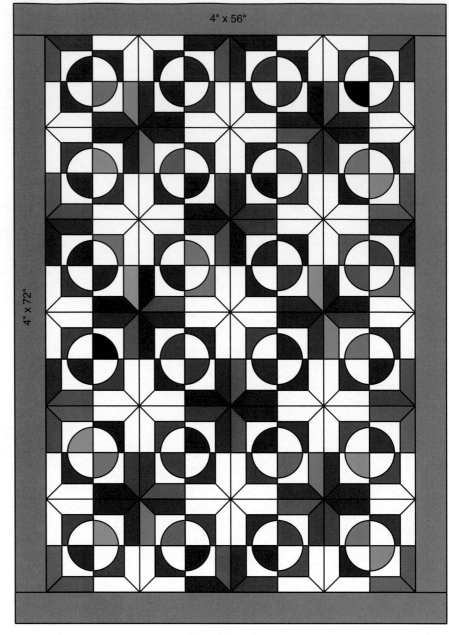

4" x 56"

4" x 72"

Something's Been Bugging Me
Placement Diagram
56" x 80"

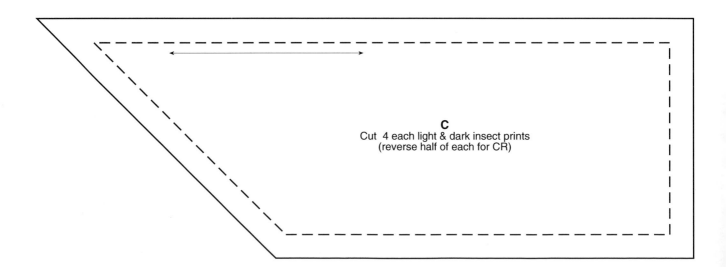

C
Cut 4 each light & dark insect prints
(reverse half of each for CR)

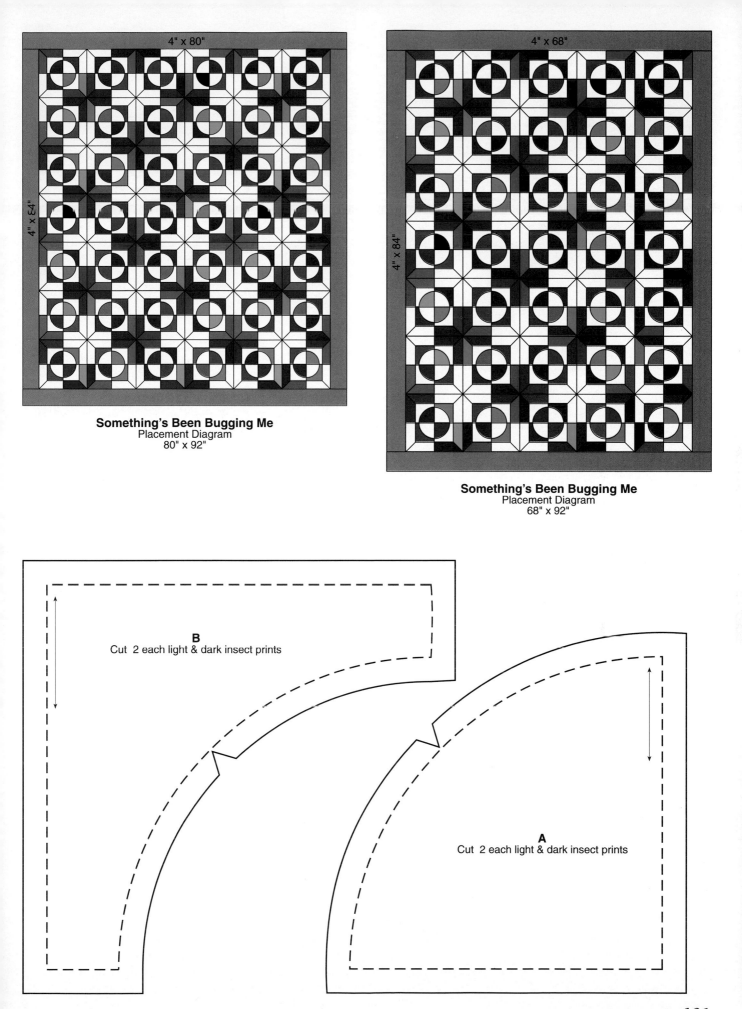

Something's Been Bugging Me
Placement Diagram
80" x 92"

Something's Been Bugging Me
Placement Diagram
68" x 92"

B
Cut 2 each light & dark insect prints

A
Cut 2 each light & dark insect prints

Garden Maze

By Judith Sandstrom

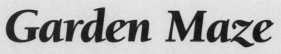

Combine the abstract look of a garden trellis with an earthy mixture of soft colors. The larger plain squares in the block centers provide a showcase for some pretty quilting designs.

Garden Maze
13 3/4" x 13 3/4" Block

Instructions

Instructions are given for the size shown in photo, with other sizes in parentheses. When only 1 number is given, it applies to all sizes.

Step 1. Cut five (3) (6) strips 6 1/4" (4 7/8") (6 1/4") by fabric width tan tone-on-tone print; subcut into 6 1/4" (4 7/8") (6 1/4") square segments for A. You will need 30 (20) (36) A squares.

Step 2. Cut eight (4) (9) strips 9 1/4" (7 1/4") (9 1/4") by fabric width rose print; subcut into 9 1/4" (7 1/4") (9 1/4") square segments. Cut each segment on both diagonals to make B triangles; you will need 120 (80) (144) B triangles.

Step 3. Cut 16 (8) (20) strips 2 1/2" (2") (2 1/2") by fabric width each green print and brown mottled.

Step 4. Staggering the strip ends as shown in Figure 1, sew each green print strip to a brown mottled strip with right sides together along length; press seams open.

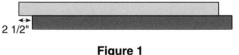

Figure 1
Stagger strip ends and sew each green print strip to a brown mottled strip.

Step 5. Cut each strip at a 45-degree angle every 2 1/2" (2") (2 1/2") as shown in Figure 2. You will need 240 (160) (288) segments.

Step 6. Pin and stitch two green/brown segments together to make a diamond unit as shown in Figure 3; press seams open. Repeat for 120 (80) (144) diamond units.

Quilt Sizes			
	Double	Crib	Queen
Finished Quilt Size	80 3/4" x 94 1/2"	45 1/2" x 55 7/8"	94 1/2" x 94 1/2"
Block Size	13 3/4" x 13 3/4"	10 3/8" x 10 3/8"	13 3/4" x 13 3/4"
Number of Blocks	30	20	36

Materials			
Tan tone-on-tone print	1 yard	1/2 yard	1 1/8 yards
Green print	1 1/4 yards	1/2 yard	1 2/3 yards
Brown mottled	1 1/4 yards	1/2 yard	1 2/3 yards
Floral print	1 1/2 yards	1/2 yard	1 3/4 yards
Rose print	2 1/8 yards	7/8 yard	2 1/2 yards
Backing	85" x 100"	49" x 60"	100" x 100"
Batting	85" x 100"	49" x 60"	100" x 100"
Self-made or purchased binding	10 1/4 yards	5 3/4 yards	11 1/4 yards
All-purpose thread to match fabrics			
Off-white quilting thread			
Basic sewing supplies and tools			

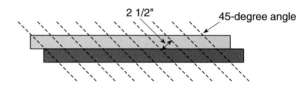

Figure 2
Cut each strip at a 45-degree angle every 2 1/2" (2") (2 1/2") as shown.

Figure 3
Pin and stitch 2 green/brown segments together to make a diamond unit.

Step 7. Stitch a diamond unit to a B triangle as shown in Figure 4; repeat for all diamond units. Press seams open.

Figure 4
Stitch a diamond unit to a B triangle.

Step 8. Pin and stitch a pieced unit to two opposite sides of an A square, leaving 1/4" free as shown in Figure 5; press seams away from A. Repeat for the remaining opposite sides of the square. Stitch remaining section of the first seam to complete one block as shown in Figure 6; press corner seams open. Repeat for 30 (20) (36) blocks.

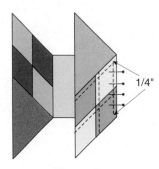

Figure 5
Pin and stitch a pieced unit to 2
opposite sides of an A square,
leaving 1/4" free as shown.

Stitch

Figure 6
Stitch remaining section of the first seam
to complete 1 block as shown.

Step 9. Join five (4) (6) blocks to make a
row; repeat for six (5) (6) rows. Press
seams in one direction. Join rows to
complete pieced center.

Step 10. Cut and piece two strips 6 1/2" x 83" (2 1/2"
x 52 3/8") (6 1/2" x 83") floral print. Sew to opposite
long sides; press seams toward strips. Cut and piece
two strips 6 1/2" x 81 1/4" (2 1/2" x 46") (6 1/2" x
95") floral print; sew to the top and bottom of the
pieced center; press seams toward strips.

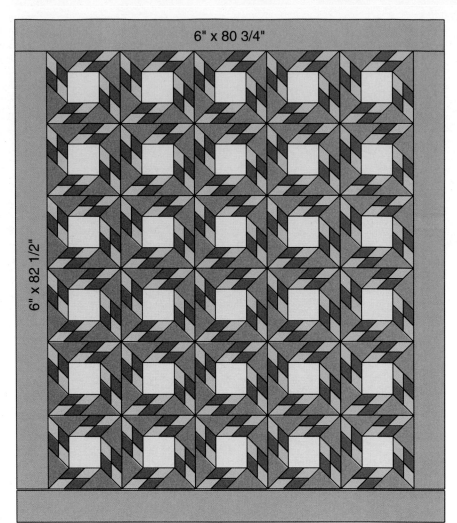

6" x 80 3/4"

6" x 82 1/2"

Garden Maze
Placement Diagram
80 3/4" x 94 1/2"

Step 11. Prepare top for quilting and finish as desired
referring to the General Instructions. **Note:** *The quilt
shown was hand-quilted using off-white quilting thread 1/4"
on inside of rose print triangles and in the center squares
using quilting design given. Reduce quilting design by 25
percent on photocopier for use on crib-size quilt.* ❥

Garden Maze
Placement Diagram
45 1/2" x 55 7/8"

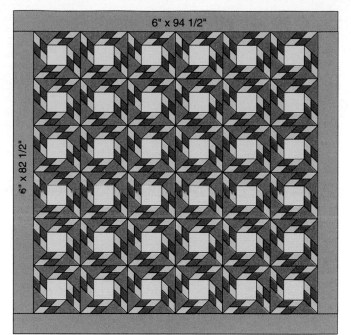

Garden Maze
Placement Diagram
94 1/2" x 94 1/2"

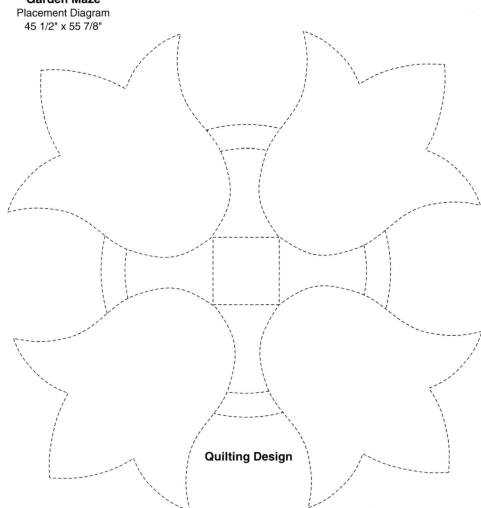

Quilting Design

Sunflower Dreams

By Marian Shenk

Appliqué and piecing combine to make a bright fan-shaped sunflower quilt using a variety of gold prints. Summer will be right around the corner in the room with this quilt on the bed.

Sunflower Fan
12" x 12" Block

Instructions

Instructions are given for the size shown in photo, with other sizes in parentheses. When only 1 number is given, it applies to all sizes.

Step 1. Cut a 20 1/2" x 32 1/2" rectangle from the length of the cream-on-cream print for center background. Fold and crease to mark center. *Note: For double and queen sizes, cut two strips each 12 1/2" x 52 1/2" and 12 1/2" x 64 1/2" from length of cream-on-cream print. Cut 14 (18) (18) 12 1/2" x 12 1/2" squares from remaining cream-on-cream print.*

Step 2. Prepare templates for pieces E and F. Cut as directed on each piece for one flower unit; repeat for three (15) (15) flower units.

Step 3. Join six F pieces referring to Figure 1 for color arrangement; repeat for three (15) (15) pieced units.

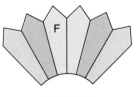

Figure 1
Join 6 F pieces.

Step 4. Sew E to the base of a pieced unit as shown in Figure 2 to complete one flower unit; repeat for three (15) (15) flower units.

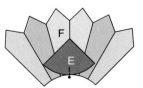

Figure 2
Sew E to the base of a pieced unit as shown to complete 1 flower unit.

Quilt Sizes			
	Lap	**Double**	**Queen**
Finished Quilt Size	52" x 64"	80" x 92"	84" x 96"
Block Size	12" x 12"	12" x 12"	12" x 12"
Number of Blocks	14	18	18

Materials			
Green print	1/8 yard	3/8 yard	3/8 yard
Brown solid	1/3 yard	1/2 yard	1/2 yard
Gold print 3	3/4 yard	1 1/8 yards	1 1/8 yards
Gold print 2	1 yard	1 1/4 yards	1 1/4 yards
Gold print 1	1 1/8 yards	1 3/8 yards	1 3/8 yards
Border stripe	2 yards	3 yards	3 yards
Cream-on-cream print	2 3/4 yards	5 1/2 yards	5 1/2 yards
Backing	56" x 68"	84" x 96"	88" x 100"
Batting	56" x 68"	84" x 96"	88" x 100"
Self-made or purchased binding	7 yards	10 yards	10 1/2 yards
All-purpose thread to match fabrics			
Off-white quilting thread			
Brown 6-strand embroidery floss			
1/4"-wide brown bias tape	3/4 yard	3 yards	3 yards
Basic sewing supplies and tools			

Step 5. Prepare templates for G and the butterfly body cut as directed on each piece for one butterfly unit, adding a seam allowance to the butterfly body when cutting for hand appliqué; repeat for two (10) (10) butterfly units.

Step 6. Join four G pieces as shown in Figure 3 for color arrangement; repeat for two (10) (10) pieced units.

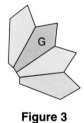

Figure 3
Join 4 G pieces.

Step 7. Prepare templates for all flowerpot pieces and leaves using pattern pieces given; cut as directed on each piece, adding a seam allowance when cutting for hand appliqué.

Step 8. Cut two 8" and one 11" length 1/4"-wide brown bias tape. Pin the 11" length on the center crease of the center background piece for center stem. Pin two leaf pieces under stem piece 5" from top end.

Hand-appliqué in place using thread to match fabrics and turning under edges of leaf pieces as you stitch.

Step 9. Pin an 8" length of brown bias tape on each side of the stitched stem piece, curving a little and referring to the Placement Diagram; pin a leaf under each stem 2" from bottom end, again referring to the Placement Diagram. Hand-appliqué in place with matching thread.

Step 10. Appliqué pot pieces on bottom ends of stems and flower units to top ends of stems, turning under edges when stitching and using thread to match fabrics.

Step 11. Arrange a butterfly unit on each top corner referring to the Placement Diagram for positioning; turn under edges and hand-appliqué in place with thread to match fabrics

Step 12. Cut two strips each 2 1/2" x 27" and 2 1/2" x 39" along length of border stripe. Sew the shorter strips to the top and bottom and longer strips to opposite sides of the appliquéd center, mitering corners. Trim excess at corner seams; set aside completed center.

Step 13. Prepare templates for pieces A–D using pattern pieces given. Cut as directed on each piece for one block; repeat for 14 (18) (18) blocks.

Step 14. To piece one Sunflower Fan block, sew B to BR as shown in Figure 4; add C and CR. Sew D to each end to complete the fan unit as shown in Figure 5. Press seams in one direction; repeat for 14 (18) (18) fan units.

Sunflower Dreams
Placement Diagram
52" x 64"

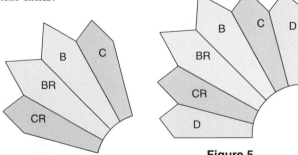

Figure 4
Sew B to BR; add C and CR.

Figure 5
Sew D to each end to complete the fan unit.

Step 15. Turn under 1/4" seam allowance on the fan blade ends; appliqué in place on a 12 1/2" x 12 1/2" cream-on-cream print square as shown in Figure 6. Repeat for all fan units.

Step 16. Turn under 1/4" on curved edge of A; appliqué in place on fan base to complete one block as shown in Figure 6; repeat for 14 (18) (18) blocks.

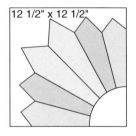

Figure 6
Turn under 1/4" seam allowance on the fan blade ends; appliqué in place on a 12 1/2" x 12 1/2" cream-on-cream print square.

Step 17. Join two blocks as shown in Figure 7; repeat. Sew a two-block unit to the top and bottom of the appliquéd center; press seams toward border stripe strips.

Figure 7
Join 2 blocks as shown.

Sunflower Dreams
Placement Diagram
80" x 92"

Sunflower Dreams
Placement Diagram
84" x 96"

Step 18. Join five blocks as shown in Figure 8 to make a row; repeat for two rows. Sew a row to opposite long sides of the appliquéd center; press seams toward border stripe strips.

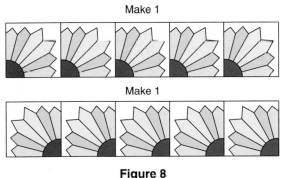

Make 1

Make 1

Figure 8
Join 5 blocks as shown to make a row.

Step 19. Cut two strips each 2 1/2" x 55" and 2 1/2" x 67" along length of border stripe. Sew the shorter strips to the top and bottom and longer strips to opposite long sides of the appliquéd and pieced center, mitering corners. Trim excess at corners; press seams toward border stripe strips. ***Note:*** *At this point the smaller-size quilt is ready to finish. Skip to Step 27.*

Step 20. Cut two each 16" and 24" lengths 1/4"-wide brown bias tape . Center and pin a shorter strip on each 12 1/2" x 52 1/2" cream-on-cream print rectangle cut in Step 1; using longer strips repeat with 12 1/2" x 64 1/2" cream-on-cream print rectangles.

Step 21. Prepare, position and pin three flower units, eight leaves and two butterfly units on each longer

rectangle referring to Figure 9. Turn under edges and hand-appliqué pieces and units in place using thread to match fabrics.

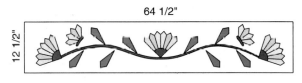

Figure 9
Prepare, position and pin 3 flower units, 8 leaves and 2 butterfly units on each longer border strip.

Step 22. Sew an appliquéd rectangle to opposite long sides of the pieced and appliquéd center; press seams toward border stripe strips.

Step 23. Repeat on shorter rectangles using three flower units, four leaves and two butterfly units as shown in Figure 10.

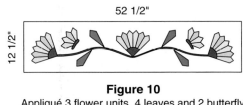

Figure 10
Appliqué 3 flower units, 4 leaves and 2 butterfly units on shorter border strips.

Step 24. Sew a Sunflower Fan block to each end of the shorter rectangles. Sew strips to the top and bottom of the pieced and appliquéd center; press seams toward border stripe strips.

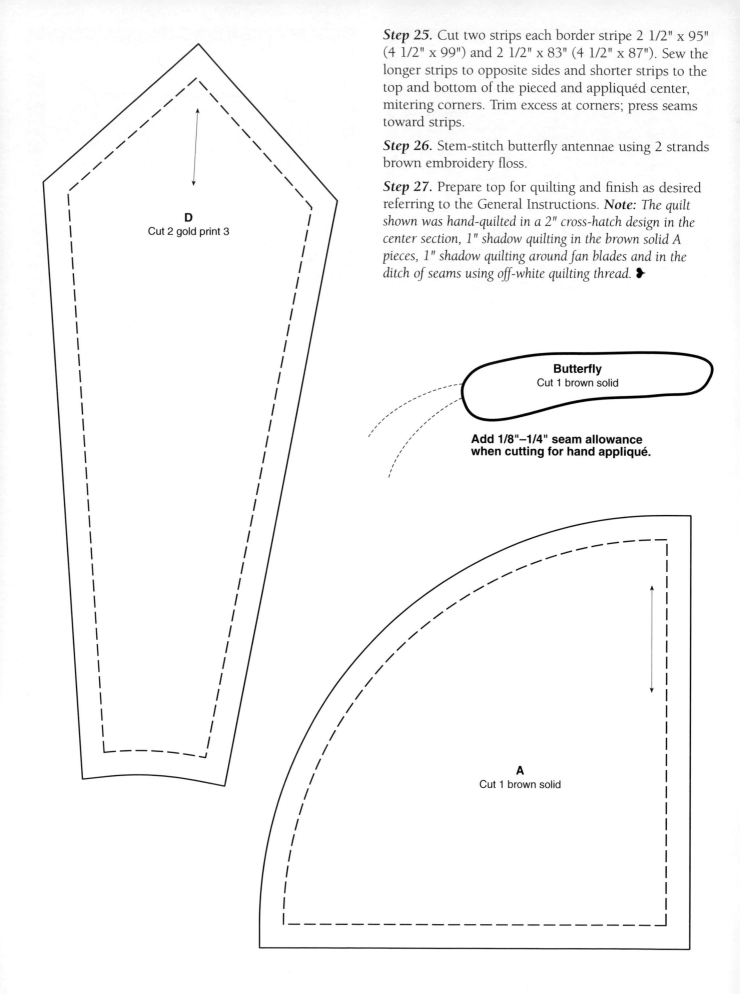

Step 25. Cut two strips each border stripe 2 1/2" x 95" (4 1/2" x 99") and 2 1/2" x 83" (4 1/2" x 87"). Sew the longer strips to opposite sides and shorter strips to the top and bottom of the pieced and appliquéd center, mitering corners. Trim excess at corners; press seams toward strips.

Step 26. Stem-stitch butterfly antennae using 2 strands brown embroidery floss.

Step 27. Prepare top for quilting and finish as desired referring to the General Instructions. *Note: The quilt shown was hand-quilted in a 2" cross-hatch design in the center section, 1" shadow quilting in the brown solid A pieces, 1" shadow quilting around fan blades and in the ditch of seams using off-white quilting thread.* ❦

D
Cut 2 gold print 3

Butterfly
Cut 1 brown solid

Add 1/8"–1/4" seam allowance when cutting for hand appliqué.

A
Cut 1 brown solid

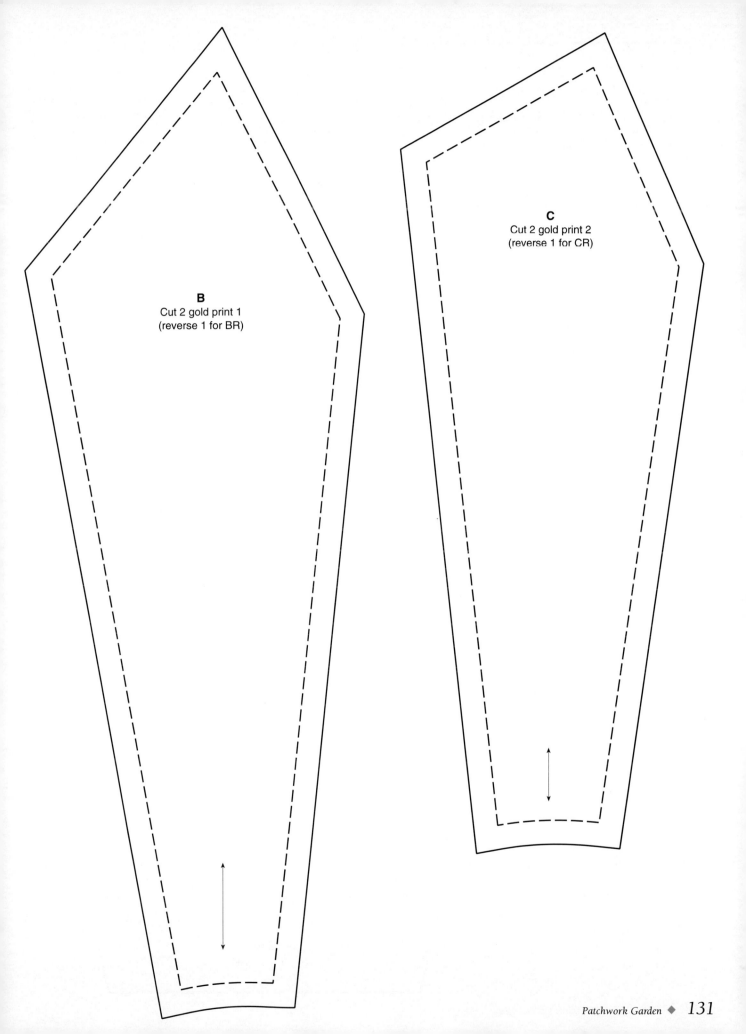

B
Cut 2 gold print 1
(reverse 1 for BR)

C
Cut 2 gold print 2
(reverse 1 for CR)

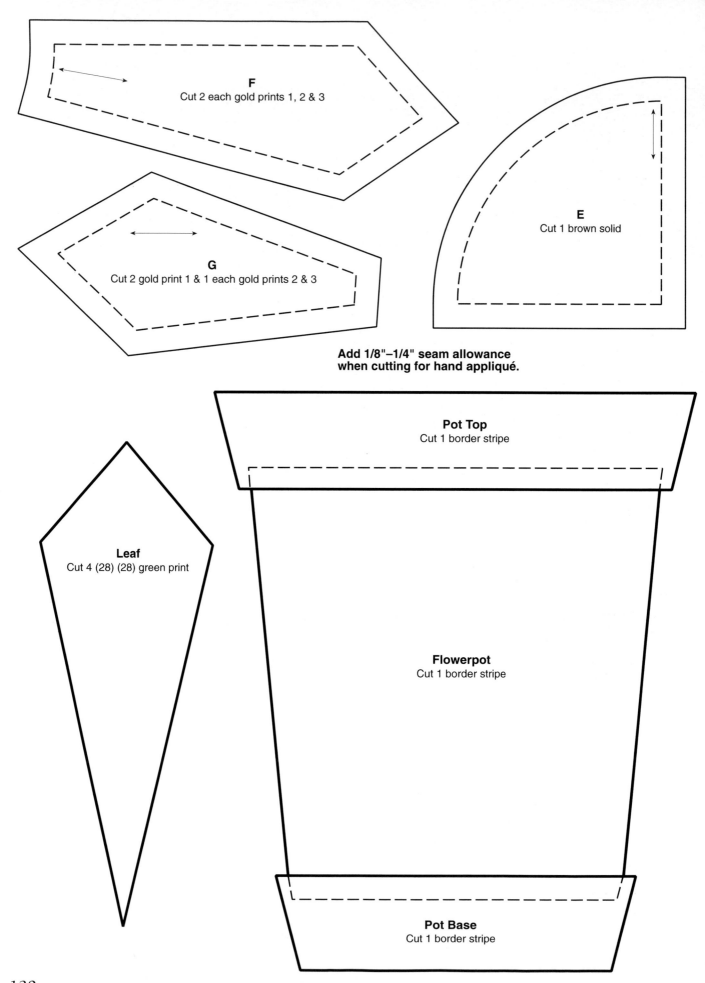

F
Cut 2 each gold prints 1, 2 & 3

G
Cut 2 gold print 1 & 1 each gold prints 2 & 3

E
Cut 1 brown solid

Add 1/8"–1/4" seam allowance when cutting for hand appliqué.

Pot Top
Cut 1 border stripe

Flowerpot
Cut 1 border stripe

Leaf
Cut 4 (28) (28) green print

Pot Base
Cut 1 border stripe

Crazy for Butterflies

By Charlyne Stewart

Make some crazy-patchwork butterflies from your favorite colors and appliqué them to a simple background pieced from a variety of blue print squares to create this quick, but colorful quilt.

Quilt Sizes

	Lap	Twin	Queen
Finished Quilt Size	56" x 72"	64" x 88"	84" x 92"
Block Size	8" x 8"	8" x 8"	8" x 8"
Number of Blocks	48	70	90

Materials

	Lap	Twin	Queen
Light blue print 1, 2, 3	5/8 yard each	7/8 yard each	1 yard each
Medium blue print 1, 2	5/8 yard each	7/8 yard each	1 yard each
Dark blue print 1	5/8 yard	7/8 yard	1 yard
Muslin	1 yard	1 1/4 yards	1 1/4 yards
Dark blue print 2	1 yard	1 yard	1 3/4 yards
Orange and yellow prints	1 1/4 yards total	1 1/2 yards total	1 3/4 yards total
Backing	60" x 76"	68" x 92"	88" x 96"
Batting	60" x 76"	68" x 92"	88" x 96"
Self-made or purchased binding	7 1/2 yards	8 3/4 yards	10 1/4 yards
Neutral color all-purpose thread			
White quilting thread			
Orange rayon thread			
Orange 6-strand embroidery floss			
Fusible transfer web	2 yards	2 3/4 yards	3 1/2 yards
Tear-off fabric stabilizer	2 yards	2 5/8 yards	3 yards

Basic sewing supplies and tools and water-erasable marker or pencil

Instructions

Instructions are given for the size shown in photo, with other sizes in parentheses. When only 1 number is given, it applies to all sizes.

Step 1. Prepare templates for butterflies using pattern pieces given.

Step 2. Cut blue print fabric squares 8 1/2" x 8 1/2" as follows: eight (12) (14) light blue print 1; eight (12) (16) light blue print 2; eight (11) (15) light blue print 3; eight (12) (16) medium blue print 1; eight (11) (14) medium blue print 2; eight (12) (15) dark blue print 1.

Step 3. Arrange the 8 1/2" x 8 1/2" blue print squares in rows referring to Figure 1 for color sequence. *Note: Refer to Placement Diagrams for twin or queen sizes.* Join squares in rows; join rows to complete pieced center. Press seams in one direction.

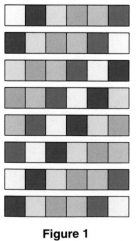

COLOR KEY
☐ Light blue print 1
☐ Light blue print 2
☐ Light blue print 3
☐ Medium blue print 1
☐ Medium blue print 2
☐ Dark blue print 1
☐ Dark blue print 2

Figure 1
Arrange squares in rows as shown.

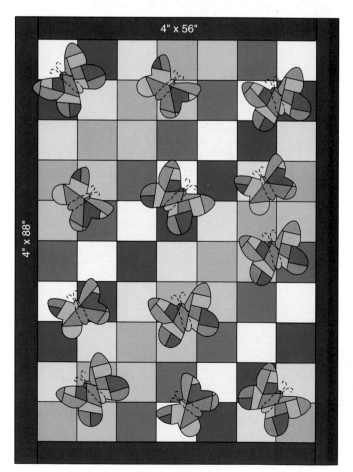

Crazy for Butterflies
Placement Diagram
84" x 92"

Crazy for Butterflies
Placement Diagram
64" x 88"

4" x 48"

4" x 72"

Crazy for Butterflies
Placement Diagram
56" x 72"

Step 4. Cut and piece two strips each 4 1/2" x 48 1/2" (4 1/2" x 56 1/2") (6 1/2" x 72 1/2") and 4 1/2" x 72 1/2" (4 1/2" x 88 1/2") (6 1/2" x 92 1/2") dark blue print 2. Sew shorter strips to the top and bottom and longer strips to opposite long sides; press seams toward strips.

Step 5. Cut five (5) (8) small and four (7) (8) large butterflies from muslin.

Step 6. Bond fusible transfer web to the wrong side of the orange and yellow print fabrics. Cut angular pieces to create a crazy-quilt pattern on the muslin butterflies as shown in Figure 2.

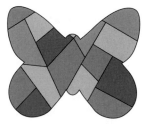

Figure 2
Cut angular pieces to
create a crazy-quilt pattern
on the muslin butterflies.

Step 7. Peel paper backing away from cut pieces; fuse shapes to the muslin butterfly shapes to completely cover muslin. Trim excess to muslin butterfly shape when finished. Repeat for all muslin shapes.

**Detail
Patterns**

Step 8. Place crazy-patchwork butterfly shapes on a piece of tear-off fabric stabilizer. Machine appliqué on all edges of each fused shape using a narrow zigzag stitch and orange rayon thread in the top of the machine and all-purpose thread in the bobbin. Repeat for all shapes. Set machine to a wider zigzag stitch and sew over first stitching lines. Trim all threads; tear away fabric stabilizer.

Step 9. Arrange the butterflies on the pieced and bordered center referring to the Placement Diagram for positioning.

Step 10. Using orange rayon thread in the top of the machine and all-purpose thread in the bobbin, machine-stitch butterflies in place using a buttonhole or wide zigzag stitch.

Step 11. Mark body shapes and antennae on each butterfly using a water-erasable marker or pencil. Machine zigzag-stitch body shapes on marked lines as in Step 10. Stem-stitch antennae using 3 strands orange embroidery floss.

Step 12. Prepare top for quilting and finish as desired referring to the General Instructions. *Note: The quilt shown was hand-quilted using the small butterfly shape in a random placement with white quilting thread.* ❧

Place line on fold

Small Butterflies
Cut 5 (5) (8) muslin

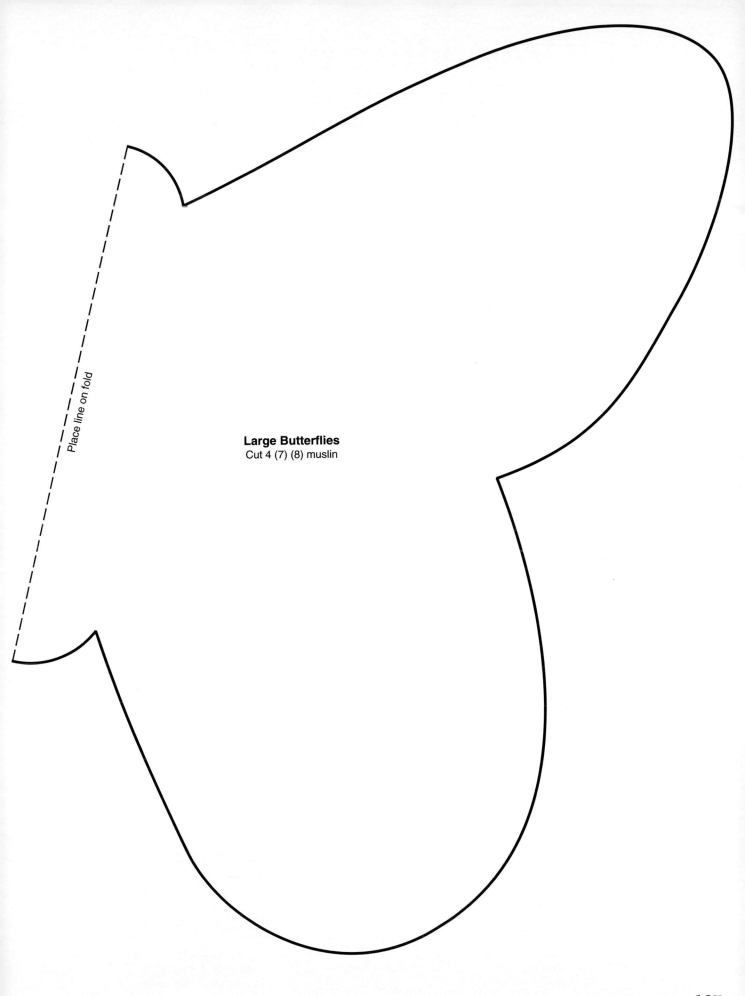

Place line on fold

Large Butterflies
Cut 4 (7) (8) muslin

Dragonflies in Flight

By Connie Rand

Dragonflies are fascinating insects. Beautiful dragonfly fabric inspired the design of this gorgeous quilt.

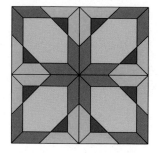

Dragonflies in Flight
12" x 12" Block

Instructions

Instructions are given for the size shown in photo, with other sizes in parentheses. When only 1 number is given, it applies to all sizes.

Step 1. Cut and piece two strips each 4 1/2" x 68 1/2" (3" x 53 1/2") (4 1/2" x 92 1/2") and 4 1/2" x 84 1/2" (3" x 72 1/2") (4 1/2" 84 1/2") dark print for inner borders. Cut and piece two strips each 6 1/2" x 68 1/2" (4 1/2" x 53 1/2") (6 1/2" x 92 1/2") and 6 1/2" x 104 1/2" (4 1/2" x 85 1/2") (6 1/2" x 104 1/2") floral print for outer borders. Set border strips aside.

Step 2. Prepare templates using pattern pieces given; cut as directed on each piece for one block. Repeat for 35 (24) (49) blocks.

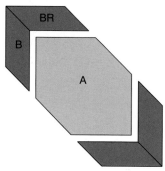

Figure 1
Sew B to BR; repeat. Set
A into the B units.

Step 3. To piece one block, sew B to BR; repeat. Set A into the B units as shown in Figure 1.

Figure 2
Sew C to C; set in D.

Quilt Sizes

	Queen	Twin	King
Finished Quilt Size	80" x 104"	61" x 85"	104" x 104"
Block Size	12" x 12"	12" x 12"	12" x 12"
Number of Blocks	35	24	49

Materials

Dark Print	2 yards	1 1/8 yards	2 1/8 yards
Pink mottled	2 1/8 yards	1 1/2 yards	2 3/4 yards
Dragonfly print	2 1/8 yards	1 1/2 yards	3 yards
Floral print	3 3/4 yards	2 1/2 yards	4 1/2 yards
Backing	84" x 108"	65" x 89"	108" x 108"
Batting	84" x 108"	65" x 89"	108" x 108"
Self-made or purchased binding	10 3/4 yards	8 1/2 yards	12 yards
Neutral color and off-white all-purpose thread			
Basic sewing supplies and tools			

Step 4. Sew C to C; set in D as shown in Figure 2. Repeat for two units.

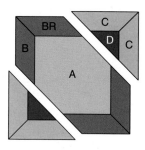

Figure 3
Sew a C-D unit to opposite
sides of the A-B unit.

Step 5. Sew a C-D unit to opposite sides of the A-B unit as shown in Figure 3; repeat for four units.

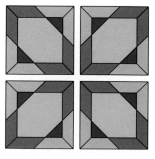

Figure 4
Join units to complete 1
Dragonflies in Flight block.

Step 6. Join units to complete one Dragonflies in Flight block as shown in Figure 4; repeat for 35 (24) (49) blocks. Press all blocks.

Step 7. Arrange blocks in seven (6) (7) rows of five (4) (7) blocks each referring to the Placement Diagram. Join blocks in rows; join rows to complete pieced center. Press seams in one direction.

Step 8. Sew longer dark print border strips to opposite long sides and shorter dark print border strips to the top and bottom of the pieced center; press seams toward strips.

Step 9. Sew shorter floral print border strips to the top and bottom and longer strips to opposite long sides of the pieced center; press seams toward strips.

Step 10. Prepare top for quilting and finish as desired referring to the General Instructions. *Note: The quilt shown was machine-quilted in the ditch of seams using off-white all-purpose thread.* ❧

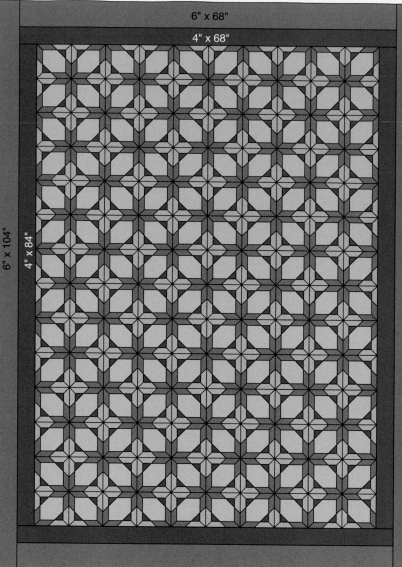

Dragonflies in Flight
Placement Diagram
80" x 104"

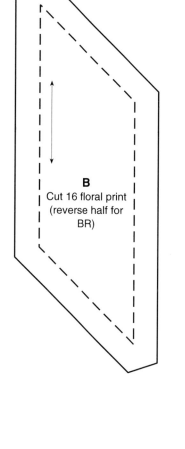

B
Cut 16 floral print
(reverse half for
BR)

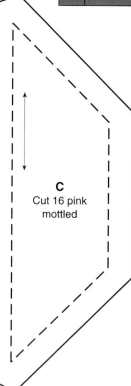

C
Cut 16 pink
mottled

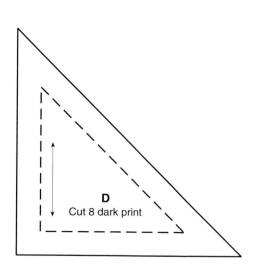

D
Cut 8 dark print

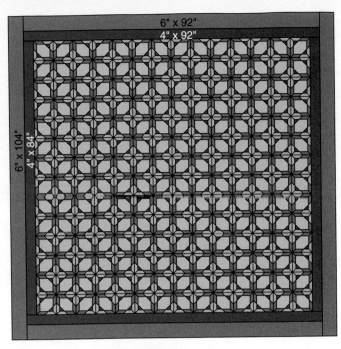

Dragonflies in Flight
Placement Diagram
104" x 104"

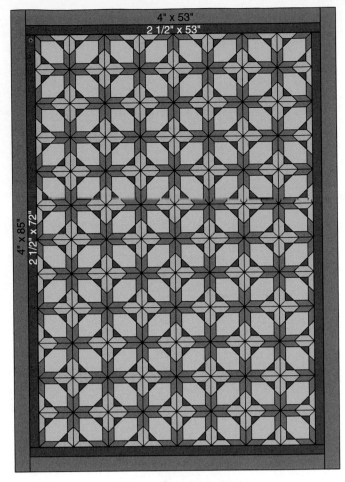

Dragonflies in Flight
Placement Diagram
61" x 85"

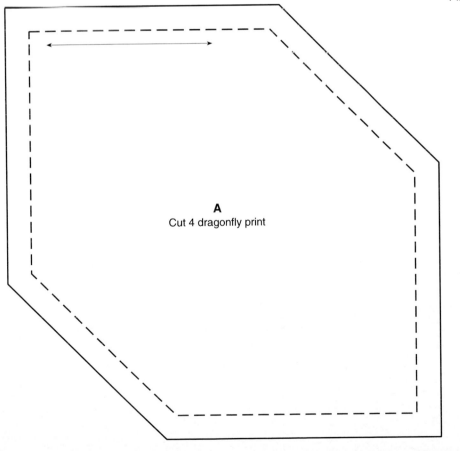

A
Cut 4 dragonfly print

Chapter Five

Quilt Upon a Star

You'll reach for the stars with the quilts in this chapter. Just as no two stars are exactly alike, so the quilts in this chapter feature a wide variety of stars, including some star designs that are out of this world. Be a star quilter with these dazzling designs.

Patriot Star

By Holly Daniels

This creative design will work up faster than you think because strip-pieced fabric sets are used for the templates.

Patriot Star
15" x 15" Block

Quilt Sizes

	Lap	Twin	King
Finished Quilt Size	55" x 55"	70" x 85"	100" x 100"
Block Size	15" x 15"	15" x 15"	15" x 15"
Number of Blocks	9	20	36

Materials

Blue print	1 1/8 yards	2 1/8 yards	3 1/2 yards
White-on-white print	1 1/4 yards	2 1/4 yards	3 1/2 yards
Red print	2 1/4 yards	4 yards	6 1/4 yards
Backing	59" x 59"	74" x 89"	104" x 104"
Batting	59" x 59"	74" x 89"	104" x 104"
Self-made or purchased binding	6 1/2 yards	9 yards	11 1/2 yards

Neutral color and navy all-purpose thread

Basic sewing supplies and tools

Instructions

Instructions are given for the size shown in photo, with other sizes in parentheses. When only 1 number is given, it applies to all sizes.

Step 1. Cut three (7) (12) strips blue print 6 1/4" by fabric width; subcut into 18 (40) (72) 6 1/4" square segments. Cut each segment on both diagonals as shown in Figure 1 to make F triangles. You will need 72 (160) (288) F triangles.

6 1/4"

6 1/4"

F

Figure 1
Cut 6 1/4" segments on both diagonals to make F triangles.

Step 2. Cut 11 (23) (37) strips blue print 1 1/8" by fabric width.

Step 3. Cut four (10) (16) strips 4 1/2" by fabric width, one (2) (3) strip 3" by fabric width and two (4) (6) strips 1 3/4" by fabric width red print.

Step 4. Cut two (4) (8) strips red print 3 7/8" by fabric width; subcut into 18 (40) (72) 3 7/8" square segments. Cut each segment on both diagonals as shown in Figure 2 to make E triangles. You will need 72 (160) (288) E triangles.

3 7/8"

3 7/8"

E

Figure 2
Cut each 3 7/8" segments on both diagonasl to make E triangles.

1" x 45"

5" x 5"

Patriot Star
Placement Diagram
55" x 55"

Step 5. Sew one 1 1/8" blue print strip to one 1 3/4" red print strip with right sides together along length as shown in Figure 3; repeat for two (4) (6) strip sets. Cut into 1 3/4" segments; you will need 36 (80) (144) blue/red segments.

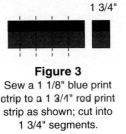

Figure 3
Sew a 1 1/8" blue print strip to a 1 3/4" red print strip as shown; cut into 1 3/4" segments.

Step 6. Cut three (5) (9) 1 1/8" blue print strips into 2 3/8" segments; you will need 36 (80) (144) segments. Sew a 2 3/8" segment to each blue/red segment to make a G unit as shown in Figure 4; repeat for 36 (80) (144) G units.

1 1/8" x 2 3/8"

Figure 4
Sew a 2 3/8" segment to each blue/red segment to make a G unit.

Step 7. Sew a 3" red print strip between two 1 1/8" blue print strips with rights sides together along length; repeat for one (2) (3) strip set. Press seams toward blue print strips. Cut into 3" segments as shown in Figure 5; you will need nine (20) (36) blue/red segments.

3"

Figure 5
Cut into 3" segments.

Step 8. Cut two (5) (8) 1 1/8" blue print strips into 4 1/4" segments; you will need 18 (40) (72) segments. Sew a 4 1/4" segment to opposite sides of each blue/red segment to make a center unit as shown in Figure 6; repeat for nine (20) (36) center units.

1 1/8" x 4 1/4"

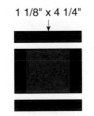

Figure 6
Sew a 4 1/4" segment to opposite sides of each blue/red segment to make a center unit.

Step 9. Sew a 1 1/8" blue print strip between two 4 1/2" red print strips with right sides together along length; repeat for two (5) (8) strip sets. Press seams toward red print strips. Make a template for A; place A on strip set, aligning lines on A with seams of blue strip as shown in Figure 7. Cut 36 (80) (144) A pieces.

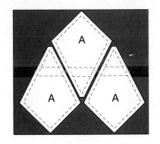

Figure 7
Place A on strip set, aligning lines on A with seams of blue strip.

Step 10. Prepare templates for pieces B, C and D using pattern pieces given. Cut as directed on each piece for one block. Repeat for nine (20) (36) blocks.

Step 11. To piece one block, sew B and BR to opposite sides of A; repeat for four A-B units. Sew an A-B unit to opposite sides of a center unit as shown in Figure 8.

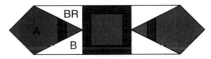

Figure 8
Sew an A-B unit to opposite sides of a center unit.

Step 12. Sew an E triangle to adjacent sides of a G unit as shown in Figure 9; repeat for four E-G units.

Figure 9
Sew an E triangle to adjacent sides of a G unit.

Step 13. Sew an E-G unit to opposite sides of a remaining A-B unit as shown in Figure 10; repeat for two units.

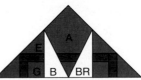

Figure 10
Sew an E-G unit to opposite sides of a remaining A-B unit.

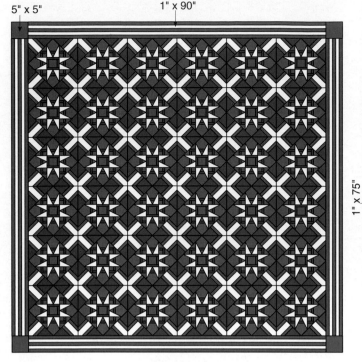

5" x 5"   1" x 90"

Patriot Star
Placement Diagram
100" x 100"

1" x 60"   5" x 5"   1" x 75"

Patriot Star
Placement Diagram
70" x 85"

Step 14. Sew the A-B-E-G units to the remaining sides of the center unit to complete the center square as shown in Figure 11.

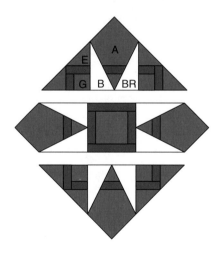

Figure 11
Sew the A-B-E-G units to the remaining sides of the center unit to complete the center square.

Step 15. Sew D and DR to opposite sides of C; repeat for four C-D units. Sew an F triangle to opposite sides of each C-D unit as shown in Figure 12.

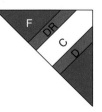

Figure 12
Sew an F triangle to opposite sides of each C-D unit.

Step 16. Sew a C-D-F unit to each side of the center square to complete one Patriotic Star block as shown in Figure 13; repeat for nine (20) (36) blocks. Press all blocks.

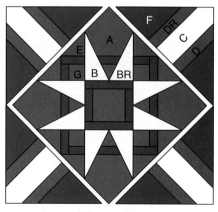

Figure 13
Sew a C-D-F unit to each side of the center square to complete 1 Patriot Star block.

Step 17. Arrange blocks in three (5) (6) rows of three (4) (6) blocks each. Join blocks in rows; join rows to complete pieced center. Press seams in one direction.

Step 18. Cut and piece four strips each 1 1/2" x 45 1/2" (1 1/2" x 75 1/2") (1 1/2" x 90 1/2") and 1 1/2" x 45 1/2" (1 1/2" x 60 1/2") (1 1/2" x 90 1/2") white-on-white print.

Step 19. Cut and piece six strips each 1 1/2" x 45 1/2"

146 ◆ *101 Made-to-Fit Quilts for Your Home*

(1 1/2" x 75 1/2") (1 1/2" x 90 1/2") and 1 1/2" x 45 1/2" (1 1/2" x 60 1/2") (1 1/2" x 90 1/2") red print.

Step 20. Sew two same-size white-on-white print strips between three same-size red print strips to make a border strip; repeat for four border strips. Press seams toward red print strips.

Step 21. Sew a border strip to opposite sides of the pieced center; press seams toward strips.

Step 22. Cut four 5 1/2" x 5 1/2" squares red print. Sew a square to opposite ends of each remaining border strip. Sew a strip to the remaining sides of the pieced center; press seams toward strips.

Step 23. Prepare top for quilting and finish as desired referring to the General Instructions. *Note: The quilt shown was machine-quilted in a meandering design through the red and blue block pieces using navy all-purpose thread.* ❧

A
Cut 4 strip-pieced units

Align with blue print strip

C
Cut 4 white-on-white print

D
Cut 8 red print
(reverse half for DR)

B
Cut 8 white-on-white print
(reverse half for BR)

Traveling Star Beams

By Leslie Beck

Star quilts are a favorite of quilt lovers. Whether for the bed or a couch cover, this bright little star makes a shining statement.

Traveling Star Beams
9" x 9" Block

Instructions

Instructions are given for the size shown in photo, with other sizes in parentheses. When only 1 number is given, it applies to all sizes.

Step 1. Cut three (4) (6) strips tan print 3 1/2" by fabric width; subcut into 3 1/2" square segments for A. You will need 30 (48) (72) A squares.

Step 2. Cut 12 (19) (28) strips white print 2" by fabric width; subcut into 2" square segments for B. You will need 240 (384) (576) B squares.

Step 3. Cut 12 (19) (28) strips white print 3 1/2" by fabric width; subcut into 2" segments for C. You will need 240 (384) (576) C rectangles.

Step 4. Cut 12 (19) (28) strips plum solid 3 1/2" by fabric width; subcut into 2" segments for D. You will need 240 (384) (576) D rectangles.

Step 5. Cut 12 (19) (28) strips rust print 2" by fabric width; subcut into 2" square segments for E. You will need 240 (384) (576) E squares.

Step 6. To piece one block, place C right sides together with D; sew on diagonal of C. Trim seam allowance to 1/4" referring to Figure 1; press open. Place D right sides together with C-D unit; stitch on diagonal of D as shown in Figure 2; trim and press open. Repeat for four D-C-D units.

Quilt Sizes			
	Lap	**Twin**	**Queen**
Finished Quilt Size	56" x 65"	65" x 83"	83" x 92"
Block Size	9" x 9"	9" x 9"	9" x 9"
Number of Blocks	30	48	72

Materials			
Gold solid	1/3 yard	3/8 yard	1/2 yard
Tan print	3/8 yard	1/2 yard	3/4 yard
Plum solid	1 1/4 yards	2 yards	3 yards
Rust print	1 5/8 yards	2 1/4 yards	2 3/4 yards
White print	2 yards	3 1/8 yards	4 3/8 yards
Backing	60" x 69"	69" x 87"	87" x 96"
Batting	60" x 69"	69" x 87"	87" x 96"
Self-made or purchased binding	7 1/4 yards	8 3/4 yards	10 1/4 yards
Neutral color and white all-purpose thread			
Rust quilting thread			
Basic sewing supplies and tools			

Step 7. Place E right sides together on one end of C; stitch on diagonal of E referring to Figure 3. Trim and press open. Repeat on opposite end of C, again referring to Figure 3; repeat for four E-C-E units.

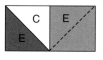

Figure 3
Place E right sides together on 1 end of C; stitch on diagonal of E; repeat on opposite end of C.

Step 8. Sew B to opposite ends of an E-C-E unit as shown in Figure 4; repeat. Sew an E-C-E unit to opposite sides of A as shown in Figure 5. Arrange units in rows as shown in Figure 6; join rows to complete block center.

Figure 4
Sew B to opposite ends of an E-C-E unit.

Figure 5
Sew an E-C-E unit to opposite sides of A.

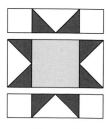

Figure 6
Arrange units in rows as shown; join to complete block center.

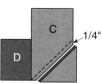

Figure 1
Trim seam allowance to 1/4".

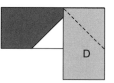

Figure 2
Stitch on diagonal of D as shown.

Step 9. Sew B to opposite ends of a D-C-D unit as shown in Figure 7; repeat. Sew a D-C-D unit to opposite sides of the block center as shown in Figure 8. Arrange units in rows; join rows to complete one Traveling Star Beams block as shown in Figure 9. Repeat Steps 6–9 to make 30 (48) (72) blocks.

Figure 7
Sew B to opposite ends of a D-C-D unit.

Figure 8
Sew a D-C-D unit to opposite
sides of the block center.

Traveling Star Beams
Placement Diagram
56" x 65"

Figure 9
Arrange units in rows; join rows to
complete 1 Traveling Star Beams block.

Step 10. Arrange blocks in six (8) (9) rows of five (6) (8) blocks each. Join blocks in rows; join rows to complete pieced center.

Step 11. Cut and piece two strips each gold solid 1 1/2" x 47 1/2" (1 1/2" x 56 1/2") (1 1/2" x 74 1/2") and 1 1/2" x 54 1/2" (1 1/2" x 72 1/2") (1 1/2" x 81 1/2"). Sew longer strips to opposite sides and shorter strips to the top and bottom; press seams toward strips.

Step 12. Cut and piece two strips each rust print 5" x 56 1/2" (5" x 74 1/2") (5" x 83 1/2"); sew to opposite long sides. Press seams toward strips. Cut two strips each rust print 5" x 56 1/2" (5" x 65 1/2") (5" x 83 1/2") sew to top and bottom. Press seams toward strips.

Step 13. Prepare top for quilting and finish as desired referring to the General Instructions. *Note: The quilt shown was machine-quilted in the ditch of block and border seams using white all-purpose thread and hand-quilted in a star design in outer borders using rust quilting thread.* ❧

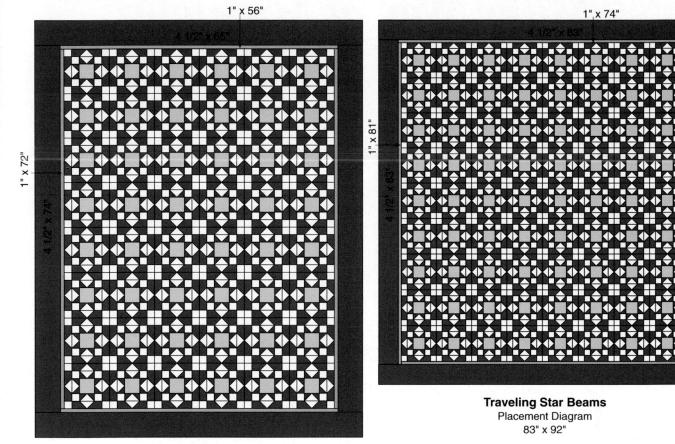

Traveling Star Beams
Placement Diagram
65" x 83"

Traveling Star Beams
Placement Diagram
83" x 92"

1" x 56"

4 1/2" x 65"

1" x 72"

4 1/2" x 74"

1" x 74"

4 1/2" x 83"

1" x 81"

4 1/2" x 83"

Milky Way at Midnight

By Willow Ann Sirch

Observing a clear night sky brilliant with twinkling stars and a love of nature inspired this striking quilt.

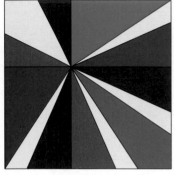

Milky Way
7 1/2" x 7 1/2" Block

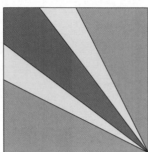

Milky Way Corner Block
6" x 6" Block

Quilt Sizes

	Lap	Twin	Queen
Finished Quilt Size	42" x 42"	72" x 87"	87" x 87"
Block Sizes	6" x 6"	6" x 6"	6" x 6"
	7 1/2" x 7 1/2"	7 1/2" x 7 1/2"	7 1/2" x 7 1/2"
Number of Blocks	20	84	104

Materials

	Lap	Twin	Queen
Black print	1/8 yard	1/8 yard	1/8 yard
Black mottled	1 yard	1 1/2 yards	1 5/8 yards
Gold metallic and solids	1 yard total	2 1/2 yards total	3 1/2 yards total
Navy prints	1 1/4 yards total	4 yards total	4 3/4 yards total
Backing	46" x 46"	76" x 91"	91" x 91"
Batting	46" x 46"	76" x 91"	91" x 91"
Self-made or purchased binding	5 1/4 yards	9 1/4 yards	10 1/4 yards
Neutral color all-purpose thread			
Navy quilting thread			
Basic sewing supplies and tools			

Project Notes

Accuracy is especially important when creating paper-piecing patterns. Photocopy machines distort images to some extent. For that reason, the foundation pattern pieces for this quilt were individually measured and marked on graph paper before being cut out.

A second method for reproducing the patterns is to trace the pattern onto a piece of tracing paper. Layer the traced design with seven or eight additional sheets of tracing paper and sew over the marked design with an unthreaded sewing machine.

If you must photocopy the patterns, be sure to copy all of them at the same time using the same machine. You will need 16 (80) (100) copies of each rectangle and four corner squares. Number the shapes on each foundation paper as on the templates. The numbers indicate the order of sewing.

Instructions

Instructions are given for the size shown in photo, with other sizes in parentheses. When only 1 number is given, it applies to all sizes.

Step 1. Copy paper-piecing patterns using patterns given and as directed on each piece.

Step 2. Measure the widest point of each shape and add an inch to the measurement; cut strips of fabric in the color marked on shape in that size. Cut the shapes from the strips, adding a 1/2" seam allowance all around.

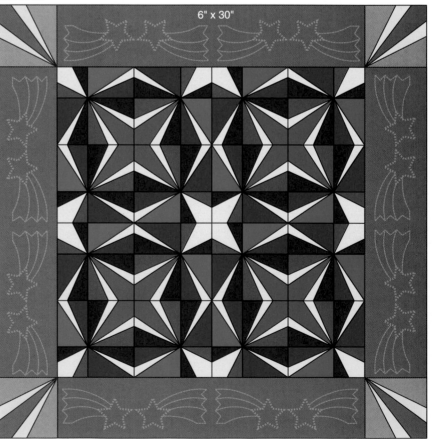

Milky Way at Midnight
Placement Diagram
42" x 42"

Step 3. Cut out the six shapes for each A pattern in their sewing order.

Step 4. Pin a numbered, photocopied and cut out paper pattern piece to each shape to identify it. Repeat for the eight B shapes for each B pattern and five for each corner block.

Step 5. Place piece 1 right side up on the unmarked side of one A foundation paper as shown in Figure 1. Holding the foundation paper with pinned piece up to a light source, check to see if piece 1 covers area marked 1 on the foundation paper. Pin piece 2 on piece 1 on the 2 side of 1 with right sides together as shown in Figure 2.

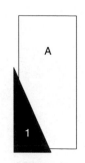

Figure 1
Place piece 1 right side up on the unmarked side of 1 A foundation paper.

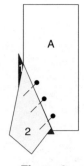

Figure 2
Pin piece 2 on piece 1 on the 2 side of 1 with right sides together.

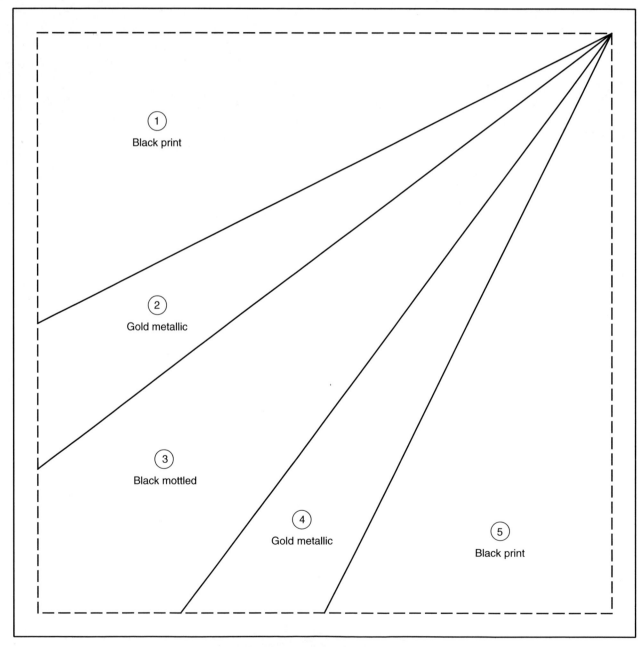

1
Black print

2
Gold metallic

3
Black mottled

4
Gold metallic

5
Black print

Corner Block Paper-Piecing Pattern
Make 4

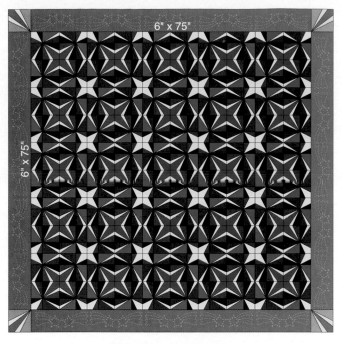

Milky Way at Midnight
Placement Diagram
87" x 87"

Step 6. With marked side of foundation paper up, sew on line between pieces 1 and 2 as shown in Figure 3. Flip piece 2 flat to be sure it covers all of area 2 on the paper; press. Trim excess seam allowance between pieces to 1/4". Continue adding pieces in this manner in numerical order until foundation piece is covered.

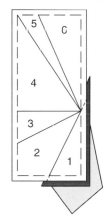

Figure 3
With marked side of foundation paper up, sew on line between pieces 1 and 2.

Step 7. Repeat for 16 (80) (100) each A and B foundation pieces and four Milky Way Corner Blocks. Trim excess of all completed units to 1/4" as marked by solid line around outside of patterns.

Step 8. Sew A and B pieces together to complete one Milky Way block as shown in Figure 4; repeat for 16 (80) (100) blocks.

Figure 4
Join A and B pieces to complete 1 Milky Way block.

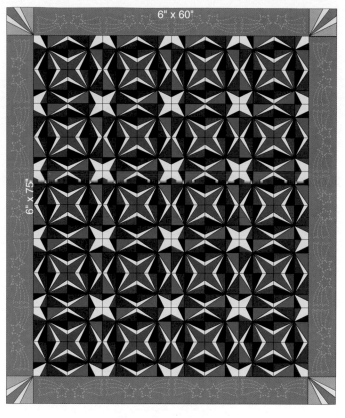

Milky Way at Midnight
Placement Diagram
72" x 87"

Step 9. Arrange blocks in four (10) (10) rows of four (8) (10) blocks each, turning blocks as necessary and referring to the Placement Diagram for arrangement of blocks. Join blocks in rows; join rows to complete the pieced center.

Step 10. Cut (and piece) two strips each black mottled 6 1/2" x 30 1/2" (6 1/2" x 60 1/2") (6 1/2" x 75 1/2"). Sew to the top and bottom of the pieced center; press seams toward strips.

Step 11. Cut (and piece) two strips each black mottled 6 1/2" x 30 1/2" (6 1/2" x 75 1/2") (6 1/2" x 75 1/2"). Sew a Milky Way Corner Block to each end of each strip; sew a strip to opposite long sides of the pieced center. Press seams toward strips.

Step 12. Remove paper from all paper-pieced units.

Figure 5
Quilt on borders as shown.

Step 13. Prepare top for quilting and finish as desired referring to the General Instructions. **Note:** *The quilt shown was hand-quilted using the quilting pattern given on border strips as shown in Figure 5 and 1/2" from seams of blocks using navy quilting thread.* ❧

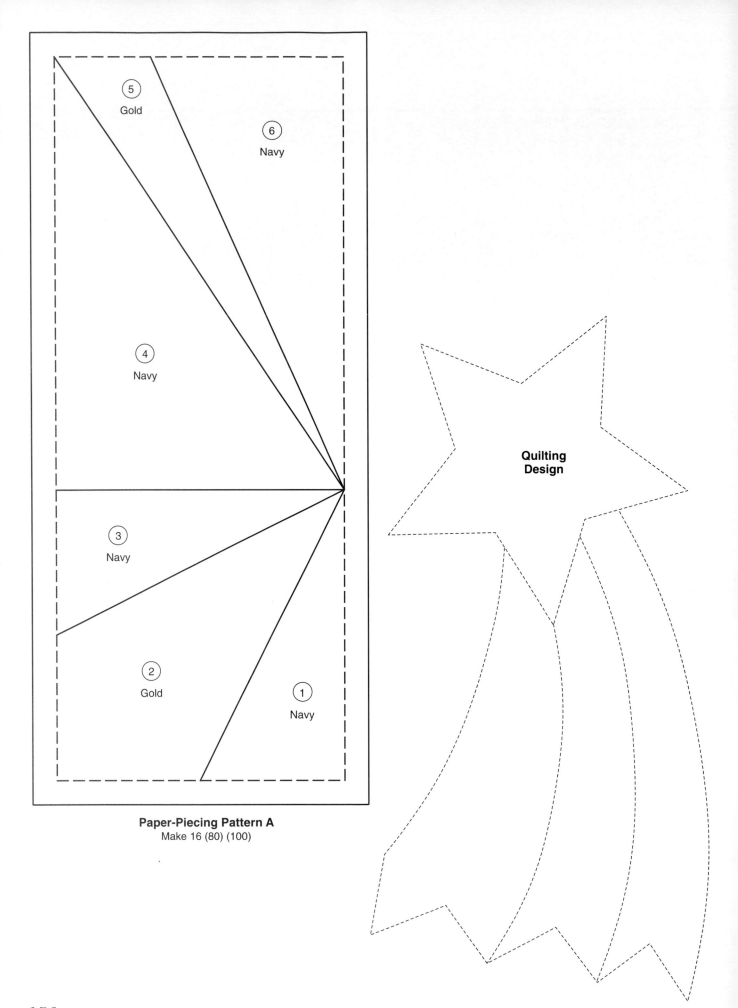

Paper-Piecing Pattern A
Make 16 (80) (100)

⑤ Gold
⑥ Navy
④ Navy
③ Navy
② Gold
① Navy

Quilting Design

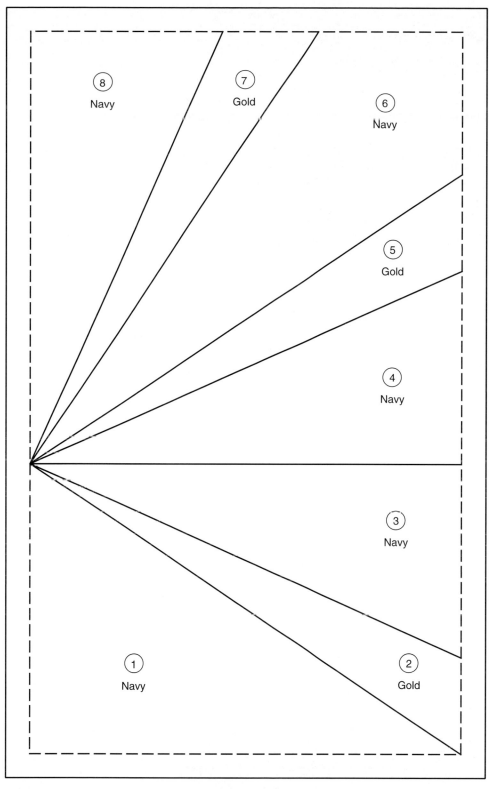

Paper-Piecing Pattern B
Make 16 (80) (100)

Golden Marble Mosaic

By Patsy Moreland

Northern Italy, near Carrara, is noted for its famous marble quarries. The marbled fabrics used in this quilt and the geometric design are a reminder of this region.

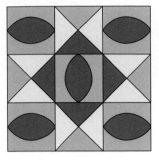

Lime Marble Mosaic
27" x 27" Block
Make 2 (3) (4)

Violet Marble Mosaic
27" x 27" Block
Make 2 (3) (5)

Project Note

The designer used the wrong side of the dark multicolored print for the inner border and the right side for the outer border. Look for fabric with good color saturation or buy different fabrics as listed to complete your version of this quilt. Lightweight interfacing is recommended in the materials list, but used dryer sheets may be substituted if recycling is important to you.

Instructions

Instructions are given for the size shown in photo, with other sizes in parentheses. When only 1 number is given, it applies to all sizes.

Step 1. Cut 12 (18) (25) squares lime green print and eight (12) (20) squares violet print 9 1/2" x 9 1/2". Fold and crease to mark centers.

Step 2. Prepare template for oval; cut as directed.

Step 3. Pin one lightweight interfacing piece to the right side of one oval; sew all around. Cut an opening in the interfacing side, being careful not to cut through fabric as shown in Figure 1; turn right side out through the opening. Press, making curved edges smooth. Repeat for all ovals.

Opening

Figure 1
Cut an opening in the interfacing side, being careful not to cut through fabric.

Step 4. Center a yellow print oval on a violet print square; machine-stitch in place using all-purpose thread to match fabric. Repeat with all yellow print ovals on violet print squares and violet print ovals on lime green print squares.

Quilt Sizes			
	Lap	**Twin**	**King**
Finished Quilt Size	69" x 69"	67" x 94"	98" x 98"
Block Size	27" x 27"	27" x 27"	27" x 27"
Number of Blocks	4	6	9

Materials			
Dark multicolored print	1 yard	3/4 yard	1 1/3 yards
Light multicolored print	1 yard	1 1/8 yards	1 1/4 yards
Yellow print	1 yard	1 1/2 yards	2 1/3 yards
Lime green print	1 1/2 yards	2 yards	3 yards
Violet print	1 1/2 yards	2 1/4 yards	3 1/2 yards
Backing	73" x 73"	71" x 98"	102" x 102"
Batting	73" x 73"	71" x 98"	102" x 102"
Self-made or purchased binding	8 1/4 yards	9 1/2 yards	11 1/2 yards
All-purpose thread to match fabrics			
Tan all-purpose thread			
Lightweight interfacing	1 3/8 yards	2 1/8 yards	3 1/4 yards
Basic sewing supplies and tools			

Step 5. Cut four (6) (9) squares each lime green and violet prints and eight (12) (18) squares yellow print 10 1/4" x 10 1/4".

Step 6. Draw lines on both diagonals on wrong side of yellow print squares. Pin a lime green print square right sides together with a yellow print square; sew 1/4" away from the marked lines on the yellow print side as shown in Figure 2; cut on the drawn lines as shown in Figure 3 to make triangle units. Repeat with all yellow and lime green print and violet print squares; press seams in one direction.

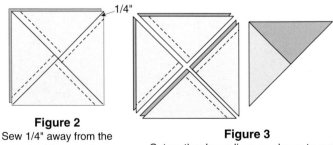
1/4"

Figure 2
Sew 1/4" away from the marked lines on the yellow print side.

Figure 3
Cut on the drawn lines as shown to make triangle units.

Step 7. Sew a lime/yellow triangle unit to a violet/yellow triangle unit as shown in Figure 4; repeat for all triangle units to make 16 (24) (36) quarter triangle/squares.

Figure 4
Sew a lime/yellow triangle unit
to a violet/yellow triangle unit.

Step 8. To piece one Violet Marble Mosaic block, sew a violet/oval square to opposite sides of a quarter triangle/square; repeat. Sew a quarter triangle/square to opposite sides of a lime/oval square. Arrange units in rows; join rows to complete one Violet Marble Mosaic block. Repeat for two (3) (5) blocks.

Step 9. To piece one Lime Marble Mosaic block, sew a lime/oval square to opposite sides of a quarter triangle/square; repeat. Sew a quarter triangle/square to opposite sides of a lime/oval square. Arrange units in rows; join rows to complete one Lime Marble Mosaic block. Repeat for two (3) (4) blocks.

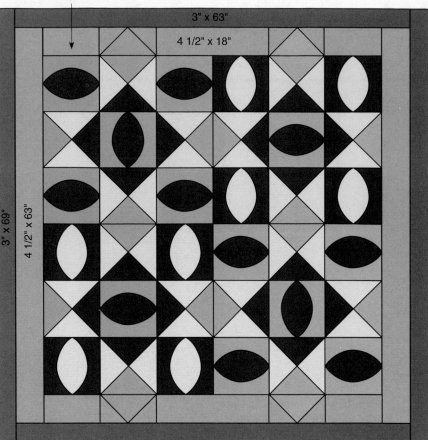

4 1/2" x 9"

3" x 63"

4 1/2" x 18"

3" x 69"

4 1/2" x 63"

Golden Marble Mosaic
Placement Diagram
69" x 69"

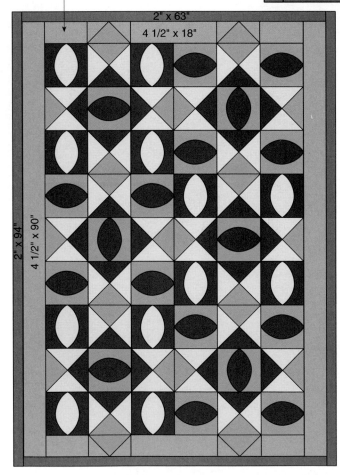

4 1/2" x 9"

2" x 63"

4 1/2" x 18"

2" x 94"

4 1/2" x 90"

Golden Marble Mosaic
Placement Diagram
67" x 94"

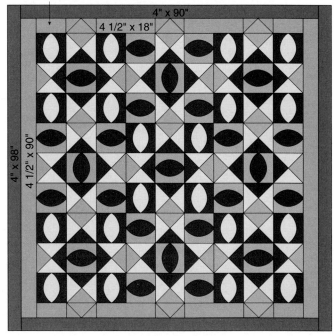

4 1/2" x 9"

4 1/2" x 18"

4" x 90"

4" x 98"

4 1/2" x 90"

Golden Marble Mosaic
Placement Diagram
98" x 98"

Step 10. Arrange blocks in rows referring to the Placement Diagram(s); join blocks in rows. Join rows to complete pieced center.

Step 11. Cut one (1) (2) square lime green print 10 1/4" x 10 1/4"; cut on both diagonals for four (4)

(6) A triangles. Cut four (4) (6) squares light multicolored print 5 3/8" x 5 3/8"; cut on one diagonal for eight (8) (12) B triangles.

Step 12. Sew B to adjacent short sides of A; repeat for four (4) (6) A-B units.

Step 13. Cut two (2) (4) rectangles light multicolored print 5" x 18 1/2". Cut four (4) (4) rectangles 5" x 9 1/2". Sew an A-B unit between 9 1/2" and 18 1/2" rectangles; repeat for two (2) (4) rectangle units.

Step 14. Sew a 9 1/2" rectangle to one end of an A-B unit; repeat for two (2) (0) rectangle units. Join rectangle units to make two border strips as shown in Figure 5; sew to top and bottom. Press seams toward strips. **Note:** *For king size, join rectangle units with remaining A-B units referring to the Placement Diagram for positioning of units.*

Step 15. Cut and piece two strips light multicolored print 5" x 63 1/2" (5" x 90 1/2") (5" x 90 1/2"). Sew to opposite long sides.

Step 16. Cut two strips each dark multicolored print 3 1/2" x 63 1/2" (2 1/2" x 63 1/2") (4 1/2" x 90 1/2") and 3 1/2" x 69 1/2" (2 1/2" x 94 1/2") (4 1/2" x 98 1/2"). Sew shorter strips to the top and bottom and longer strips to opposite sides; press seams toward strips.

Step 17. Prepare top for quilting and finish as desired referring to the General Instructions. **Note:** *The quilt shown was machine-quilted in a meandering design using tan all-purpose thread.* ❧

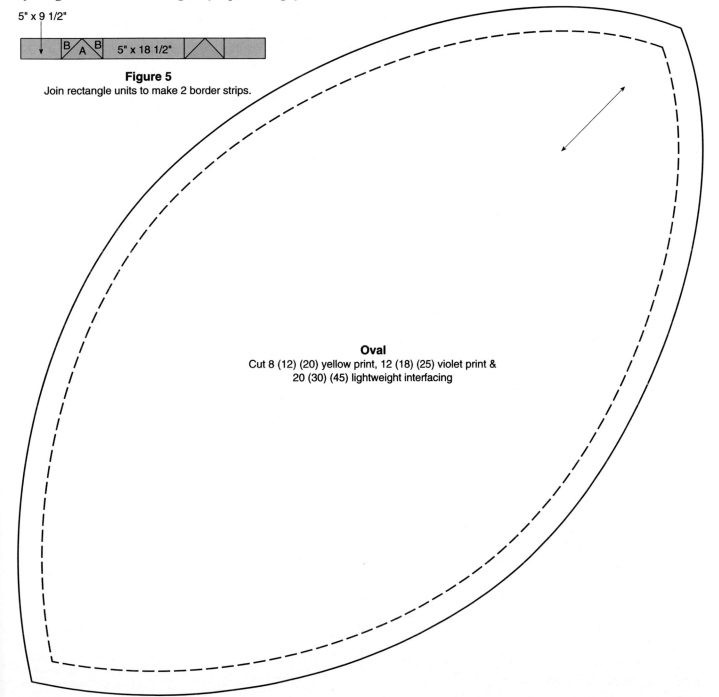

5" x 9 1/2"

B A B   5" x 18 1/2"

Figure 5
Join rectangle units to make 2 border strips.

Oval
Cut 8 (12) (20) yellow print, 12 (18) (25) violet print &
20 (30) (45) lightweight interfacing

Royal Nine-Patch Stars

By Marian Shenk

Nine-Patch blocks become star blocks with the addition of four points. Two different blocks are created for this colorful quilt.

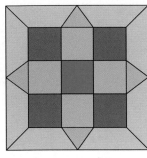

Four Squares
13" x 13" Block

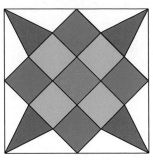

Nine-Patch Star
13" x 13" Block

Project Note

Yardage listed in materials chart for border stripe fabric assumes there are four 4"-wide finished, same-stripe motifs and four 2"-wide finished, same-stripe motifs along length of the fabric. Adjust the yardage if this is not available in fabric.

Instructions

Instructions are given for the size shown in photo, with other sizes in parentheses. When only 1 number is given, it applies to all sizes.

Step 1. Cut two strips each 4 1/2" x 50" (4 1/2" x 80") (4 1/2" x 105") and 4 1/2" x 50" (4 1/2" x 90") (4 1/2" x 105") from length of border stripe; set aside.

Step 2. Prepare templates using pattern pieces given. Cut as directed on each piece for one block.

Step 3. To piece one Nine-Patch Star block, sew a green print A between two blue print A's; repeat. Sew a mauve print A between two green print A's. Join the A units to complete the Nine-Patch center as shown in Figure 1.

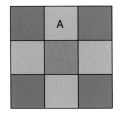

Figure 1
Join the A units to complete the
Nine-Patch center.

Step 4. Sew C between B and BR; repeat for four B-C units. Sew a B-C unit to each side of the Nine-Patch center as shown in Figure 2 to complete one Nine-Patch Star block; repeat for five (15) (25) blocks.

Step 5. To piece one Four Squares block, sew a green print F between two purple mottled F's; repeat. Sew a blue print F between two green print F's. Join the F units to complete the Nine-Patch center as shown in Figure 3.

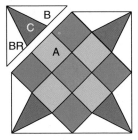

Figure 2
Sew a B-C unit to each side
of the Nine-Patch center.

Figure 3
Join the F units to complete
the Nine-Patch center.

Step 6. Sew D between two E pieces; repeat for four D-E units. Sew a D-E unit to each side of the Nine-Patch center, mitering corners as shown in Figure 4 to complete one Four Squares block; repeat for four (15) (24) blocks.

Figure 4
Sew a D-E unit to each side of
the Nine-Patch center, mitering
corners as shown to complete
1 Four Squares block.

	Quilt Sizes		
	Lap	**Double**	**King**
Finished Quilt Size	47" x 47"	73" x 86"	99" x 99"
Block Size	13" x 13"	13" x 13"	13" x 13"
Number of Blocks	9	30	49
Materials			
Mauve print	1/6 yard	1/3 yard	3/8 yard
Blue print	1/2 yard	1 yard	1 1/3 yards
Purple mottled	1/2 yard	1 1/4 yards	1 3/4 yards
Green print	5/8 yard	1 1/2 yards	2 1/2 yards
Cream-on-cream print	2/3 yard	1 2/3 yards	2 7/8 yards
Border stripe	1 1/2 yards	4 1/2 yards	7 yards
Backing	51" x 51"	77" x 90"	103" x 103"
Batting	51" x 51"	77" x 90"	103" x 103"
Self-made or purchased binding	5 3/4 yards	9 1/4 yards	11 1/2 yards
Neutral color all-purpose thread			
Off-white quilting thread			
Basic sewing supplies and tools			

Step 7. Join two (3) (4) Nine-Patch Star blocks and one (2) (3) Four Squares block to make a row referring to the Placement Diagram for positioning of blocks; repeat for two (3) (4) rows. Press seams in one direction.

Step 8. Join two (3) (4) Four Squares blocks with one (2) (3) Nine-Patch Star block to make a row again referring to the Placement Diagram; press seams in one direction. *Note: For double and king sizes, repeat to make (3) (3) rows.*

Step 9. Join the rows referring to the Placement Diagram to complete pieced center; press seams in one direction.

Step 10. Sew border strips cut in Step 1 to sides and top and bottom of pieced center, mitering corners; press seams toward strips. *Note: Try to make mitered seams on each corner fall in the same motif to create identical corner designs on all four corners. Refer to photo of sample project.*

Step 11. Prepare top for quilting and finish as desired referring to the General Instructions. *Note: The quilt shown was hand-quilted in the ditch of all seams and around motifs in the border stripe using off-white quilting thread.* ❧

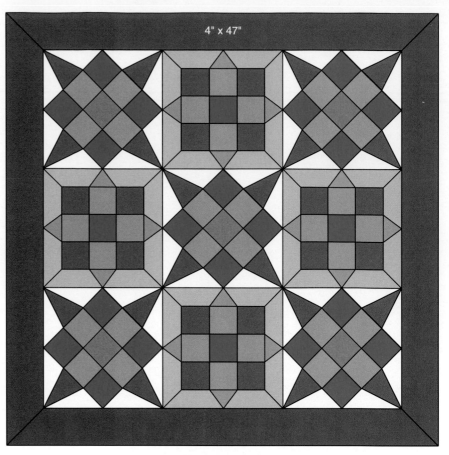

Royal Nine-Patch Stars
Placement Diagram
47" x 47"

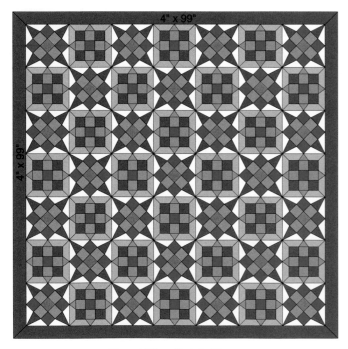

Royal Nine-Patch Stars
Placement Diagram
99" x 99"

Royal Nine-Patch Stars
Placement Diagram
73" x 86"

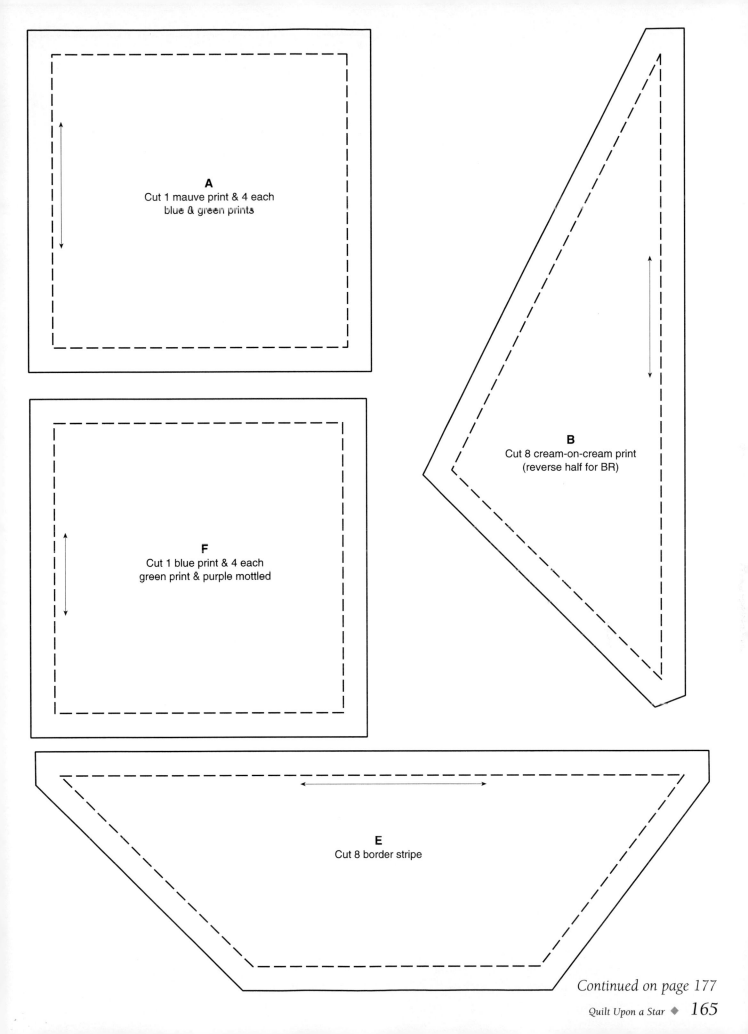

A
Cut 1 mauve print & 4 each
blue & green prints

B
Cut 8 cream-on-cream print
(reverse half for BR)

F
Cut 1 blue print & 4 each
green print & purple mottled

E
Cut 8 border stripe

Continued on page 177

Striped Stars

By Connie Rand

Stripes and pinwheels unite to form these bright yellow and blue stars. Sew your own galaxy.

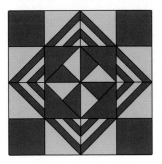
Striped Square
12" x 12" Block

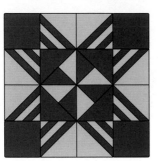
Striped Star
12" x 12" Block

Quilt Sizes			
	Lap	**Twin**	**Queen**
Finished Quilt Size	44" x 56"	64" x 88"	88" x 100"
Block Size	12" x 12"	12" x 12"	12" x 12"
Number of Blocks	12	24	42
Materials			
Yellow print	1 3/4 yards	3 3/4 yards	6 yards
Blue print	2 1/2 yards	4 1/2 yards	7 1/4 yards
Backing	48" x 60"	68" x 92"	92" x 104"
Batting	48" x 60"	68" x 92"	92" x 104"
Self-made or purchased binding	6 yards	9 yards	11 yards
Navy all-purpose thread			
Basic sewing supplies and tools			

Instructions

Instructions are given for the size shown in photo, with other sizes in parentheses. When only 1 number is given, it applies to all sizes.

Step 1. Prepare templates using pattern pieces given; cut as directed on each piece for one block. Repeat for 12 (24) (42) blocks.

Step 2. Cut 28 (56) (96) strips each 1" by fabric width yellow and blue prints. Sew two blue print strips to two yellow print strips along length with right sides together to make a strip set as shown in Figure 1; press seams in one direction. Repeat for 14 (28) (48) strip sets.

Figure 1
Sew 2 blue print strips to 2 yellow print strips along length with right sides together to make a strip set as shown.

Step 3. Place B template on strip set aligning strip seams with lines on template as shown in Figure 2. Cut as directed on piece for one block; repeat for two blocks.

Figure 2
Place B template on strip set aligning strip seams with lines on template as shown.

Step 4. To piece one Striped Star block, sew a striped B to yellow print B as shown in Figure 3; repeat for eight B units. Join B units, again referring to Figure 3.

Step 5. Join yellow and blue print A triangles to make a pinwheel unit as shown in Figure 4. Sew a blue print B to each side of the pinwheel unit.

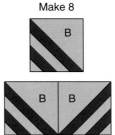

Figure 3
Sew a striped B to a yellow print B; repeat for 8 units. Join B units.

Figure 4
Join yellow and blue print A triangles to make a pinwheel unit.

Step 6. Join a B unit with two C squares as shown in Figure 5; repeat. Arrange units in rows; join rows to complete one Striped Star block as shown in Figure 6. Repeat to make six (12) (21) Striped Star blocks.

Figure 5
Join a B unit with 2 C squares.

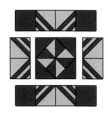

Figure 6
Arrange units in rows; join rows to complete 1 Striped Star block as shown.

Step 7. To piece one Striped Square block, repeat Steps 4–6 except join striped B with yellow print B to make B units as shown in Figure 7 and arrange units in rows as shown in Figure 8. Repeat to make six (12) (21) Striped Square blocks.

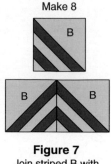

Make 8

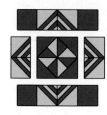

Figure 7
Join striped B with
yellow print B to make
B units as shown.

Figure 8
Arrange units in rows as shown to
complete 1 Striped Square block.

Step 8. For all sizes, cut and piece two strips each 4 1/2" x 44 1/2" (4 1/2" x 64 1/2") (4 1/2" x 88 1/2") and 4 1/2" x 48 1/2" (4 1/2" x 80 1/2") (4 1/2" x 92 1/2") blue print. Sew the longer strips to opposite long sides and the shorter strips to the top and bottom.

Step 9. For twin and queen sizes, cut and piece two strips each (2" x 51 1/2") (2" x 75 1/2") and (2" x 72 1/2") (2" x 84 1/2") blue print. Cut and piece two strips each (3" x 56 1/2") (3" x 80 1/2") and (3" x 75 1/2") (3" x 87 1/2") yellow print. Sew longer strips to opposite sides and shorter strips to top and bottom.

Step 10. Prepare top for quilting and finish as desired referring to the General Instructions. *Note: The quilt shown was machine-quilted in the ditch of seams using navy all-purpose thread.* ❧

4" x 44"

4" x 48"

Striped Stars
Placement Diagram
44" x 56"

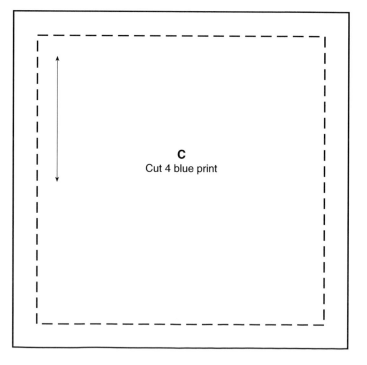

C
Cut 4 blue print

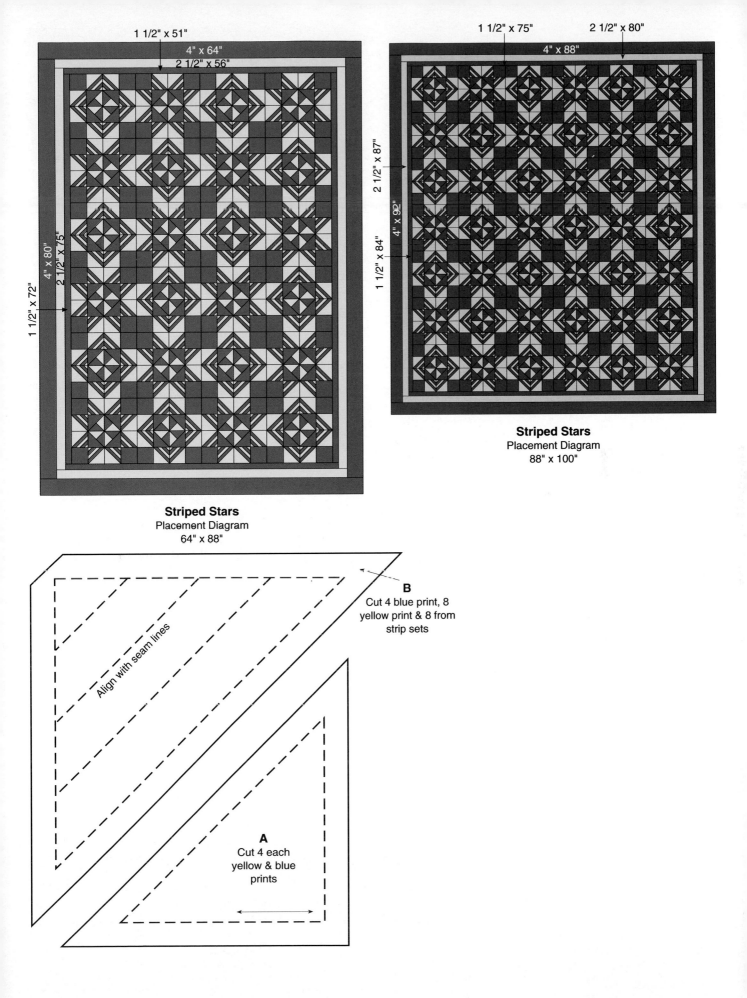

1 1/2" x 51"

4" x 64"

2 1/2" x 56"

1 1/2" x 72"

4" x 80"

2 1/2" x 75"

Striped Stars
Placement Diagram
64" x 88"

1 1/2" x 75"

2 1/2" x 80"

4" x 88"

2 1/2" x 87"

4" x 92"

1 1/2" x 84"

Striped Stars
Placement Diagram
88" x 100"

Align with seam lines

B
Cut 4 blue print, 8
yellow print & 8 from
strip sets

A
Cut 4 each
yellow & blue
prints

Playful Stars

By Carla Schwab

Bright blue and gold combine to make this quick-to-stitch quilt for a bed centerpiece or cover.

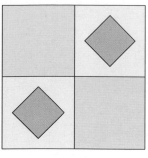

Four-Patch
9" x 9" Block

Playful Star
9" x 9" Block

Instructions

Instructions are given for the size shown in photo, with other sizes in parentheses. When only 1 number is given, it applies to all sizes.

Step 1. Cut four (9) (14) strips each medium yellow solid and yellow print 5" by fabric width. Sew a solid strip to a print strip along length with right sides together to make a strip set; repeat for four (9) (14) strip sets. Press seams in one direction.

Step 2. Cut each strip set into 5" segments. You will need 32 (70) (112) segments. Join two segments to make a Four-Patch unit; repeat for 16 (35) (56) Four-Patch units.

Step 3. Cut three (5) (8) strips dark yellow print 2 3/4" by fabric width; subcut into 32 (70) (112) 2 3/4" square segments. Turn under 1/4" seam allowance all around each square. Center and hand-appliqué a square on both medium yellow solid squares of each Four-Patch unit to complete Four-Patch blocks referring to the block drawing for positioning of square.

Step 4. Cut five (7) (9) strips blue print 9 1/2" by fabric width; subcut into 20 (28) (34) 9 1/2" square segments.

Step 5. Make templates for star and tail pieces; cut as directed on each piece, adding 1/8"–1/4" seam allowance all around when cutting. Prepare pieces for appliqué; hand-appliqué on blue print squares referring to the block drawing for positioning.

Quilt Sizes			
	Lap	**Twin**	**Queen**
Finished Quilt Size	56 1/2" x 56 1/2"	65 1/2" x 83 1/2"	83 1/2" x 92 1/2"
Block Size	9" x 9"	9" x 9"	9" x 9"
Number of Blocks	36	63	90

Materials			
Dark yellow print	1/3 yard	1/2 yard	3/4 yard
Light yellow solid	3/4 yard	7/8 yard	1 yard
Medium yellow solid	1 yard	1 1/3 yards	2 yards
Blue print	1 1/2 yards	2 yards	2 1/2 yards
Yellow print	2 yards	3 1/8 yards	4 yards
Backing	57" x 57"	66" x 84"	84" x 93"
Batting	57" x 57"	66" x 84"	84" x 93"
Neutral color all-purpose thread			
Yellow quilting thread			
Basic sewing supplies and tools			

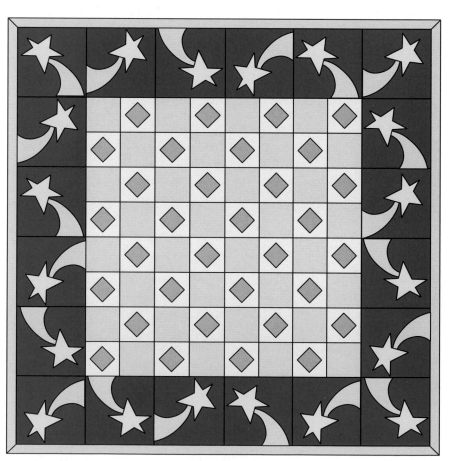

Playful Stars
Placement Diagram
56 1/2" x 56 1/2"

Step 6. Join four (5) (7) Four-Patch blocks to make a row as shown in Figure 1; repeat for four (7) (8) rows. Join rows to complete pieced center; press seams in one direction.

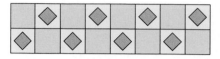

Figure 1
Join 4 Four-Patch blocks to make a row.

Step 7. Join four (7) (8) Star blocks as shown in Figure 2 to make a side border strip; repeat for two strips. Sew a pieced strip to opposite sides of the pieced center; press seams toward border strips.

Figure 2
Join 4 Star blocks as shown to
make a side border strip.

Step 8. Join six (7) (9) Star blocks as shown in Figure 3; repeat for two strips. Sew a pieced strip to the top and bottom of the pieced center; press seams toward border strips.

Figure 3
Join 6 Star blocks as shown.

Step 9. Cut and piece two strips each yellow print 4" x 61 1/2" (4" x 70 1/2") (4" x 88 1/2"). Sew a strip to the top and bottom.

Step 10. Cut and piece two strips each yellow print 4" x 61 1/2" (4" x 88 1/2") (4" x 97 1/2"). Sew strips to opposite sides, mitering corners.

Step 11. Prepare top for quilting referring to the General Instructions. Cut backing and batting 1" smaller than the quilt top all around. Quilt as desired by hand or machine. *Note: The quilt shown was hand-quilted diagonally through Four-Patch blocks and machine-quilted around stars and tails using yellow quilting thread.*

Step 12. Turn under edge of yellow print border strips 1/4"; turn to backside, leaving 1 1/4" showing on quilt front. Hand-stitch folded-under section to the quilt back to finish. ❧

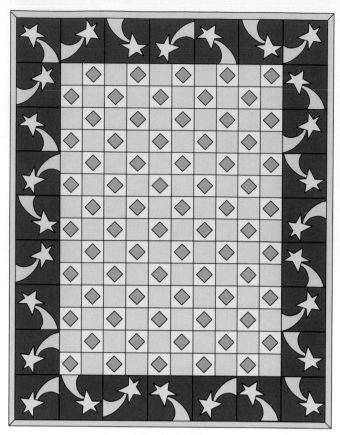

Playful Stars
Placement Diagram
65 1/2" x 83 1/2"

Playful Stars
Placement Diagram
83 1/2" x 92 1/2"

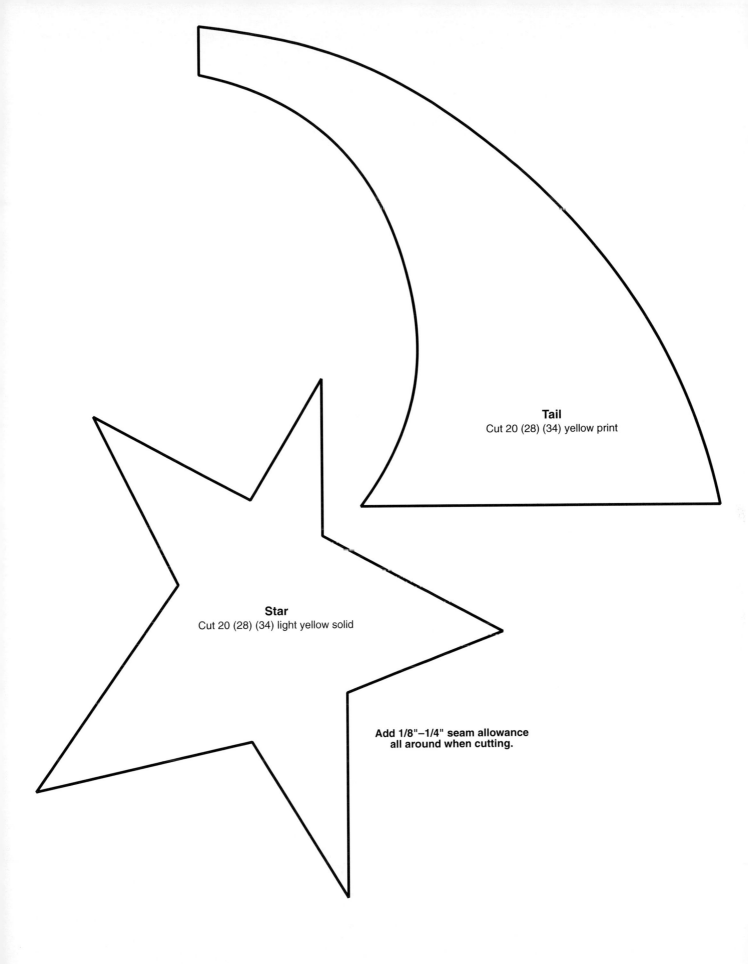

Tail
Cut 20 (28) (34) yellow print

Star
Cut 20 (28) (34) light yellow solid

**Add 1/8"–1/4" seam allowance
all around when cutting.**

Octagon Stars

By Connie Rand

When the pieced blocks are joined in rows, a star design is formed between the octagon shapes. Two templates create this simple, yet interesting pattern.

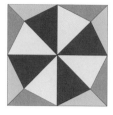

Octagon Stars
12" x 12" Block

Instructions

Instructions are given for the size shown in photo, with other sizes in parentheses. When only 1 number is given, it applies to all sizes.

Step 1. Prepare templates using pattern pieces given; cut as directed on each piece for one block. Repeat for 35 (42) (49) blocks.

Step 2. To piece one block, sew a fern print A to a lavender print B as shown in Figure 1. Sew a purple print AR to a green print BR, again referring to Figure 1.

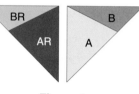

Figure 1
Sew a fern print A to a lavender B; sew a purple print AR to a green BR.

Quilt Sizes			
	Twin	**Queen**	**King**
Finished Quilt Size	73" x 97"	85" x 97"	97" x 97"
Block Size	12" x 12"	12" x 12"	12" x 12"
Number of Blocks	35	42	49

Materials			
Lavender print	1 1/2 yards	1 3/4 yards	2 yards
Green print	2 1/8 yards	2 1/2 yards	2 3/4 yards
Fern print	3 yards	3 1/8 yards	3 3/4 yards
Purple print	3 1/8 yards	4 3/8 yards	5 yards
Backing	77" x 101"	89" x 101"	101" x 101"
Batting	77" x 101"	89" x 101"	101" x 101"
Self-made or purchased binding	10 yards	10 1/2 yards	11 1/4 yards
Neutral color and lavender all-purpose thread			
Basic sewing supplies and tools			

Step 3. Sew A-B to AR-BR as shown in Figure 2; repeat for four units. Join units to make one Octagon Stars block as shown in Figure 3; repeat for 35 (42) (49) blocks.

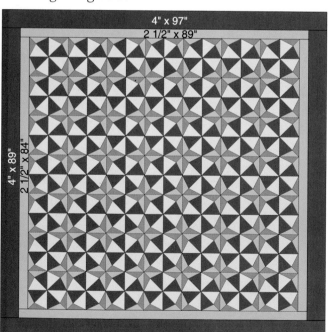

Octagon Stars
Placement Diagram
97" x 97"

Octagon Stars
Placement Diagram
85" x 97"

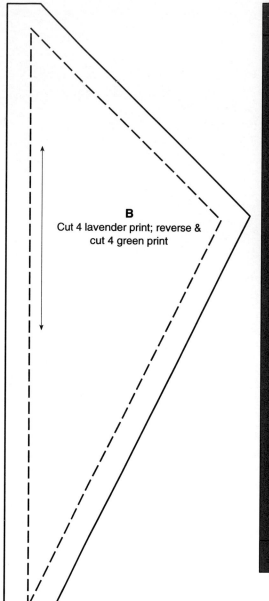

B
Cut 4 lavender print; reverse &
cut 4 green print

Octagon Stars
Placement Diagram
73" x 97"

4" x 73"

2 1/2" x 65"

4" x 89"

2 1/2" x 84"

Figure 2
Sew A-B to AR-BR.

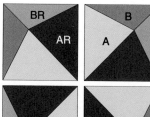

Figure 3
Join 4 units to make 1
Octagon Stars block.

Step 4. Join blocks in seven (7) (7) rows of five (6) (7) blocks each; press seams in one direction. Join the rows to complete pieced center; press seams in one direction.

Step 5. Cut and piece two strips each 3" x 65 1/2" (3" x 77 1/2") (3" x 89 1/2") and 3" x 84 1/2" (3" x 84 1/2") (3" x 84 1/2") green print. Sew longer strips to opposite long sides and shorter strips to the top and bottom. Press seams toward strips.

Step 6. Cut and piece two strips each 4 1/2" x 73 1/2" (4 1/2" x 85 1/2") (4 1/2" x 97 1/2") and 4 1/2" x 89 1/2" (4 1/2" x 89 1/2") (4 1/2" x 89 1/2") purple print. Sew longer strips to opposite long sides and shorter strips to the top and bottom. Press seams toward strips.

Step 7. Prepare top for quilting and finish as desired referring to the General Instructions. **Note:** *The quilt shown was machine-quilted in the ditch of all seams using lavender all-purpose thread.* ❧

Octagon Stars

A
Cut 4 fern print;
reverse & cut 4
purple print

Royal Nine-Patch Stars
Continued from page 165

D
Cut 4 green print

C
Cut 4 purple mottled

Quiltmaking Basics

Materials & Supplies

Fabrics

Fabric Choices. Quilts and quilted projects combine fabrics of many types, depending on the project. It is best to combine same-fiber-content fabrics when making quilted items.

Buying Fabrics. One hundred percent cotton fabrics are recommended for making quilts. Choose colors similar to those used in the quilts shown or colors of your own preference. Most quilt designs depend more on contrast of values than on the colors used to create the design.

Preparing the Fabric for Use. Fabrics may be prewashed or not, depending on your preference. Whether you do or don't, be sure your fabrics are colorfast and won't run onto each other when washed after use.

Fabric Grain. Fabrics are woven with threads going in a crosswise and lengthwise direction. The threads cross at right angles—the more threads per inch, the stronger the fabric.

The crosswise threads will stretch a little. The lengthwise threads will not stretch at all. Cutting the fabric at a 45-degree angle to the crosswise and lengthwise threads produces a bias edge which stretches a great deal when pulled (Figure 1).

If templates are given with patterns in this book, pay careful attention to the grain lines marked with arrows. These arrows indicate that the piece should be placed on the lengthwise grain with the arrow running on one thread. Although it is not necessary to examine the fabric and find a thread to match to,

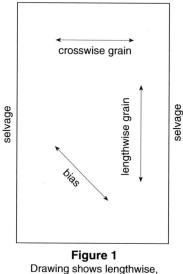

Figure 1
Drawing shows lengthwise, crosswise and bias threads.

it is important to try to place the arrow with the lengthwise grain of the fabric (Figure 2).

Thread

For most piecing, good-quality cotton or cotton-covered polyester is the thread of choice. Inexpensive polyester threads are not recommended because they can cut the fibers of cotton fabrics.

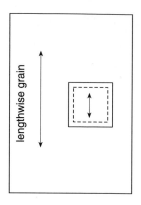

Figure 2
Place the template with marked arrow on the lengthwise grain of the fabric.

Choose a color thread that will match or blend with the fabrics in your quilt. For projects pieced with dark and light color fabrics choose a neutral thread color, such as a medium gray, as a compromise between colors. Test by pulling a sample seam.

Batting

Batting is the material used to give a quilt loft or thickness. It also adds warmth.

Batting size is listed in inches for each pattern to reflect the size needed to complete the quilt according to the instructions. Purchase the size large enough to cut the size you need for the quilt of your choice.

Some qualities to look for in batting are drapeability, resistance to fiber migration, loft and softness.

If you are unsure which kind of batting to use, purchase the smallest size batting available in the type you'd like to try. Test each sample on a small project. Choose the batting that you like working with most and that will result in the type of quilt you need.

Tools & Equipment

There are few truly essential tools and little equipment required for quiltmaking. The basics include needles (hand-sewing and quilting betweens), pins (long, thin sharp pins are best), sharp scissors or shears, a thimble, template materials (plastic or cardboard), marking tools (chalk marker, water-erasable pen and a No. 2 pencil are a few) and a quilting frame or hoop. For piecing and/or quilting by machine, add a sewing machine to the list.

Other sewing basics such as a seam ripper, pincushion, measuring tape and an iron are also necessary. For choosing colors or quilting designs for your quilt, or for designing your own quilt, it is helpful to have graph paper, tracing paper, colored pencils or markers and a ruler on hand.

For making strip-pieced quilts, a rotary cutter, mat and specialty rulers are often used. We recommend an ergonomic rotary cutter, a large self-healing mat and several rulers. If you can choose only one size, a 6" x 24" marked in 1/8" or 1/4" increments is recommended.

Construction Methods

Templates

Traditional Templates. While many quilt instructions in this book use rotary-cut strips and quick-sewing methods, a few patterns require templates. Templates are like the pattern pieces used to sew a garment. They are used to cut the fabric pieces which make up the quilt top. There are two types—templates that include a 1/4" seam allowance and those that don't.

Choose the template material and the pattern. Transfer the pattern shapes to the template material with a sharp No. 2 lead pencil. Write the pattern name, piece letter or number, grain line and number to cut for one block or whole quilt on each piece as shown in Figure 3.

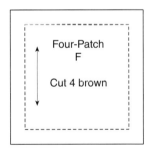

Figure 3
Mark each template with the pattern name and piece identification.

Some patterns require a reversed piece (Figure 4). These patterns are labeled with an R after the piece letter; for example, A and AR. To reverse a template, first cut it with the labeled side up and then with the labeled side down. Compare these to the right and left fronts of a blouse. When making a

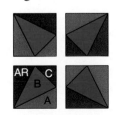

Figure 4
This pattern uses reversed pieces.

garment, you accomplish reversed pieces when cutting the pattern on two layers of fabric placed with right sides together. This can be done when cutting templates as well.

If cutting one layer of fabric at a time, first trace the template onto the backside of the fabric with the marked side down; turn the template over with the marked side up to make reverse pieces.

Appliqué patterns given in this book do not include a seam allowance. Most designs are given in one drawing rather than individual pieces. This saves space while giving you the complete design to trace on the background block to help with placement of the pieces later. Make templates for each shape using the drawing for exact size. Remember to label each piece as for piecing templates.

For hand appliqué, add a seam allowance when cutting pieces from fabric. You may trace the template with label side up on the right side of the fabric if you are careful to mark lightly. The traced line is then the guide for turning the edges under when stitching.

If you prefer to mark on the wrong side of the fabric, turn the template over if you want the pattern to face the same way it does on the page.

For machine appliqué, a seam allowance is not necessary. Trace template onto the right side of the fabric with label facing up. Cut around shape on the traced line.

Piecing

Hand-Piecing Basics. When hand-piecing it is easier to begin with templates which do not include the 1/4" seam allowance. Place the template on the wrong side of the fabric, lining up the marked grain line with lengthwise or crosswise fabric grain. If the piece does not have to be reversed, place with labeled side up. Trace around shape; move, leaving 1/2" between the shapes, and mark again.

When you have marked the appropriate number of pieces, cut out pieces, leaving 1/4" beyond marked line all around each piece.

To piece, refer to assembly drawings to piece units and blocks, if provided. To join two units, place the patches with right sides together. Stick a pin in at the beginning of the seam through both fabric patches,

Figure 5
Stick a pin through fabrics to match the beginning of the seam.

matching the beginning points (Figure 5); for hand-piecing, the seam begins on the traced line, not at the edge of the fabric (see Figure 6).

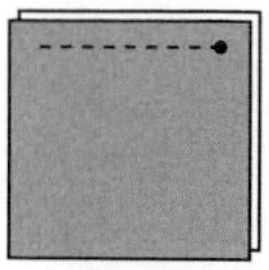

Figure 6
Begin hand-piecing at seam, not at the edge of the fabric. Continue stitching along seam line.

Thread a sharp needle; knot one strand of the thread at the end. Remove the pin and insert the needle in the hole; make a short stitch and then a backstitch right over the first stitch.

Continue making short stitches with several stitches on the needle at one time. As you stitch, check the back piece often to assure accurate stitching on the seam line. Take a stitch at the end of the seam; back-stitch and knot at the same time as shown in Figure 7.

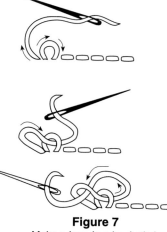

Figure 7
Make a loop in a backstitch to make a knot.

Seams on hand-pieced fabric patches may be finger-pressed toward the darker fabric.

To sew units together, pin fabric patches together, matching seams. Sew as above except where seams meet; at these intersections, backstitch, go through seam to next piece and backstitch again to secure seam joint.

Not all pieced blocks can be stitched with straight seams or in rows. Some patterns require set-in pieces. To begin a set-in seam on a star pattern, pin one side of the square to the proper side of the star point with right sides together, matching corners. Start stitching at the seam line on the outside point; stitch on the marked seam line to the end of the seam line at the center referring to Figure 8.

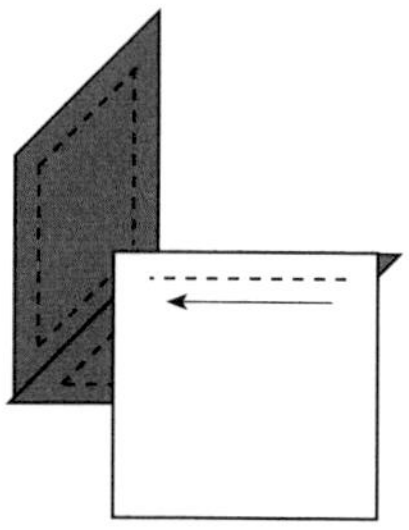

Bring around the adjacent side and pin to the next star point, matching seams. Continue the stitching line from the adjacent seam through corners

Figure 8
To set a square into a diamond point, match seams and stitch from outside edge to center.

and to the outside edge of the square as shown in Figure 9.

Machine-Piecing.
If making templates, include the 1/4" seam allowance on the template for machine-piecing. Place template on the wrong side of the fabric as for hand-piecing except butt pieces against one another when tracing.

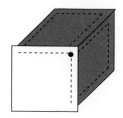

Figure 9
Continue stitching the adjacent side of the square to the next diamond shape in 1 seam from center to outside as shown.

Set machine on 2.5 or 12–15 stitches per inch. Join pieces as for hand-piecing for set-in seams; but for other straight seams, begin and end sewing at the end of the fabric patch sewn as shown in Figure 10. No backstitching is necessary when machine-stitching.

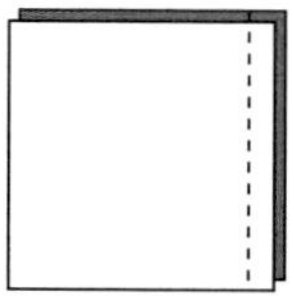

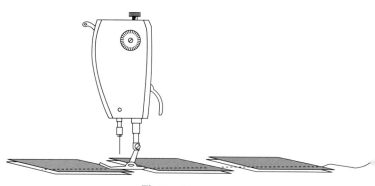

Figure 10
Begin machine-piecing at the end of the piece, not at the end of the seam.

Join units as for hand-piecing referring to the piecing diagrams where needed. Chain piecing (Figure 11—sewing several like units before sewing other units) saves time by eliminating beginning and ending stitches.

Figure 11
Units may be chain-pieced to save time.

When joining machine-pieced units, match seams against each other with seam allowances pressed in opposite directions to reduce bulk and make perfect matching of seams possible (Figure 12).

Figure 12
Sew machine-pieced units with seams pressed in opposite directions.

Cutting

Quick-Cutting. Quick-cutting and piecing strips are recommended for making many of the projects in this book. Templates are completely eliminated; instead, a rotary cutter, plastic ruler and mat are used to cut fabric pieces.

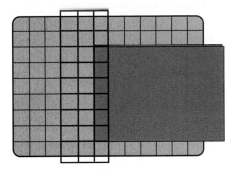

Figure 13
Fold fabric and straighten as shown.

When rotary-cutting strips, straighten raw edges of fabric by folding fabric in fourths across the width as shown in Figure 13. Press down flat; place ruler on fabric square with edge of fabric and make one cut from the folded edge to the outside edge. If fabric is not straightened, a wavy strip will result as shown in Figure 14.

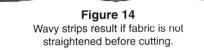

Figure 14
Wavy strips result if fabric is not straightened before cutting.

Always cut away from your body, holding the ruler firmly with the non-cutting hand. Keep fingers away from the edge of the ruler as it is easy for the rotary cutter to slip and jump over the edge of the ruler if cutting is not properly done.

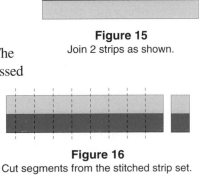

Figure 15
Join 2 strips as shown.

For many strip-pieced blocks two strips are stitched together as shown in Figure 15. The strips are stitched, pressed and cut into segments as shown in Figure 16.

Figure 16
Cut segments from the stitched strip set.

The cut segments are arranged as shown in Figure 17 and stitched to complete, in this example, one Four-Patch

block. Although the block shown is very simple, the same methods may be used for more complicated patterns.

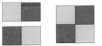

Figure 17
Arrange cut segments to make a Four-Patch block.

The direction to press seams on strip sets is important for accurate piecing later. The normal rule for pressing is to press seams toward the darker fabric to keep the colors from showing through on lighter colors later. For joining segments from strip sets, this rule doesn't always apply.

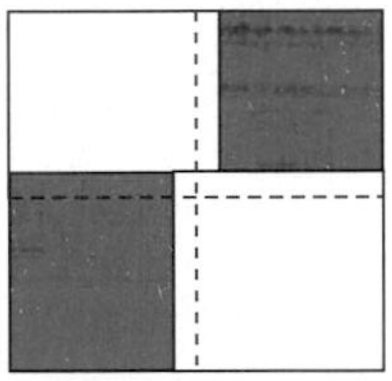

It is best if seams on adjacent rows are pressed in opposite directions. When aligning segments to stitch rows together, if pressed properly, seam joints will have a seam going in both directions as shown in Figure 18.

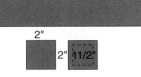

Figure 18
Seams go in both directions at seam joints.

If a square is required for the pattern, it can be subcut from a strip as shown in Figure 19.

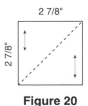

Figure 19
If cutting squares, cut proper-width strip into same-width segments. Here, a 2" strip is cut into 2" segments to create 2" squares. These squares finish at 1 1/2" when sewn.

If you need right triangles with the straight grain on the short sides, you can use the same method, but you need to figure out how wide to cut the strip. Measure the finished size of one short side of the triangle. Add 7/8" to this size for seam allowance. Cut fabric strips this width; cut the strips into the same increment to create squares. Cut the squares on the diagonal to produce triangles. For example, if you need a triangle with a 2" finished height, cut the strips 2 7/8" by the width of the fabric. Cut the strips into 2 7/8" squares. Cut each square on the diagonal to produce the correct-size triangle with the grain on the short sides (Figure 20).

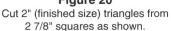

Figure 20
Cut 2" (finished size) triangles from 2 7/8" squares as shown.

Triangles sewn together to make squares are called

half-square triangles or triangle/squares. When joined, the triangle/square unit has the straight of grain on all outside edges of the block.

Another method of making triangle/squares is shown in Figure 21. Layer two squares with right sides

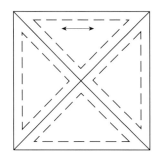

Figure 21
Mark a diagonal line on the square; stitch 1/4" on each side of the line. Cut on line to reveal stitched triangle/squares.

together; draw a diagonal line through the center. Stitch 1/4" on both sides of the line. Cut apart on the drawn line to reveal two stitched triangle/squares.

If you need triangles with the straight of grain on the diagonal, such as for fill-in triangles on the outside edges of a diagonal-set quilt, the procedure is a bit different.

To make these triangles, a square is cut on both diagonals; thus, the straight of grain is on the longest or diagonal side (Figure 22). To figure out the size to cut the square, add 1 1/4" to the needed finished size of the longest

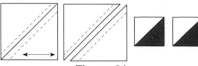

Figure 22
Add 1 1/4" to the finished size of the longest side of the triangle needed and cut on both diagonals to make a quarter-square triangle.

side of the triangle. For example, if you need a triangle with a 12" finished diagonal, cut a 13 1/4" square.

If templates are given, use their measurements to cut fabric strips to correspond with that measurement. The template may be used on the strip to cut pieces quickly. Strip cutting works best for squares, triangles, rectangles and diamonds. Odd-shaped templates are difficult to cut in multiple layers using a rotary cutter.

Foundation Piecing

Foundation Piecing. Paper or fabric foundation pieces are used to make very accurate blocks, provide stability for weak fabrics, and add body and weight to the finished quilt.

Temporary foundation materials include paper, tracing paper, freezer paper and removable interfacing. Permanent foundations include utility fabrics, non-woven interfacing, flannel, fleece and batting.

Methods of marking foundations include basting

lines, pencils or pens, needlepunching, tracing wheel, hot-iron transfers, copy machine, premarked, stamps or stencils.

There are two methods of foundation piecing—under-piecing and top-piecing. When under-piecing, the pattern is reversed when tracing. We have not included any patterns for top-piecing. *Note: All patterns for which we recommend paper piecing are already reversed in full-size drawings given.*

To under-piece, place a scrap of fabric larger than the lined space on the unlined side of the paper in the No. 1 position. Place piece 2 right sides together with piece 1; pin on seam line, and fold back to check that the piece will cover space 2 before stitching.

Stitch along line on the lined side of the paper—fabric will not be visible. Sew several stitches beyond the beginning and ending of the line. Backstitching is not required as another fabric seam will cover this seam.

Remove pin; finger-press piece 2 flat. Continue adding all pieces in numerical order in the same manner until all pieces are stitched to paper. Trim excess to outside line (1/4" larger all around than finished size of the block).

Tracing paper can be used as a temporary foundation. It is removed when blocks are complete and stitched together. To paper-piece, copy patterns using a copy machine or trace each block individually. Measure the finished paper foundations to insure accuracy in copying.

Appliqué

Appliqué is the process of applying one piece of fabric on top of another for decorative or functional purposes.

Making Templates. Most appliqué designs given here are shown as full-size drawings for the completed designs. The drawings show dotted lines to indicate where one piece overlaps another. Other marks indicate placement of embroidery stitches for decorative purposes such as eyes, lips, flowers, etc.

For hand appliqué, trace each template onto the right side of the fabric with template right side up. Cut around shape, adding a 1/8"–1/4" seam allowance.

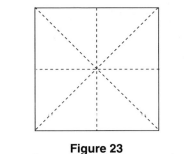

Figure 23
Fold background to mark centers as shown.

Before the actual appliqué process begins, cut the background block and prepare it for stitching. Most appliqué designs are centered on the block. To find the center of the background square, fold it in half and in half again; crease with your fingers. Now unfold and fold diagonally and crease; repeat for other corners referring to Figure 23. Center-line creases help position the design. If centering the appliqué design is important, an X has been placed on each drawing to mark the center of the design. Match the X with the creased center of the background block when placing pieces.

If you have a full-size drawing of the design, as is given with most appliqué designs in this book, it might help you to draw on the background block to help with placement. Transfer the design to a large piece of tracing paper. Place the paper on top of the design; use masking tape to hold in place. Trace design onto paper.

If you don't have a light box, tape the pattern on a window; center the background block on top and tape in place. Trace the design onto the background block with a water-erasable marker or chalk pencil. This drawing will mark exactly where the fabric pieces should be placed on the background block.

Hand Appliqué. Traditional hand appliqué uses a template made from the desired finished shape without seam allowance added.

After fabric is prepared, trace the desired shape onto the right side of the fabric with a water-erasable marker, light lead or chalk pencil. Leave at least 1/2" between design motifs when tracing to allow for the seam allowance when cutting out the shapes.

When the desired number of shapes needed has been drawn on the fabric pieces, cut out shapes leaving 1/8"–1/4" all around drawn line for turning under.

Turn the shape's edges over on the drawn or stitched line. When turning the edges under, make sharp corners

sharp and smooth edges smooth. The fabric patch should retain the shape of the template used to cut it.

When turning in concave curves, clip to seams and baste the seam allowance over as shown in Figure 24.

Figure 24
Concave curves should be clipped before turning as shown.

During the actual appliqué process, you may be layering one shape on top of another. Where two fabrics overlap, the underneath piece does not have to be turned under or stitched down.

If possible, trim away the underneath fabric when the block is finished by carefully cutting away the background from underneath and then cutting away unnecessary layers to reduce bulk and avoid shadows from darker fabrics showing through on light fabrics.

For hand appliqué, position the fabric shapes on the background block and pin or baste them in place. Using a blind stitch or appliqué stitch, sew pieces in place with matching thread and small stitches. Start with background pieces first and work up to foreground pieces. Appliqué the pieces in place on the background in numerical order, if given, layering as necessary.

Machine Appliqué. There are several products available to help make the machine-appliqué process easier and faster.

Fusible transfer web is a commercial product similar to iron-on interfacings except it has two sticky sides. It is used to adhere appliqué shapes to the background with heat. Paper is adhered to one side of the web.

To use, dry-iron the sticky side of the fusible product onto the wrong side of the chosen fabric. Draw desired shapes onto the paper and cut them out. Peel off the paper and dry-iron the shapes in place on the background fabric. The shape will stay in place while you stitch around it. This process adds a little bulk or stiffness to the appliquéd shape and makes hand quilting through the layers difficult.

For successful machine appliqué a tear-off stabilizer is recommended. This product is placed under the background fabric while machine appliqué is being done. It is torn away when the work is finished. This kind of stabilizer keeps the background fabric from pulling during the machine-appliqué process.

During the actual machine-appliqué process, you will be layering one shape on top of another. Where two fabrics overlap, the underneath piece does not have to be turned under or stitched down.

Thread the top of the machine with thread to match the fabric patches or with threads that coordinate or contrast with fabrics. Rayon thread is a good choice when a sheen is desired on the finished appliqué stitches. Do not use rayon thread in the bobbin; use all-purpose thread.

Set your machine to make a zigzag stitch and practice on scraps of similar weight to check the tension. If you can see the bobbin thread on the top of the appliqué, adjust your machine to make a balanced stitch. Different-width stitches are available; choose one that will not overpower the appliqué shapes. In some cases these appliqué stitches will be used as decorative stitches as well and you may want the thread to show.

If using a stabilizer, place this under the background fabric and pin or fuse in place. Place shapes as for

Tips & Techniques

Before machine-piecing fabric patches together, test your sewing machine for positioning an accurate 1/4" seam allowance. There are several tools to help guarantee this. Some machine needles may be moved to allow the presser-foot edge to be a 1/4" guide.

A special foot may be purchased for your machine that will guarantee an accurate 1/4" seam. A piece of masking tape can be placed on the throat plate of your sewing machine to mark the 1/4" seam. A plastic stick-on ruler may be used instead of tape with the same results.

hand-appliqué and stitch all around shapes by machine.

When all machine work is complete, remove stabilizer from the back referring to the manufacturer's instructions.

Putting It All Together

Many steps are required to prepare a quilt top for quilting, including setting the blocks together, adding borders, choosing and marking quilting designs, layering the top, batting and backing for quilting, quilting or tying the layers and finishing the edges of the quilt.

As you begin the process of finishing your quilt top, strive for a neat, flat quilt with square sides and corners, not for perfection—that will come with time and practice.

Finishing the Top

Settings. Most quilts are made by sewing individual blocks together in rows which, when joined, create a design. There are several other methods used to join blocks. Sometimes the setting choice is determined by the block's design. For example, a house block should be placed upright on a quilt, not sideways or upside down.

Plain blocks can be alternated with pieced or appliquéd blocks in a straight set. Making a quilt using plain blocks saves time; half the number of pieced or appliquéd blocks are needed to make the same-size quilt as shown in Figure 1.

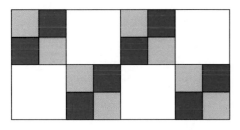

Figure 1
Alternate plain blocks with pieced blocks to save time.

Adding Borders. Borders are an integral part of the quilt and should complement the colors and designs used in the quilt center. Borders frame a quilt just like a mat and frame do a picture.

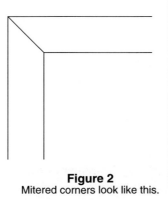

Figure 2
Mitered corners look like this.

If fabric strips are added for borders, they may be mitered or butted at the corners as shown in Figures 2 and 3.

To determine the size for butted-border strips, measure across the center of the completed quilt top from one side raw edge to the other side raw edge. This measurement will include a 1/4" seam allowance. Cut two border strips that length by the chosen width of the border. Sew these strips to the top and bottom of the pieced center referring to Figure 4. Press the seam allowance toward the border strips.

Measure across the completed quilt top at the center, from top raw edge to bottom raw edge, including the two border strips already added. Cut two border strips that length by the chosen width of the border. Sew a strip to each of the two remaining sides as shown in Figure 4. Press the seams toward the border strips.

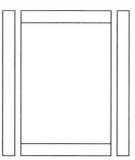

Figure 3
Butted corners look like this.

Figure 4
Sew border strips to opposite sides; sew remaining 2 strips to remaining sides to make butted corners.

To make mitered corners, measure the quilt as before. To this add twice the width of the border and 1/2" for seam allowances to determine the length of the strips. Repeat for opposite sides. Center and sew on each strip, stopping

Figure 5
For mitered corner, stitch strip, stopping 1/4" from corner seam.

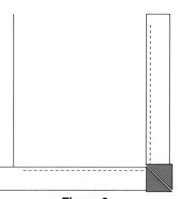

Figure 6
Fold and press corner to make a 45-degree angle.

stitching 1/4" from corner, leaving the remainder of the strip dangling.

Press corners at a 45-degree angle to form a crease. Stitch from the inside quilt corner to the outside on the creased line. Trim excess away after stitching and press mitered seams open (Figures 5–7).

Press seam open

Figure 7
Trim away excess from underneath when stitching is complete. Press seams open.

Carefully press the entire quilt top. Avoid pulling and stretching while pressing, which would distort shapes.

Getting Ready to Quilt

Choosing a Quilting Design. If you choose to hand- or machine-quilt your finished top, you will need to choose a design for quilting.

There are several types of quilting designs, some of which may not have to be marked. The easiest of the unmarked designs is in-the-ditch quilting. Here the quilting stitches are placed in the valley created by the seams joining two pieces together or next to the edge of an appliqué design. There is no need to mark a top for in-the-ditch quilting. Machine quilters choose this option because the stitches are not as obvious on the finished quilt (Figure 8).

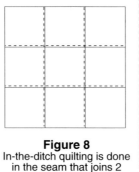
Figure 8
In-the-ditch quilting is done in the seam that joins 2 pieces.

Outline-quilting 1/4" or more away from seams or appliqué shapes is another no-mark alternative (Figure 9) which prevents having to sew through the layers made by seams, thus making stitching easier.

If you are not comfortable eyeballing the 1/4" (or other distance), masking tape is available in different widths and is helpful

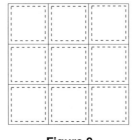
Figure 9
Outline-quilting 1/4" away from seam is a popular choice for quilting.

to place on straight-edge designs to mark the quilting line. If using masking tape, place the tape right up against the seam and quilt close to the other edge.

Meander or free-motion quilting by machine fills in open spaces and doesn't require marking. It is fun and easy to stitch as shown in Figure 10.

Marking the Top for Quilting or Tying. If you choose a fancy or all-over design for quilting, you will

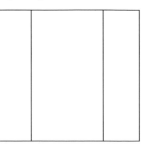
Figure 10
Machine meander quilting fills in large spaces.

need to transfer the design to your quilt top before layering with the backing and batting. You may use a sharp medium-lead or silver pencil on light background fabrics. Test the pencil marks to guarantee that they will wash out of your quilt top when quilting is complete; or be sure your quilting stitches cover the pencil marks. Mechanical pencils with very fine points may be used successfully to mark quilts.

Manufactured quilt-design templates are available in many designs and sizes and are cut out of a durable plastic template material which is easy to use.

To make a permanent quilt-design template, choose a template material on which to transfer the design. See-through plastic is the best as it will let you place the design while allowing you to see where it is in relation to your quilt design without moving it. Place the design on the quilt top where you want it and trace around it with your marking tool. Pick up the quilting template and place again; repeat marking.

No matter what marking method you use, remember—the marked lines should never show on the finished quilt. When the top is marked, it is ready for layering.

Preparing the Quilt Backing. The quilt backing is a very important feature of your quilt. In most cases, the materials list for each quilt in this book gives the size requirements for the backing, not the yardage needed. Exceptions to this are when the backing fabric is also used on the quilt top and yardage is given for that fabric.

A backing is generally cut at least 4" larger than the quilt top or 2" larger on all sides. For a 64" x 78" finished quilt, the backing would need to be at least 68" x 82".

To avoid having the seam across the center of the quilt backing, cut or tear

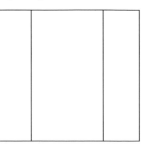
Figure 11
Center 1 backing piece with a piece on each side.

one of the right-length pieces in half and sew half to each side of the second piece as shown in Figure 11.

Quilts that need backing more than 88" wide may be pieced in horizontal pieces as shown in Figure 12.

Layering the Quilt Sandwich.
Layering the quilt top with the batting and backing is time-consuming. Open the batting several days before you need it and place over a bed or flat on the floor to help flatten the creases caused from its being folded up in the bag for so long.

Iron the backing piece, folding in half both vertically and horizontally and pressing to mark centers.

If you will not be quilting on a frame, place the backing right side down on a clean floor or table. Start in the center and push any wrinkles or bunches flat. Use masking tape to tape the edges to the floor or large clips to hold the backing to the edges of the table. The backing should be taut.

Place the batting on top of the backing, matching centers using fold lines as guides; flatten out any wrinkles. Trim the batting to the same size as the backing.

Fold the quilt top in half lengthwise and place on top of the batting, wrong side against the batting, matching centers. Unfold quilt and, working from the center to the outside edges, smooth out any wrinkles or lumps.

To hold the quilt layers together for quilting, baste by hand or use safety pins. If basting by hand, thread a long thin needle with a long piece of unknotted white or off-white thread. Starting in the center and leaving a long tail, make 4"–6" stitches toward the outside edge of the quilt top, smoothing as you baste. Start at the center again and work toward the outside as shown in Figure 13.

Figure 12
Horizontal seams may be used on backing pieces.

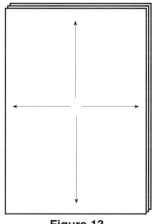
Figure 13
Baste from the center to the outside edges.

If quilting by machine, you may prefer to use safety pins for holding your quilt sandwich together. Start in the center of the quilt and pin to the outside, leaving pins open until all are placed. When you are satisfied that all layers are smooth, close the pins.

Quilting

Hand Quilting. Hand quilting is the process of placing stitches through the quilt top, batting and backing to hold them together. While it is a functional process, it also adds beauty and loft to the finished quilt.

To begin, thread a sharp between needle with an 18" piece of quilting thread. Tie a small knot in the end of the thread. Position the needle about 1/2" to 1" away from the starting point on quilt top. Sink the needle through the top into the batting layer, but not through the backing. Pull the needle up at the

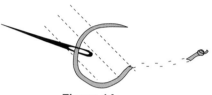
Figure 14
Start the needle through the top layer of fabric 1/2"–1" away from quilting line with knot on top of fabric.

Tips & Techniques
Knots should not show on the quilt top or back. Learn to sink the knot into the batting at the beginning and ending of the quilting thread for successful stitches.

When you have nearly run out of thread, wind the thread around the needle several times to make a small knot and pull it close to the fabric. Insert the needle into the fabric on the quilting line and come out with the needle 1/2" to 1" away, pulling the knot into the fabric layers the same as when you started. Pull and cut thread close to fabric. The end should disappear inside after cutting. Some quilters prefer to take a backstitch with a loop through it for a knot to end.

Making 12–18 stitches per inch is a nice goal, but a more realistic goal is seven to nine stitches per inch. If you cannot accomplish this right away, strive for even stitches—all the same size—that look as good on the back as on the front.

You will perfect your quilting stitches as you gain experience, your stitches will get better with each project and your style will be uniquely your own.

starting point of the quilting design. Pull the needle and thread until the knot sinks through the top into the batting (Figure 14).

Some stitchers like to take a backstitch at the beginning while others prefer to begin the first stitch here. Take small, even running stitches along the marked quilting line (Figure 15). Keep one hand positioned underneath to feel the needle go all the way through to the backing.

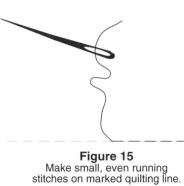

Figure 15
Make small, even running
stitches on marked quilting line.

Machine Quilting. Successful machine quilting requires practice and a good relationship with your sewing machine.

Prepare the quilt for machine quilting in the same way as for hand quilting. Use safety pins to hold the layers together instead of basting with thread.

Presser-foot quilting is best used for straight-line quilting because the presser bar lever does not need to be continually lifted.

Set the machine on a longer stitch length (3 or eight to 10 stitches to the inch). Too tight a stitch causes puckering and fabric tucks, either on the quilt top or backing. An even-feed or walking foot helps to eliminate the tucks and puckering by feeding the upper and lower layers through the machine evenly. Before you begin, loosen the amount of pressure on the presser foot.

Special machine-quilting needles work best to penetrate the three layers in your quilt.

Decide on a design. Quilting in the ditch is not quite as visible, but if you quilt with the feed dogs engaged, it means turning the quilt frequently. It is not easy to fit a rolled-up quilt through the small opening on the sewing machine head.

Meander quilting is the easiest way to machine-quilt—and it is fun. Meander quilting is done using an appliqué or darning foot with the feed dogs dropped. It is sort of like scribbling. Simply move the quilt top around under the foot and make stitches in a random pattern to fill the space. The same method may be used to outline a quilt design. The trick is the same as in hand-quilting; you are

striving for stitches of uniform size. Your hands are in complete control of the design.

If machine-quilting is of interest to you, there are several very good books available at quilt shops that will help you become a successful machine quilter.

Tied Quilts, or Comforters. Would you rather tie your quilt layers together than quilt them? Tied quilts are often referred to as comforters. The advantage of tying that it takes so much less time and the required skills can be learned quickly.

If a top will be tied, choose a thick, bonded batting—one that will not separate during washing. For tying, use pearl cotton, embroidery floss, or strong yarn in colors that match or coordinate with the fabrics in your quilt top.

Decide on a pattern for tying. Many quilts are tied at the corners and centers of the blocks and at sashing joints. Try to tie every 4"–6". Special designs can be used for tying, but most quilts are tied in conventional ways. Begin tying in the center and work to the outside edges.

To make the tie, thread a large needle with a long thread (yarn, floss or crochet cotton); do not knot. Push the needle through the quilt top to the back, leaving a 3"–4" length on top. Move the needle to the next position without cutting thread. Take another stitch through the layers; repeat until thread is almost used up.

Cut thread between stitches, leaving an equal amount of thread on each stitch. Tie a knot with the two thread ends. Tie again to make a square knot referring to Figure 16.

Trim thread ends to desired length.

Finishing the Edges

After your quilt is tied or quilted, the edges need to be finished. Decide how you want the edges of

Figure 16
Make a square knot as shown.

your quilt finished before layering the backing and batting with the quilt top.

Without Binding—Self-Finish. There is one way to eliminate adding an edge finish. This is done before quilting. Place the batting on a flat surface. Place the pieced top right side up on the batting. Place the backing right sides together with the pieced top. Pin and/or baste the layers together to hold flat referring to page 187.

Begin stitching in the center of one side using a 1/4" seam allowance, reversing at the beginning and end of the seam. Continue stitching all around and back to the beginning side. Leave a 12" or larger opening. Clip corners to reduce excess. Turn right side out through the opening. Slipstitch the opening closed by hand. The quilt may now be quilted by hand or machine.

The disadvantage to this method is that once the edges are sewn in, any creases or wrinkles that might form during the quilting process cannot be flattened out. Tying is the preferred method for finishing a quilt constructed using this method.

Bringing the backing fabric to the front is another way to finish the quilt's edge without binding. To accomplish this, complete the quilt as for hand or machine quilting. Trim the batting *only* even with the front. Trim the backing 1" larger than the completed top all around.

Turn the backing edge in 1/2" and then turn over to the front along edge of batting. The folded edge may be machine-stitched close to the edge through all layers, or blind-stitched in place to finish.

The front may be turned to the back. If using this method, a wider front border is needed. The backing and batting are trimmed 1" smaller than the top and the top edge is turned under 1/2" and then turned to the back and stitched in place.

One more method of self-finish may be used. The top and backing may be stitched together by hand at the edge. To accomplish this, all quilting must be stopped

1/2" from the quilt-top edge. The top and backing of the quilt are trimmed even and the batting is trimmed to 1/4"–1/2" smaller. The edges of the top and backing are turned in 1/4"–1/2" and blind-stitched together at the very edge.

These methods do not require the use of extra fabric and save time in preparation of binding strips; they are not as durable as an added binding.

Binding. The technique of adding extra fabric at the edges of the quilt is called binding. The binding encloses the edges and adds an extra layer of fabric for durability.

To prepare the quilt for the addition of the binding, trim the batting and backing layers flush with the top of the quilt using a rotary cutter and ruler or shears. Using a walking-foot attachment (sometimes called an even-feed foot attachment), machine-baste the three layers together all around approximately 1/8" from the cut edge.

The list of materials given with each quilt in this book often includes a number of yards of self-made or purchased binding. Bias binding may be purchased in packages and in many colors. The advantage to self-made binding is that you can use fabrics from your quilt to coordinate colors.

Double-fold, straight-grain binding and double-fold, bias-grain binding are two of the most commonly used types of binding.

Double-fold, straight-grain binding is used on smaller projects with right-angle corners. Double-fold, bias-grain binding is best suited for bed-size quilts or quilts with rounded corners.

To make double-fold, straight-grain binding, cut 2"-wide strips of fabric across the width or down the length of the fabric totaling the perimeter of the quilt plus 10". The strips are joined as shown in Figure 17 and pressed in half wrong sides together along the length using an iron on a cotton setting with no steam.

Lining up the raw edges, place the binding on the top of the quilt and begin sewing (again using the walking foot) approximately 6" from the beginning of the binding strip. Stop sewing 1/4"

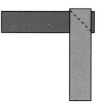

Figure 17
Join binding strips in a diagonal seam to eliminate bulk as shown.

from the first corner, leave the needle in the quilt, turn and sew diagonally to the corner as shown in Figure 18.

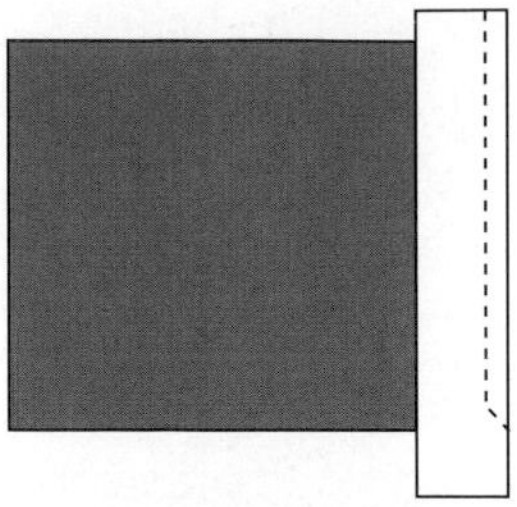

Figure 18
Sew to within 1/4" of corner; leave needle in quilt, turn and stitch diagonally off the corner of the quilt.

Fold the binding at a 45-degree angle up and away from the quilt as shown in Figure 19 and back down flush with the raw edges. Starting at the top raw edge of the quilt, begin sewing the next side as shown in Figure 20. Repeat at the next three corners.

As you approach the beginning of the binding strip, stop stitching and overlap the binding 1/2" from the edge; trim. Join the two ends with a 1/4" seam allowance and press the seam open. Reposition the joined binding along the edge of the quilt and resume stitching to the beginning.

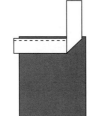

Figure 19
Fold binding at a 45-degree angle up and away from quilt as shown.

To finish, bring the folded edge of the binding over the raw edges and blind-stitch the binding in place over the machine-stitching line on the backside. Hand-miter the corners on the back as shown in Figure 21.

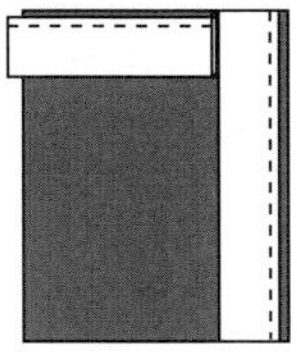

Figure 20
Fold the binding strips back down, flush with the raw edge, and begin sewing.

If you are making a quilt to be used on a bed, you will want to use double-fold, bias-grain bindings because the many threads that cross each other along the fold at the edge of the quilt make it a more durable binding.

Cut 2"-wide bias strips from a large square of fabric. Join the strips as illustrated in Figure 17 and press the seams open. Fold the beginning end of the bias strip 1/4" from the raw edge and press. Fold the joined strips in half along the long side, wrong sides together, and press with no steam (Figure 22).

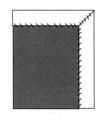

Figure 21
Miter and stitch the corners as shown.

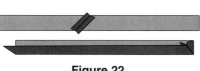

Figure 22
Fold end in and press strip in half.

Follow the same procedures as previously described for preparing the quilt top and sewing the binding to the quilt top. Treat the corners just as you treated them with straight-grain binding.

Since you are using bias-grain binding, you do have the option to just eliminate the corners if this option doesn't interfere with the patchwork in the quilt. Round the corners off by placing one of your dinner plates at the corner and rotary-cutting the gentle curve (Figure 23).

Figure 23
Round corners to eliminate square-corner finishes.

As you approach the beginning of the binding strip, stop stitching and lay the end across the beginning so it will slip inside the fold.

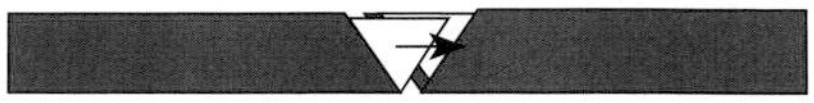

Figure 24
End the binding strips as shown.

Cut the end at a 45-degree angle so the raw edges are contained inside the beginning of the strip (Figure 24). Resume stitching to the beginning. Bring the fold to the back of the quilt and hand-stitch as previously described.

Overlapped corners are not quite as easy as rounded ones, but a bit easier than mitering. To make overlapped corners, sew binding strips to opposite sides of the quilt top. Stitch edges down to finish. Trim ends even.

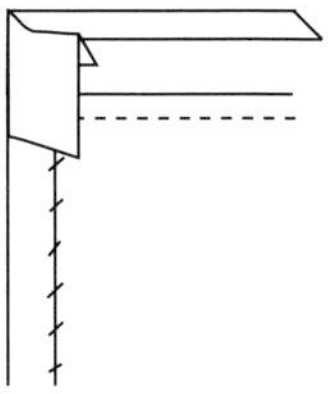

Sew a strip to each remaining side, leaving 1 1/2"–2" excess at each end. Turn quilt over and fold end in even with previous finished edge as shown in Figure 25.

Figure 25
Fold end of binding even with previous edge.

Fold binding in toward quilt and stitch down as before, enclosing the previous bound edge in the seam as shown in Figure 26. It may be necessary to trim the folded-down section to reduce bulk.

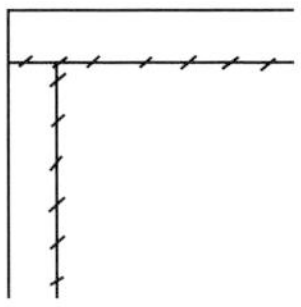

Figure 26
An overlapped corner is not quite as neat as a mitered corner.

Making Continuous Bias Binding

Instead of cutting individual bias strips and sewing them together, you may make continuous bias binding.

Cut a square 18" x 18" from chosen binding fabric. Cut the square once on the diagonal to make two triangles as shown in Figure 27. With right sides together, sew the two triangles together with a 1/4" seam allowance as shown in Figure 28; press seam open to reduce bulk.

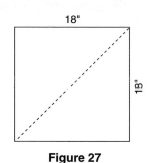

18"

18"

Figure 27
Cut 18" square on the diagonal.

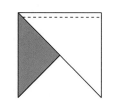

Figure 28
Sew the triangles together.

Mark lines every 2 1/4" on the wrong side of the fabric as shown in Figure 29. Bring the short ends together, right sides together, offsetting one line as shown in Figure 30 to make a tube; stitch. This will seem awkward.

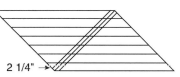

2 1/4"

Figure 29
Mark lines every 2 1/4".

Begin cutting at point A as shown in Figure 31; continue cutting along marked line to make one continuous strip. Fold strip in half along length with wrong sides together; press. Sew to quilt edges as instructed previously for bias binding.

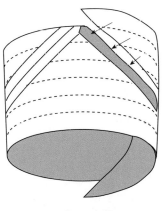

Figure 30
Sew short ends together, offsetting lines to make a tube.

Final Touches

If your quilt will be hung on the wall, a hanging sleeve is required. Other options include purchased plastic rings or fabric tabs. The best choice is a fabric sleeve, which

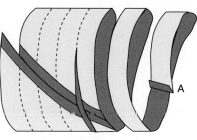

Figure 31
Cut along marked lines, starting at A.

will evenly distribute the weight of the quilt across the top edge, rather than at selected spots where tabs or rings are stitched, keep the quilt hanging straight and not damage the batting.

To make a sleeve, measure across the top of the finished quilt. Cut an 8"-wide piece of muslin equal to that length—you may need to seam several muslin strips together to make the required length.

Fold in 1/4" on each end of the muslin strip and press. Fold again and stitch to hold. Fold the muslin strip lengthwise with right sides together. Sew along the long side to make a tube. Turn the tube right side out; press with seam at bottom or centered on the back.

Hand-stitch the tube along the top of the quilt and the bottom of the tube to the quilt back making sure the quilt lies flat. Stitches should not go through to the front of the quilt and don't need to be too close together as shown in Figure 32.

Slip a wooden dowel or long curtain rod through the sleeve to hang.

When the quilt is finally complete, it should be signed and dated. Use a permanent pen on the back of

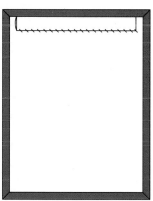

Figure 32
Sew a sleeve to the top back of the quilt.

the quilt. Other methods include cross-stitching your name and date on the front or back or making a permanent label which may be stitched to the back.

Special Thanks

We would like to thank the talented quilt designers whose works are
featured in this collection.

Leslie Beck
Nine-Patch Posies, 102
Pinwheels in the Breeze, 105
Traveling Star Beams, 148

Kathy Brown
Bugs in My House, 46

Barbara Clayton
Bears Gone Fishing, 35
Pinwheels & Garland, 66

Michele Crawford
Spring Bouquet, 108

Holly Daniels
Whirlybird Bed Quilt, 8
Flannel Four-Patch, 27
Baton Rouge Baby Quilt, 32
Reflections, 70
Bluebell Medallion, 112
Patriot Star, 144

Lucy Fazely
Hunter's Star, 74

Leslie Hartsock
Garden Friends, 14
Rocket in Outer Space, 41

Sue Harvey
Tied With a Bow, 49
Sunburst Medallion, 77

Sandra Hatch
Nine-Patch Rectangle, 20
Flying Geese Strippy, 23

Patsy Moreland
Scrappy Pieced Puzzle, 82
Golden Marble Mosaic, 158

Connie Rand
Something's Been Bugging Me, 118
Dragonflies in Flight, 138
Striped Stars, 166
Octagon Stars, 174

Jill Reber
Peppermint Twist, 86
Rainbow of Tumbling Blocks, 92

Judith Sandstrom
Garden Maze, 122

Carla Schwab
Two-Patch Quilt, 10
Good Night Good Earth, 54
Desert Courtyard, 89
Playful Stars, 170

Marian Shenk
Sunflower Dreams, 126
Royal Nine-Patch Stars, 162

Willow Sirch
Milky Way at Midnight, 152

Charlyne Stewart
Crazy for Butterflies, 133

Beth Wheeler
Snowball Castles, 60

Johanna Wilson
Crossroads, 96

Fabrics & Supplies

Page 23: Flying Geese Strippy—
Mountain Mist quilt batting from
The Stearns Technical Textiles Co.,
Mission Valley fabrics and machine-
quilting by Dianne Hodgekin

Page 32: Baton Rouge Baby Quilt—
HeatnBond Lite iron-on adhesive

Page 41: Rocket in Outer Space—
Pellon Quilter's Fleece, Stitch-n-Tear
tear-off fabric stabilizer and Wonder-
Under fusible transfer web, rayon
threads from Sulky of America and
Fiskars rotary cutter, mat and ruler

Page 49: Tied With a Bow—505
Spray & Fix basting spray and Warm
& White cotton batting from The
Warm Co.

Page 74: Hunter's Star—Kaufman

Fine Fabrics, Warm & Natural cotton
batting, Sew/Fit cutting mat and Snap-
Shot Ruler and machine-quilting by
Tyler's Machine Quilting Service

Page 86: Peppermint Twist—Master
Piece 45 ruler and Static Stickers

Page 92: Rainbow of Tumbling
Blocks—Master Piece 45 ruler and
Static Stickers

Page 102: Nine-Patch Posies—Warm
& Natural cotton batting from The
Warm Co. and Aleene's Hot Stitch
Fusible Web No. 17-8

Page 105: Pinwheels in the Breeze—
Warm & Natural cotton batting from
The Warm Co.

Page 108: Spring Bouquet—Warm

& Natural Soft & Bright batting

Page 112: Bluebell Medallion—
HeatnBond Lite iron-on adhesive

Page 122: Garden Maze—Hobbs
Heirloom cotton batting, DMC needles and quilting thread, and Fiskars
rotary cutter, ruler and mat

Page 133: Crazy for Butterflies—
rayon threads from Sulky of America
and DMC embroidery floss

Page 148: Traveling Star Beams—
Warm & Natural cotton batting from
The Warm Co.

Page 158: Golden Marble Mosaic—
Warm & Natural cotton batting from
The Warm Co., fabrics from
Hoffman International Fabrics and
Benartex Inc.